More
Heavenly Gems

Written and Compiled

By

Rayola Kelley

Hidden Manna Publications
P.O. Box 3572
Oldtown, ID. 83822

More Heavenly Gems

Except where otherwise indicated, all Scripture quotations in this book are taken from the King James Version of the Bible.

The (*) signifies a word whose definition can be found in the glossary located in the back of this book.

Dedication:

I want to dedicate this book of
spiritual gems to a
special group of women:
Carol Stribling, Sandi Johnson,
Betty Allen, Faye Moore,
and Nyla Ray

You have been my friends:
(ready to explore spiritual depths and heights),
You have been my sisters:
(allowing me to laugh and cry with you),
You have been "good" soldiers:
(lifting my arms up in prayer),
and above all
You have been special gems:
(adding untold riches to my life).

Special Appreciation

I want to thank Sandee Lloyd for taking time to edit this book, Jeannette Haley for sharing her ministry and life stories with me, while wading through each of my books to ensure completion, Kitty Miller for her ongoing support of the various projects of our ministry, Betty Allen for providing valuable material for this book, Maureen Human for giving me permission to once again use her poems.

I especially want to acknowledge the fact that God has richly blessed me with the various sources that provide these priceless gems. Without Him my body would be a lifeless shell, my soul a hopeless train wreck, and my spirit, a shriveled up prune. I am so thankful for the presence of the eternal and abundant life of His Son, and that His Spirit illuminates these treasures to enrich my life; and then affords me the opportunity to share them with others.

Table of Contents

INTODUCTION

Some would wonder why fill another empty chest (pages) with treasures from heaven? My answer is: can we have too many overflowing spiritual treasure chests, or too many glorious gems that would enrich our lives beyond measure? Clearly, God's gems are eternal, ongoing, and ever flowing from His throne.

Inspirational gems reveal how God can miraculously preserve the beauty and intent of His treasures in spite of the material He has to work with. Many years ago after recognizing the treacherous ways of my pride, I asked the Lord to keep me from touching His glory. I was aware how sometimes the touch of humanity can put a questionable mark upon the Lord's gems. He has been faithful to answer such a prayer by constantly showing the failure and weakness of my humanity.

Through the years I have realized that whatever writing ability that I now possess, has gone through much transformation, but it still clearly reveals my human side.   In spite of the imperfections which come along with being human, the inspired writings, poems, and stories, reveal the touch of heaven. It is truly the inspiration of the Spirit of the Living God, and His work on the imperfect gems that bring out the luster of His glory and the reflection of His Son. However crude and lacking man's writing may be, despite the prevalent flaws that cause humanity to miss the mark, still the touch of heaven adds value and substance to it. I have long learned that the wisdom which transforms comes from heaven.   The knowledge that stirs up that which is excellent comes from the ongoing revelation of Christ, and the gems which have enriched the lives of His people, all have passed through His sanctifying hands to be brought forth for His glory and purpose.

Clearly, the Lord desires to enrich our lives with His heavenly gems. He has provided each of us with a treasure map (His Word) that leads us to many priceless treasures. He has given us a spiritual compass (the Holy Spirit) to guide us to such possessions. The beauty of these treasures is that the cloud of witnesses which have gone before us, have acquired such gems through faith and obedience. They in turn, shared these inspirational nuggets with the following generations, establishing a richer and fuller inheritance and witness *(Hebrews 6:12; 12:1)*. And faithful to His ways, the Lord continues to multiply these gems as they pass from vessel to vessel.

Heaven's gems adorn our earthly lives. Like lustrous sapphire, His grace embellishes us with favor undeserved. His redeeming power, the covenant in his blood glows red in the likeness of rubies, and his mercies bedeck His beloved ones as beryl. The fruitful ways of His Spirit glimmer as emerald's splendor, while His truths radiate in our lives with the clarity of the loveliest of diamonds.

Each gem I encounter in my journey, I find myself wanting to share with others to enrich their lives with the eternal revelation of God. Oh, to see Jesus being reflected in each nugget brings such joy and liberty to my spirit. To experience the richness of His promises satisfies the longings of my soul. To know His presence brings such comfort to my weary mind, and to land upon His faithful and abiding ways establishes a greater assurance that He is the immovable Rock of the ages.

One of the predominant themes throughout this book is that of missionary work. As in the previous two books, along with each "nugget" the author and source is identified. Those imparted to this author, are signified by my initials RJK. Unmarked stories also have been formatted and recorded by me.

My heart in providing these treasures is to enrich, edify, and encourage others in ways that are transforming in attitude, life-changing in service, prove excellent in their ways, and glorious in their fruits and manifestations.

THE MASTER

He sees the sculptured face on the silent rock.
The potential of a lump of clay,
The image on the blank canvas,
The beauty of an encrusted gem,
The form in the tree,
The symphony on an empty music sheet.

He is the Sculptor with a fine chisel,
A Potter with a magnificent touch,
An Artist with an exquisite ability with colors,
A *Lapidary who knows how to bring out
   the value of a gem,
A Wood Carver who knows how to whittle,
A Composer who knows the endless rhythm of heaven.

He is the Lord God of heaven, Creator of all,
He took the hardness of sin
   and broke its hold on my life.
Like clay, He molded my soul with His redemption
   and brought out its purpose.
Like a canvas, He resurrected my spirit with new life
   and made it beautiful.
Like a gem, He brought out the luster in my new heart,
   to once again reflect the glory of heaven.
Like a dead tree, He once again brought life to me,
   and transformed me.
Like a music note, He wrote on my heart a new song,
   a lovely song of praise, hope, and victory.

As Creator, He masterfully brought out my possibilities,
As Savior, my way of salvation;
As God, my destination of hope;
As Lord, my life of service;
As King, my future;
As Teacher, my walk.

As Master, Jesus took the chisel of adversity
   to bring out my potential,
The potter's wheel to shape me in His likeness,

More Heavenly Gems

The paint brush to bring forth His image in my life,
The Sword of His Word to whittle away the old life,
   to bring forth the new life.
Heavenly tools to polish and establish His reflection in me,
The instruments to play the sweet harmony
   of heavenly praises and honor in my heart towards Him.

For He is a capable Master...a humble...a worthy...a gracious
   ...an honorable Master,
Becoming MY precious Master
   ...Mastering ALL my life in blessed communion!

-RJK

THE ISSUE OF SALVATION

The Prodigal

The pastor had nearly succumbed to the harsh elements after losing his way in the Smokey Mountains of Tennessee during a snowstorm. He had lost consciousness as hypothermia set in, gripping his body with icy claws of death.

But instead of waking up on the other side of eternity, he awoke to a crackling fire. A bearded man was leaning over him, swearing because he would not open his mouth. It was at that time that the pastor wondered if he was, indeed, on the other side of eternity, only in the wrong place.

When the pastor finally gained his senses, he recognized the man who had brought the much-needed aid and saved his life. The man, a notorious outlaw, admitted to hating God. Due to the loss of his son two decades prior, he had made a covenant that he would never welcome any person who represented this God, under his roof. So rabid was his hatred, that he beat his wife nearly to death, just for giving a coin to a preacher.

Yet, for some reason this bearded man was showing compassion to this preacher. He had even sat up with him through the night, seeing to his care, providing whatever ministrations were necessary to pull the preacher through his tenuous ordeal.

The pastor tried to show his appreciation by leaving the fellow with some money, but the man refused it. As the pastor picked up his saddlebags from the bedside and started towards the door, something gripped his conscience. The command was clear, *"You must try again."*

Putting aside the conflict raging within his soul, the pastor finally walked over to the man and in a voice that trembled with emotion, the pastor said, "Mr. Woods, I have a little book that I want to read from, and I'd like to talk to a Friend of mine before I go. Will you let me?"

Without turning to face the preacher, Woods turned to his wife and gave the pastor permission to go ahead. The pastor began to read about the lost sheep that was found and then commenced to read the story of the prodigal son. It was during the story of the prodigal son that Jake Woods finally turned around to face the pastor and seemed to take interest in what was being said. It was as if he was saying, "What are you talking about me for?" It was well known that Jake had sneered in the face of the messenger who had brought news that his dying father wished to see him.

Upon the ending of the story of the Prodigal Son, the pastor dropped to his knees and took hold of God with one hand and reached out to Jake Woods with the other hand. The pastor struggled for that simple key that would unlock whatever door guarded the prodigal's heart. Then the pastor remembered the great hospitality that Jake and his wife had shown him. His prayer towards God was simple. The pastor reminded God that this couple had taken him in and showed kindness. He went on to say: "But ever since they have had a house Jesus Christ has stood at their door with outstretched bleeding hands and with thorn-crowned brow, and they have slammed the door in His face. Lord, help Jake Woods to invite Jesus Christ to come in today."

When the pastor was done, Woods was sitting on the floor, looking at the doorway. The pastor followed the gaze of Woods to the open door but only saw the sunshine and the melting snow. After an interval of silence, Woods said, "Come in." Then turning to the pastor, he added, "He came in," as much as to say, "You can't throw it up to me anymore."

Woods followed the pastor to the gate and asked him if he had another one of those little books. He shared how his pap used to read about that wayward son, whom he acknowledged that he was like. He added that perhaps he could find someone else to read that story to him because he would like to hear it again.

The pastor gave him the Bible, and Woods added that his wife might come hear the pastor preach the next time he was in the area.

10

The pastor had preached in the area various times before to a few good souls. However, when he arrived at the meeting place after his encounter with Jake Woods, the whole campus seemed to be covered with people. The first man to greet the pastor right after he got off his horse was Jake Woods.

The pastor soon learned it was Jake Woods who brought the people to hear him preach. It was later that Jake's wife Nancy, told the pastor that something was wrong with Jake and to call the mourners, because he could not be long for this world.

When the pastor inquired as to what she was talking about. Nancy explained through tears that he was a different man and that he had actually been good to her.

The pastor gave his sermon to the people. He powerfully preached about the One who came seeking the lost to save them. Upon completion of his sermon, the preacher began to invite the lost to come forward to receive, but Jake Woods jumped to his feet and went down the aisle, speaking in a voice that drowned out the pastor's.

This is what Woods said, "Men and women, come on! Doc's telling you the truth; for I saw that Man when Doc prayed in my house. When I opened my eyes He was standing in the door with His hands stretched out, and there were holes in them with blood running out. I saw thorns on His head, too. And I told Him to come in and He came, and I haven't been the same man since."

The net of salvation had surely been let down that day and many were allowing themselves to be caught by the loving arms of God. In fact, they came until it seemed they all would come. It was a miracle. (ISL, pgs. 37-42)

Jake Woods reminds us that before any of us were enfolded in the net of salvation, we were prodigals, lost sheep that strayed far away from the sheepfold of our great, loving Shepherd and Father. We have in fact become enemies to the One who wanted to reach out to embrace us in the promises of heaven. In our fierce independence, we often would shun any overtures from Him in utter contempt and mockery. But praise God, for every believer, they know that the Shepherd found each of us, lost and desperate to find our real home. And, like the prodigal in Jesus' parable, when we turned to come back,

11

our loving Father was there to enfold us into His arms as we were clothed with a robe of righteousness and sealed with His Holy Spirit.

It was meet that we should make merry, and be glad: for this thy brother was dead, and is alive again; and was lost, and is found (Luke 15:32).

♦ Our Lord is the literal road which a sinner must take if he is to reach heaven, and Jesus thus becomes the method by which he is saved.
-Kenneth S. Wuest
(GN, pg. 89)

♦ Evangelical repentance is a change of willing, of feeling, *and of life, in respect to God.* Repentance always implies abhorrence of sin. It is willing and feeling as God does in respect to sin. It of course involves the love of God, and an abhorrence of sin.
-Charles Finney
(LRR, pg. 349)

♦ God never speaks to His people of sin except with the purpose of saving them from it. The same light that shows the sin will show the way out of it. The same power that condemns will give the power to rise up and conquer.
-Andrew Murray
(AP, Mar. 18)

♦ You can never cleanse sin; you can never purify sin; you can never be strong if in sin; you will never have a vision while in sin. Revelation stops when sin comes in. The human spirit must come to an end, but the Spirit of Christ must be alive and active.
-Smith Wigglesworth
(SWD, Feb. 3)

♦ He hated wickedness, so much that He bled to wound it to the heart; He died that it might die; He was buried that He might bury it in His tomb; and He rose that He might for ever trample it beneath His feet.
-Charles Spurgeon
(MES, May. 29 (M))

♦ Who by His death saves from the *penalty of sin*—by His resurrection, saves us from the *power* of sin and Who at His coming, will save us from the entire *presence* of sin.

-Herbert Lockyer Sr.
(DP, pg. 508)

♦ God's eternity and man's mortality join to persuade us that faith in Jesus Christ is not optional. For every man it must be Christ or eternal tragedy. Out of eternity our Lord came into time to rescue His human brethren whose moral folly had made them not only fools of the passing world but slaves of sin and death as well.

-A. W. Tozer
(KH, pg. 42)

***

Return, O wanderer, now return,
    And seek thy Father's face;
Those new desires which in thee burn
    Were kindled by His grace.

Return, O wanderer, now return,
    And wipe the falling tear:
Thy Father calls,--no longer mourn;
    'Tis love invites thee near.

-William Benco Collyer
1782-1854
(KH, pg. 96)

And he arose, and came to his father. But when he was yet a great way off, his father saw him, and had compassion, and ran, and fell on his neck, and kissed him (Luke 15:20).

♦ We can never come to any growth in the knowledge of God until we are ready to admit that we personally deserve the wrath of God...We do not believe that any human being is truly saved until he has seen that truth in all its stark and naked reality.

-Donald Grey Barnhouse
(IW, pg. 117)

13

♦ Education and culture are not enough; you must be born again.
-R. A. Torrey
(PWH, pg. 102)

♦ There never was and never will be any one saved by any thing but truth as the means. Truth is the outward means the outward motive, presented first by man and then by the Holy Spirit.
-Charles Finney
(LRR, pg.167)

♦ Put your faith in the Lord Jesus as your personal Saviour, and you will find that God the Father chose you to salvation, God the Holy Spirit brought you to the act of faith, and the Son cleansed you from sin in His precious blood.
-Kenneth Wuest
(BNT, pg. 23)

♦ What is salvation? It is the breaking in of divine light. The veiling of that light meant perdition.
-Watchman Nee
(WN, Dec. 15)

♦ It is salvation in Christ, or it is no salvation at all.
-R. A. Torrey
(RA, pg. 93)

♦ Salvation is not something we achieve, it is something we receive.
-Unknown
(BB)

♦ We shall yet with joy draw water out of the wells of salvation, though now for a season we have to pass by the noxious streams of sin and sorrow.
-Charles Spurgeon
(MES, May 31 (M))

♦ "Man, know thyself," is a wise *aphorism, but to know God as *our* God is truer wisdom for man cannot know himself aright until he knows God as Savior.

-Herbert Lockyer Sr.
(DP, pg. 371)

***

To see the great King of heaven stooping from his height, and condescending himself to offer terms of reconciliation to his rebellious creatures—

To see offended majesty courting the offenders to accept of pardon—

To see God persuading, entreating, and beseeching men to return to him with such earnestness and importunity as if his very life were bound up in them, and his own happiness depended on theirs—

To see the adorable Spirit of God, with infinite long-suffering and gentleness, submitting to the contempt and insults of such miserable, despicable wretches as sinful mortals are—Is not this amazing?

-Valentine Nalson
17th Century
(DP, pg. 481)

For the Son of man is not come destroy men's lives, but to save them. (Luke 9:56a).

♦ Many refuse salvation because they know they cannot continue to live in the same old ways; therefore, they do not invite Christ to their homes.

-Smith Wigglesworth
(SWD, May 17)

♦ Facts, real or supposed, should be used to show the truth. Truths not illustrated, are generally just as well calculated to convert sinners as a mathematical demonstration.

-Charles Finney
(LRR, pg.199)

♦ Jesus tells us, "Repent or perish." There is no salvation without repentance. R. A. Torrey said this about repentance, "The Greek word for repentance means "an afterthought" or "change of mind." To repent, then, means to change your mind. But change your mind about what? About three things: about God, about Jesus Christ, and about sin. (PWH, pg. 204)

♦ Without Christ you are like a sheep without its shepherd; like a tree without water at its roots; like a *sere leaf in the tempest—not bound to the tree of life.

-Charles Spurgeon
(MES, Jan. 19 (M))

Are You Born Again?

"Except a man be born again, he cannot see the kingdom of heaven." This was Jesus statement to the inquiring Nicodemus. The Pharisee recognized that Jesus was from God, but would he be able to accept Jesus' explanation of what it would mean for him to be received in the kingdom of God.

Jesus related the spiritual birth to the natural birth. In the natural birth we are born into the present world, but we have been born into the fallen Adamic race. In the present fallen state of sin, each of us stand with a death sentence over us, condemned to die in our miserable state of separation from God.

As a result, God provided the solution through the death, burial, and resurrection of His Son. By receiving Christ we will be born again. However, we must become identified in His death. This means we will be dead to the influences of the "old sinful, selfish" disposition in us, for it was left in the grave. However, because of the power of God we will be given resurrection power that will rise up in us a new man, by the Spirit of God. The life in this new man is the life of Christ which is eternal and abundant. As this new man is formed in us by the Spirit, we will begin to manifest the glory of this new life to those around us.

It is vital that we discern whether we are displaying this new life in us. Here is a quick summary of how this life will manifest itself. This information was acquired from a Bible that belongs to my friend, Betty Allen:

1. New awareness of right and wrong. (John 16:8-11; Romans 7)
2. Hunger for God's Word. (Job 23:12; Jeremiah 15:16; Hebrews 5:7)
3. Desire new life. (2 Corinthians 5:17)
4. Increase in being tested. (Luke 6:22; Timothy 3:12)
5. Fellowship and Love (1 John 4:7-13)
6. Desire to share Christ with others (Psalm 107:2; 1 Peter 3:15)

Jesus answered and said unto him, Verily, verily, I say unto thee, Except a man be born again, he cannot see the kingdom of God (John 3:3).

♦ To be our Savior, Jesus had to be *fully* God and *fully* man, not a hybrid composed of half of each.

-Dave Hunt

♦ It was the searchlight, or the floodlight of God, so to speak, playing upon that dreary and obscure spot of the great world which God so loved that He sent His only Begotten Son to redeem it.

-F. Ellsworth Powell
(KG, pgs. 6, 7)

♦ Admire the grace which saves thee—the mercy which spares thee—the love which pardons thee!

-Charles Spurgeon
(MES, Jun. 16 (E))

♦ *Salvation!* What music sweeter than the music of a thousand worlds is in this word! But for the *wicked*, there can be nothing but condemnation all the time they fail to seek the Savior, the statutes reveal.

-Herbert Lockyer Sr.
(DP, pg. 603)

♦ To be saved by the power of God is to be brought from the realm of the ordinary into the extraordinary, from the natural into the divine.

-Smith Wigglesworth
(SWD, Feb. 8)

♦ But however contrary to the doctrines of the Church of England, yet our pulpits ring of nothing more than doing no one any harm, living honestly, loving your neighbor as yourselves, and do what you can, and then Christ is to make up the deficiency; this is making Christ to be half a savior, and man the other part.

-George Whitefield
(GW, pg. 61)

♦ Ordinarily, there are three agents employed in the work of conversion, and one instrument. The agents are God,--some person who brings the truth to bear on the mind, --and the sinner himself. The instrument is the truth. There are *always two* agents, God and the sinner, employed and active in every case of genuine conversion.

-Charles Finney
(LRR, pg.18)

***

Did Christ o'er sinners weep
    And should our cheeks be dry?
Let tears of penitential grief
    Flow forth from every eye.
He shed those tears for me
    And His atoning blood,
And shall I fail to weep for those
    Who're wandering far from God?

-Selected

Then said Jesus, Father, forgive them; for they know not what they do. And they parted his raiment, and cast lots (Luke 23:34).

♦ The presence of Jesus is the assurance of eternal salvation, because He lives, we shall live also.

-Charles Spurgeon
(MES, Sept. 18 (E))

♦ ...a Christian eternal life begins, not on the day a man enters heaven, but on the day eternal life enters into the man through the new birth.

-Donald Grey Barnhouse
(IW, pg. 39)

♦ He chose the most unlikely material He could find. He gets more glory to Himself by choosing red clay into which He has breathed the breath of lives and conforming that inferior material into the very image of His Son than if He had taken hold of angels for salvation.

-Kenneth Wuest
(BNT, pg. 101)

♦ And in this *chequered work we are brought to an establishment of these four things; so that we are witnesses for God and His truth, in that we are sinners of the deepest dye, destitute of all power in ourselves or in others, that there is salvation in no other name under heaven but in Jesus Christ, and that He is our only able, willing, and all-sufficient Saviour.

-John Rusk
(FT, pg. 81)

Prayer: O Lord, we pray, that these sinners may be solemn, that they may have a deep sense of their sinfulness, that they may go home impressed with their lost condition, that they may attempt nothing in their own strength, that they may not lose their convictions and that, in thine own time and way, they may be brought out into the glorious light and liberty of the sons of God.

-Charles Finney
(LRR, pg. 340)

♦ The inquirer is not to seek sorrow, but the Savior.

-D. L. Moody

♦ We are saved by an incorruptible power—a process always refining, a grace always enlarging, a glory always increasing.

-Smith Wigglesworth
(SWD, May 21)

♦ But men are to be converted, not by physical force, or by a change wrought in their nature or constitution by creative power, but by the truth made effectual by the Holy Spirit. Conversion is yielding to the truth.

-Charles Finney
(LRR, pg. 318)

♦ The grace which does not make a man better than others is a worthless counterfeit. Christ saved His people, not in their sins, but from them.

-Charles Spurgeon
(MES, Feb. 8 (E))

***

To Save the World

How can we save a dying world?
    That problem has been solved Above:
The key is found in Calvary,
    The only way is LOVE!

-Mrs. Booth-Clibborn

For God so loved the world, that he gave his only begotten Son, that whosoever believeth in him should not perish, but have everlasting life (John 3:16).

♦ Salvation by the works of the law is a frail and broken vessel whose shipwreck is sure; but the covenant vessel fears no storms, for the blood ensures the whole. The blood of Jesus made His testament valid.

-Charles Spurgeon
(MES, Nov. 6 (E))

♦ God's salvation is an oversize salvation. It is shock proof, strain proof, unbreakable, all sufficient. It is equal to every emergency, for it flows from the heart of an infinite God, freely bestowed and righteously given through the all-sufficient sacrifice of our Lord on the Cross.

-Kenneth S. Wuest
(GN, pg. 82)

♦ The subject of holiness will not bring salvation, *but rather true salvation will result in the work of holiness.*

-RJK

♦ A man cannot come to Christ and retain sin. You have to choose between Jesus Christ and sin.

-R. A. Torrey
(RA, pg. 185)

♦ If God should attempt to relieve sinners, and save them without humbling their pride and turning them from their sins, he could not do it.

-Charles Finney
(LRR, pg. 318)

♦ God's love for a lost race was called out of His heart by the preciousness of each lost soul, precious because He finds in that lost soul His own image, though that image is marred by sin, and precious, because that lost soul is made of material that God through salvation can transform into the very image of Christ.

-Kenneth S. Wuest
(GTL, pg. 66)

♦ Jesus knew that when He came to the end of the Cross, He would forever save all those who would believe.

-Smith Wigglesworth
(SWD, (TFT) Oct. 23)

♦ My sins were scourges which lacerated those blessed shoulders, and crowned with thorn those bleeding brows; my sins cried "Crucify Him! Crucify Him!" and laid the cross upon His gracious shoulders.

-Charles Spurgeon
(MES, Apr. 9 (M))

***

Have I an object, Lord, below
Which would divide my heart with Thee?
Which would divert its even flow
In answer to Thy constancy?
O Teach me quickly to return,
And cause my heart afresh to burn.

Have I a hope, however dear,
Which would defer Thy coming, Lord—
Which would detain my spirit here
Where naught can lasting joy afford?
From it, my Savior, set me free
To look and long and wait for Thee.

Be Thou the object bright and fair
To fill and satisfy the heart,
My hope to meet Thee in the air,
And nevermore from Thee to part;
That I may undistracted be
To follow, serve, and wait for Thee.

-G. W. Frazer
(1840-1896)
(SOA, pg. 56)

If the Son therefore shall make you free, ye shall be free indeed (John 8:36).

♦ ...let not the business of the world make you unmindful of your souls; but in all your moral actions, in the business of life, let all be done with a view to the glory of God, and the salvation of your souls.

-George Whitefield
(GW, pg. 67)

♦ Shall we be satisfied with being saved ourselves, if we are not concerned about the perishing around us?

-Selected

♦ Arguments will never save souls.

-Unknown

♦ No nation can die while there are true hearts ready to be put out like a puff of vapor for its salvation.

-Herbert Lockyer, Sr.
(DP, pg. 383)

♦ Regeneration is a subject which lies at the very basis of salvation, and we should be very diligent to take heed that we really are "born again," for there are many who fancy they are, who are not.

-Charles Spurgeon
(MES, Mar. 6 (M))

A Crown for the Occasion

I recently discover that there are two words translated in the Greek for the word, "crown." There is "diadema" in which we get our word, "diadem" and "stephanos." Diadema referred to a blue band of ribbon marked with white, which the Persian kings used to bind on a turban or tiara, pointing to royalty.

Stephanos points to a different type of crown. It is described as a victor's crown that was obtained in some type of victory. For example, a stephanos would be awarded to those who participated in the first Olympics. (BNT, pg. 62)

Jesus will have won two crowns. A stephanos came in the form of a crown of thorns. Even though it was crude, it pointed to the victory of the cross. But, when He comes back He will be wearing the crown of royalty. It will declare Him to be the King of kings and the Lord of lords.

As Christians, we will receive crowns. However, to receive the diadema of God's kingdom, we must first obtain the stephanos, the crown of victory. This requires us to be overcomers in this present world. Although we will cast all crowns at our Lord's feet, we must realize that each crown identifies us to the work of Christ's redemption and His Spirit. It is by His Spirit we will acquire the stephanos, but when we pass from this world to the next we will receive the diadema that has been established by His redemption and identifies us to His kingdom and our inheritance: that of eternal life.

Henceforth there is laid up for me a crown of righteousness, which the Lord, the righteous judge, shall give me at that day: and not to me only, but unto all them that love his appearing (2 Timothy 4:8).

♦ Do you care? We feel for them, but feelings will not save souls; it cost God Calvary to win us.
-Unknown

♦ The sinner must come to Jesus, not to works, ordinances, or doctrines, but to a personal Redeemer, who His own self bare our sins in His own body on the tree.
-Charles Spurgeon
(MES, Dec. 31 (M))

♦ If we are to walk as He walked, **(1 Jn. 2:6)**, then our hearts must willingly follow Him along the dusty roads of suffering humanity; through the valleys of humiliation and persecution; up the steep, barren, and rocky slopes of temptation; across stormy seas of loneliness and frustration; into the hypocrisy and judgmentalism of the religious systems; into the bizarre world of the demon-possessed; up mountain heights of fleeting moments of ecstasy and revelation; through the dark night of the soul in the Garden of Gethsemane; into the tormenting hands of lost men, and finally up a hill called Calvary. But, remember, the promise is eternal life!
-Jeannette Haley

♦ Human life has an end; divine life has only a beginning.
-Smith Wigglesworth
(SWD, (TFT) Apr. 8)

***

Escape for thy life;
Look not behind thee,
Neither stay thou in all the plain;
Escape to the mountain,
Lest thou be consumed.

-Charles Spurgeon
(MES, Dec. 31 (E))

And to wait for his Son from heaven, whom he raised from the dead, even Jesus, which delivered us from the wrath to come (1 Thessalonians 1:10).

♦ While you aim at great things for the Lord, yet keep in view the arithmetic of heaven's exultant joy—"joy over ONE sinner that repenteth."

-Weibrecht

♦ It is soap, soup, and then salvation. The man is easier to reach if his physical needs are cared for, and his mind and heart are at rest.

-Kenneth S. Wuest
(GTL, pg. 120)

♦ And thus all through the sacred writings are we to understand Jesus Christ as the God-man, two natures in one Person. As man, He suffered; as God, he merited; and His divinity stamps an eternal dignity and eternal merit on all His sufferings for us men and our salvation.

-John Rusk
(FT, pg. 84)

♦ There is many a man who thinks that perhaps it may be a foolish thing not to accept Christ, and admit the folly of it, but he has never realized the guilt of it.

-R. A. Torrey
(RA, pg. 90)

The Vision

The wisest man in the Old Testament, Solomon, stated that people without any vision will perish. In the past I have meditated on such a notion. What does it mean to have a vision? After all, we have been gifted with the ability to see in some way. Therefore, to have a vision is not a matter of being able to necessarily see with the eye. It entails something that will see into the spiritual realm.

For a person to have a valid vision, certain criteria must be present. The first criterion is that it must come from above: it must come from God. If a vision does not cause one to look upward to receive a greater revelation in regard to the reality and matters of the kingdom of God, then it must be deemed untrustworthy.

The second criterion is that it must be bigger than self. So much of people's perspective never gets past the small arenas of self and this present world. Such vision is bound to the physical, indifferent to the spiritual, and captive to the fleshly.

The third criterion is that it will cause a sense of responsibility and urgency. We must do something with what we see. It will change the direction of our passion, transform us in our thinking, and convert us towards a new agenda and emphasis.

The fourth and final criterion is that it must be in line with the Holy Spirit and His Word. Visions from above will be inspired by heaven but must be confirmed by His Word. If it does not maintain the character of God and the intent of His Word it must be discarded.

I have had a few visions but the one that stands out the most to me I received while sitting in a church pew during a funeral. Before me were two caskets, and in them were the lifeless bodies of a young married couple. The woman was in the last year of her teens and the man was in his early 20s. Their lives had been cut short by a motorcycle accident.

I had worked with the young woman in her earlier teenage years. She was very rough around the edges and her coarse language verified the fact that her environment and lifestyle was void of any reality of God. She would habitually use Jesus' name like it was a common word that had no real significance except as a slang

26

expression followed by or integrated in her animated opinions and feelings.

After a few days of listening to her trash my Lord's name, I made statement that I had heard in the past, "He has nothing to do with it!" The first time I made my declaration, she stopped with a shock look on her face. From that point on when she used Jesus' name, she was met with the same statement.

Through the unusual exchange we developed a relationship. She grew to respect me and I grew to like her. We had a mutual understanding between us that was chiseled in silence, but made obvious by how she disciplined her tongue around me.

Eventually, our paths parted and even though we lived in a small community they only crossed a couple of times within a matter of three years. The first time I encountered her I was busy working, and she happily came up to me to say hello. To my disappointment I could see she was drunk. She was a happy drunk and displayed great excitement in seeing me. Once again in her excitement, she used the name of Jesus. As before, I reminded her that He had nothing to do with it.

My statement immediately seemed to produce a sobriety in her. She looked at me with such a genuine apologetic countenance and said, "Rayola, I am so sorry, I know He is your friend."

The second time was when I was walking down the sidewalk in our small town. She was coming in the opposite direction. I had heard that she had become pregnant and that she and her boyfriend had married. As we came face to face, I could see she bore the weight of the world on her shoulders. It was obvious that there were problems in her life and that because of them the strength of her youth was giving way to that which was causing her to become old before her time.

Since I was on company time the most I could do was exchange typical greetings of, "Hi, how are you." Like many individuals, she lied a bit when she said she was okay. However, I could tell by her countenance that she felt lost or even trapped in a whirlwind of uncertainty and hopelessness.

Sitting in the church pew, my encounters with her played themselves out on the screen of my mind. It is at those times the regrets of "if only" can consume a person. Granted, I had shared my testimony with those I worked with, which included her, but I never really sat down and talked to her personally about Christ. "If only" I had taken the time to talk to her the day I met her on the sidewalk.

The "if only" are speculations of "what could have been", but the truth is that it was "what it was." We cannot turn back the clock in terms of speculating about possible lost opportunities. As I looked upon the shell of what represented her life, I had to honestly face what is, knowing nothing will change the present reality.

It was at that time a deep, silent cry raised up like a phoenix out the depths of my soul. "Oh God, is she in hell?" A vision immediately swept across the screen of my mind, gripping my soul with *exigency. I saw the broad path that led to hell. I could see people coming from many directions and emerging onto the wide road. It was obvious they were blinded to the chasm they were walking towards. I had a grave sense that I knew some of the people on the path. As the different people stepped off the edge of the path into utter darkness, I could see the flames reach up and pull each one into the depth of the abyss, and it was at that time I heard their screams.

I discerned that God was not showing me whether she was in hell or not. The pastor told how her husband who had a Christian background had attended an evangelistic meeting that very night. He was in despair about his life and family, for he and his wife had separated. When an altar call was made he went forward to recommit his life to the Lord.

That same night the young man had called his estranged wife to get their family back together. They were on their way to pick up their son when they both entered into eternity. No one knows what transpired between the young couple in the time they were together. Perhaps, he shared Christ with her and a memory from the past of another time when the name of Jesus ceased to be a byword and finally was attached to a Man who could bring hope, life, reconciliation. Perhaps restoration became her personal reality. Only eternity will make such mysteries known.

Meanwhile, I sat in the pew with a vision that could not be shaken. The Lord was showing me the urgency of my commission. I could not be casual about it for souls were indeed on the line. Another cry came from the depths of my being, "Lord, do not let anyone pass me by that wants to hear your message of salvation."

I have long learned that the reality of hell will not keep the unbeliever out of its grasp any more than the promise of heaven will keep a believer on the narrow path. Granted, both hell and heaven are a reality. One is the reality of damnation and the other one is the revelation of life. What will keep a sinner from going to hell is the revelation and conviction of being lost and the promise of life that is found in Christ Jesus. The only way a believer will continue on the narrow path is because he or she loves the Lord Jesus.

Hell is not an incentive to be saved and heaven in not the sustaining motivation to stay the course of righteousness. It is all about relationship with God, coming to place of reconciliation because nothing else makes sense. It is about knowing that one must be prepared to face eternity and it is only in and through Jesus Christ, that one can be ensured of possessing the blissful promise of eternal life that will be lived out in the presence of His unending glory.

And fear not them which kill the body, but are not able to kill the soul; but rather fear him which is able to destroy both soul and body in hell (Matthew 10:28).

THE ATTRIBUTES AND WAYS OF GOD

The Friend of the Wounded

Jesus is clear about how sin wounds each of us. It has made us poor in spirit and barren in our souls. It has broken our hearts with the spears of hatred and the darts of rejection. It has taken each of us captive with the chains of condemnation and put us behind bars of hopelessness. It has caused us to live in utter darkness, creating blindness that only the healing light of heaven can penetrate. And, it has bruised our inner being in such a way that we are left in despair, sorrow, and agony.

When we think of the ways of sin, we cannot help but realize the conflict it causes in our souls and within relationships in the home, society, nation, and world. The wills of people collide because of sin while factions of society war against each other in total lawlessness, and nations stage a "cat and mouse" game to arrogantly and cleverly entrap and subdue one another.

Where can people who, wounded by a world gone mad with sin, find healing and resolution for the unseen and visible scars? A man by the name of James Check discovered the answer to the matter while in France during the throes of WW1.

Doubt and disdain, those were the predominant feelings of George Casey, in respect to the rumors of the "Comrade in White", said to have helped wounded soldiers, even in the midst of gunfire, at places such as Nancy, Argonne, Soissons, and Ypres. When his friend, George Casey had asked him if he had seen the Friend of the Wounded, he could only give him a queer look.

The next day during a battle, Check was shot through both legs. By God's mercy he fainted and fell into some sort of hole, hiding him from the eyes of the Germans. Even though he was in great pain, he dared not move or make a sound and give himself away to the enemy. He waited for night to fall, knowing that there were a company of men who would run any risk in the darkness to locate and save a wounded comrade.

Night came and Check did hear a step, but it did not sound like what he would expect from those seeking out the wounded. It was quiet and firm, as if neither darkness nor death could check those unhindered feet.

The figure that he saw coming towards him shimmered of white in the darkness. As his mind tried to grasp what he was seeing, he guessed that it was the Comrade in White. At that moment the German rifle-fire began. There was no way that the bullets would ever miss such an easy target, but the Comrade in White flung out his arms as though in entreaty. He spoke, but Check could only remember the beginning and the ending of what He was saying, The beginning was "If thou hadst known" –and the ending was, "but now they are hid from Thine eyes."

Check fainted again and when he came to, he found he was in a cave by a stream, and the Comrade in White was tending to his wounds. Even though Check was in great pain, he experienced great happiness in the presence of this compassionate comrade. He was aware that as long as the hand touched him and the eyes of the comrade showed pity, Check found contentment and did not care about the matters of life or death.

Check noticed that there was a wound in the comrade's hand. The Comrade's wound seemed to be more awful than any that the bitter war could inflict. "You are wounded, too," Check said faintly.

The comrade gently replied that it was an old wound, but it was troubling Him of late. Check also noticed that the same cruel mark was on His feet. It was only then that he knew who the Comrade in White was: The living Christ!

In the passionate foolishness of his youth, Check had put Christ out of his life. Now in his plight he longed to speak to Him and thank

Him, but no words came. Then the Lord spoke to him, "Lie here today by the water. I will come for you tomorrow. I have work for you to do and you will do it for Me." (ISL, pgs. 30-32)

The Lord is closer to us than our very breath. He desires to walk with us, but sadly for most of us it is only after the battles of life bring us down is He able to come to us as the One who needs to become our "Comrade." To allow Christ to become such a comrade, we must be cut off at the legs of self-sufficiency and brought low to the ditch of hopelessness. As the Comrade in White stated, "If only the unbelieving and the skeptic knew who He was and what He had in store for those who will but believe."

At the end of "if onlys" is the vast reality of people who are blinded by the god of this world. They are in darkness and all their attempts to wipe out the light of truth and hope will prove to be in vain. For some it takes life and death matters to take the veil from their eyes so that they can see the reality of God, so they can see His heart and what He desires to do for each of us in our desperate plight.

The Spirit of the Lord is upon me, because he hath anointed me to preach the gospel to the poor; he hath sent me to heal the brokenhearted, to preach deliverance to the captives, and recovering of sight to the blind, to set at liberty them that are bruised, To preach the acceptable year of the Lord (Luke 4:18-19).

♦ Jesus' ministry is one of reconciliation, not one that majors in religious knowledge, activities, or experiences.

-RJK

♦ Because God is sovereign, and we are not, do not expect "predictability" to be the norm in the ministry.

-Jeannette Haley

♦ God in His wisdom plans the test, and limits the temptation. God in His love sends the test, and permits the temptation. God in His grace meets the test, and overcome the temptation.

-Kenneth S. Wuest
(GN, pg. 17)

♦ Communion with Jesus is a richer gem than ever glittered in imperial diadem. Union with the Lord is a coronet of beauty outshining all the blaze of imperial pomp.

-Charles Spurgeon
(MES, Jul. 26 (E))

♦ Mystical visions should not be sought. God's method is not mystical, but He communicates with us through mind and spirit. It is perilously easy to engage in self-hypnotism.

-J. Oswald Sanders
(POG, pg. 99)

♦ Supernatural phenomena were given at the discretion of the divine wisdom. It is not for us to ask that God will guide us in some miraculous way. If, in His wisdom, He knows that such means are what we need, He will surely give them.

-Elisabeth Elliot
(POG, pg. 99)

♦ The *Father's* name is *great,* for He is our Source, the Creator of all; the *Son's* name is *terrible,* for He is to be our Judge; and the name of the *Holy Spirit* is *holy,* for He it is Who bestows sanctification. But these three adjectives, *great, terrible,* and *holy,* portray different aspects of the Divine character, whether terrible or tender, pardoning or punishing.

-Herbert Lockyer Sr.
(DP, pg. 364)

♦ Modesty may demure at so rash a thought, but audacious faith dares to believe the Word and claim friendship with God. We do God more honor by believing what He has said about Himself and having the courage to come boldly to the throne of grace than by hiding in self-conscious humility among the trees of the garden.

-A. W. Tozer
(KH, pg. 100)

♦ As our Maker, we should kneel adoringly before Him, bowing to His will in our lives. If He purposes that we suffer for a season, we bow to that in reverence.

-Bob Sorge
(FDA, pg. 35)

♦ God's order is always: first, His Word; second, belief in His Word; third, experience or feeling.

-R. A. Torrey
(PWH, pg. 228)

♦ It is not the design of preaching, to make men easy and quiet, but to make them ACT.

-Charles Finney
(LRR, pg.190)

♦ What is unequivocal in God's wisdom becomes ambiguous to man's intelligence.

-Abraham J. Heschel
(TP, pg. 225)

♦ The Lord will not accept crumbs, leftovers, or tainted, compromising worship or service. He is God, and He is the one who determines the character and truth as to what He will accept from mere man.

-RJK

♦ If you expect any revelation of God apart from holiness, you will have only a mixture. Holiness opens the door to all the treasures of God.

-Smith Wigglesworth
(SWD, May 30)

♦ Facts are the finger of God.

-J. Oswald Sanders
(POG, pg. 130)

♦ Humility is so essential to the right state of our souls that one cannot live a reasonable or pious life without it.

-William Law
(DHL, pg. 192)

♦ Jesus' College is the only one in which God's truth can be really learned; other schools may teach us what is to be believed, but Christ's alone can show us how to believe it.

-Charles Spurgeon
(MES, Jan. 19 (E))

***

If Thou shouldst call me to resign
What most I prize, it ne'er was mine,
I only yield Thee what was Thine:
Thy will be done!

-Charlotte Elliott
(SOA, pg. 57)

Jesus saith unto them, My meat is to do the will of him that sent me, and to finish his work (John 4:34).

♦ God is able to change the foulest sinner into the purist saint.

-Jeannette Haley

♦ If there be no defect in his being, there can be none in his working; if his nature be pure holiness, all his way must be perfect faithfulness.

-John Flavel
(RR, pg. 110)

♦ God didn't do anything new in Job, He just did something very deep in him...Satan wants your pain to get you offended at God; God wants your pain to press you into His face with a fervency that will produce change in you.

-Bob Sorge
(FDA, pg.42, 43)

♦ Jesus did not propound a set of laws for His people to follow. He gave them great moral and spiritual principles that they would have to apply themselves to the circumstances of life.

-J. Oswald Sanders
(POG, pg. 42)

♦ An idea or a theory of God can easily become a substitute for God, impressive to the mind when God as a living reality is absent from the soul.

-Abraham J. Heschel
(TP, pg. 286)

♦ The hardest circumstances are just lifting places into the grace of God.

-Smith Wigglesworth
(SWD, (TFT) Feb. 28)

♦ Your piety is worthless unless it leads you to wish that the same mercy which has been extended to you may bless the whole world.

-Charles Spurgeon
(MES, Aug. 6 (E))

Prayer: Do good in thy good pleasure unto us, O Lord. Act towards us not as we deserved but as it becomes Thee, being the God Thou art. So shall we have nothing to fear in this world or in that which is to come. Amen.

-A. W. Tozer
(KH, pg. 82)

♦ This is the advice that J. Oswald Sanders was given by his father, "When you are seeking guidance, there are three words that are important. The first is *wait!* The second is *wait!* The third is *wait!* Sanders goes on to say, "Don't allow anyone to pressure you into action when you are not sure." (POG, pg. 140)

♦ All the powers of the soul are strengthened by exercise...If the mind is not exercised, the brain will not grow, and the man will become an idiot. If the affections are not exercised he will become a stoic.

-Charles Finney
(LRR, pg. 381)

♦ Some of the promises God made go back to the first man He created, but they are not worn out by millenniums of use, for Divine faithfulness in the fulfillment of promises endured forever.

-Herbert Lockyer Sr.
(DP, pg. 573)

♦ Grace takes its rise far back in the heart of God, in the awful and incomprehensible abyss of His being; but the channel through which it flows out to men is Jesus Christ, crucified and risen.

-A. W. Tozer
(KH, pg. 93)

♦ The great promise of the Father until the coming of Christ was the coming atoning Savior and King. When Jesus came and died His atoning death upon the cross of Calvary and arose and ascended to the right hand of the Father, then the second great promise of the Father was the Holy Spirit, to take the place of our absent Lord.

-R. A. Torrey
(PWH, pg. 56)

♦ Sometimes God imprisons His servants in a prison of obedience so that they have a platform to speak into the lives of those in a prison of disobedience.

-Bob Sorge
(FDA, pg.52)

♦ The circumstances surrounding our lives are not accidental but are devised by an all-wise and loving Father, who knows how best we can glorify Him and yet at the same time achieve our own highest good. When this becomes a conviction, believed and accepted, then every part of life becomes significant, and life itself becomes one long voyage of discovery of God and our own true selves.

-J. Oswald Sanders
(POG, pg. 11)

♦ Mercy and Truth are often joined together in Scripture to prove that the Lord reveals Himself to His people not only in mercy but truth also. His mercy is bounded by His truth, so that none may either presume Him more merciful than His truth or word declared, and also that none may despair because of their great sins that His mercy is not *gratis, according to the truth of His promise.

-Herbert Lockyer Sr.
(DP, pg. 515)

♦ Only glass can reflect God's light without distortion. For sand to become glass, it must be processed by fire. Revelation exposes us to the light and fire of God.

-Manfred Haller
(CA, pg. 26)

♦ God's grace is that matchless, wonderful, marvelous, act on His part when He out of the spontaneous infinite love of His heart steps down from His judgment throne in heaven to take upon Himself the guilt of our sin and the penalty which is justly ours, doing this not for His friends but for His enemies.

-Kenneth S. Wuest
(GN, pg. 81)

♦ Tribulation produces perseverance" – to those who respond properly to tribulation that is. It is incredibly tempting to give up when the pressure is on, but God designs that we persevere in the midst of the pressure. This is where the fire is. The heat is turned up when the pressure doesn't abate, and we're called of God to persevere. It's unabated heat and pressure, and it's the stuff of which diamonds are made.

-Bob Sorge
(FDA, pg. 59)

♦ God's purpose is not to turn out facsimiles, but to develop and mature the unique personality of each of His children. He wants you to be you, not someone else—but a much better you, of course.

-J. Oswald Sanders
(POG, pg. 12)

His Workmanship

Man is forever trying to figure out God. However, the Bible is clear that we can know His ways, but we cannot know His mind. It is clear that we can discover Him in the patterns established through His Word, but we cannot comprehend the depths of His work and the heights of His glory. We are indeed limited by what we can know in our finite state, unable to see clearly in our flesh, and incapable or always hearing because of our fickle (fallen) condition. The Apostle Paul summarized our condition in this way, "But as it is written, Eye hath not seen, nor ear heard, neither have entered into the heart of man, the things which God hath prepared for them that love him" (*1 Corinthians 2:9*).

The Bible is also clear that God has one purpose in mind, to conform us to the image of His Son (*Romans 8:29*). Depending on who we are, we will reflect that image in different ways, but nevertheless, people will be able to distinguish that it is His life, His reflection, and His glory that they are encountering and witnessing.

In the first part of this book, I wrote a poem about how the Lord is a master craftsman in all that He does. There is no variance in His ways and no deviation in His accomplishments. However, man has a tendency to either judge, downplay, criticize, or explain away the works of God. This is especially true when it comes to the work He does in others. In essence, we end up trying to play the Holy Spirit in other people' lives.

Admittedly, I have judged the work He has done in others. My judgment was based on the board of self-righteousness that rested comfortably in the center of my eye (*Matthew 7:1-5*). In my mind if a person did not see a matter the way I saw it, preached the personal cause I was preaching at the time, and choosing the particular band wagon that I was riding high on, I judged them as inferior or just plain wrong.

The Lord was merciful to pull out the board in my eye so that I could see how far away from the mark of His ways I had veered in my self-righteousness. Needless to say, it was a humbling time for me, but it also worked in me compassion. Compassion is able to turn into a ministry of consolation. Ultimately, it comes from a state of empathy that has become active in compassion. Compassion enters in and truly becomes identified with the place or position which another finds himself or herself in his or her own life. However, compassion usually comes off the heels of humility and suffering.

Since that time, I have learned that God takes each of us down different paths. He also uses different tools to work the very life, attitude, ways, and glory of His Son in our life. Since He deals with us individually, we must not take liberty to judge how He is working the life of His Son in others. Such judgment could in turn be meted out to us (*Luke 6:38*). For example, as a great artist, the Lord might be using a paintbrush on you, but He might be using a chisel on someone else. You do not have a right to judge the other person because God is using a chisel of conflict on him or her while He is presently using a paintbrush of persuasion on you.

It goes without saying that if He is using a chisel on you, but you see He is using the fiery ovens of affliction, a chainsaw of despair on others, or the indelible ink of illness on someone else, that you must not falsely judge the vessel as being inferior or wrong, or His work as being that of Satan and consequences for some deviation in character.

It is not up to us to judge in such ways. We are called to be ministers of His life which will clearly bring consolation, hope, spiritual healing, and deliverance to one's spirit and soul. Therefore, next time as believers, when we go to judge the work of God in another person, we need to stop and seek His perspective. Instead of identifying what we think is wrong with the present picture, we need to seek God's face to find out how to become an instrument of edification to the work that God is doing in the individual, thereby, becoming co-laborers with Him and ultimately bringing glory to Him.

For we are his workmanship, created in Christ Jesus unto good works, which God hath before ordained that we should walk in them (Ephesians 2:10).

♦ What praise should be ours for Him Who became the smitten Rock at Calvary, even Jesus, Who opened a fountain for sins and uncleanness!

-Herbert Lockyer, Sr.
(DP, pg. 341)

♦ He will lead you into nothingness, but when you are in nothingness, you will be in power. He will lead you into weakness, but when you are in weakness, God will be with you in might.

Everything that seems weak from a human perspective will be under the control of divine power.

-Smith Wigglesworth
(SWD, (TFT) Feb. 21)

♦ All Providences are doors to trial. Even our mercies, like roses have their thorns. Men may be drowned in seas of prosperity as well as in rivers of affliction. Our mountains are not too high, and our valleys are not too low for temptations: trials lurk on all roads.

-Charles Spurgeon
(MES, Sept. 3 (E))

♦ Often eager planners like myself have to wait. God's delays might have wonderful unseen factors that make the fulfillment all the more wonderful and complete. Often the very process of delay and disappointment help us to sift our motives and turn our eyes to the Lord in a way they were not when we first formulated our plans.

-Part of a letter from a missionary executive
(POG, pg. 141)

♦ The man who is the most fully taught of God is the very one who will be most ready to listen to what God has taught others.

-R. A. Torrey
(PWH, pg. 136)

♦ Personal suffering opens to us the portal of identifying with God in His great passion for mankind.

-Bob Sorge
(FDA, pg.72)

♦ If we desperately want to know what God is like, all we have to do is to look at Jesus. He is the perfect revelation of God's character and the perfect model for our emulation.

-J. Oswald Sanders
(POG, pg. 25)

♦ If we would have God on our side, we must take care to be on His side.

-Herbert Lockyer Sr.
(DP, pg. 521)

♦ Repentance, though necessary, is not meritorious but a condition for receiving the gracious gift of pardon which God gives of His goodness.

-A. W. Tozer
(KH, pg. 83)

♦ Being in favor with God implies, of course, that we are pardoned and favored by him, for the sake of our Lord and Saviour Jesus Christ. Pardon is favor, and implies the renunciation of rebellion against God.

-Charles Finney
(LRR, pg. 429)

♦ These four attributes are the robes God invests Himself with:
Justice defends His subjects, and acts in a right way towards every one.
Judgment restrains rebels, and preserves from injuries.
Mercy shows compassion, pardons, supports the weak.
Truth performs all that God has promised.

-Herbert Lockyer, Sr.
(DP, pg. 301)

♦ God's ability will not flourish without my availability.

-Unknown
(BB)

Prayer: "Oh Lord Jesus, search my heart. Help me to truly repent of all that is not of You. Restore my relationship with You and others. Lord, I want to know You in greater ways and walk with You in truth and righteousness. Thank You for the sword of Your Word which sets me free and cuts asunder the weights I need not carry! In Your Holy Name I pray. Amen."

♦ It is always helpful to us to fix our attention on the Godward aspect of Christian work; to realize that the work of God does not mean so much man's work for God, as God's own work through man.

-Hudson Taylor
(VCK, pg. 12)

♦ God doesn't lead us into the valley, however, to keep us there. His purpose is to refine us in the valley of delayed answers and then bring us forth into the sunlight of maturity and fruitfulness...You don't go out of the valley; you grow out of the valley.

-Bob Sorge
(FDA, pg.15)

♦ God leads, but He does not override the will of man. In guidance there will always be a need for our mental and spiritual exercise.

J. Oswald Sanders
(POG, pg. 46)

♦ God alone sees the heart—the heart alone sees God.

-Herbert Lockyer Sr.
(DP, pg. 543)

♦ God never works needless miracles; if His purposes can be accomplished by ordinary means. He will not use miraculous agency.

-Charles Spurgeon
(MES, Sept. 17 (E))

♦ God is not in a hurry. He cannot do things with us until we are trained and ready for them.

-James Fraser
(MR, pg. 102)

♦ Remember this: you never lose as much as when you lose your peace.

-Smith Wigglesworth
(SWD, (TFT) Aug. 3)

♦ One of the reasons we can't hear from God, when the darkness descends, is that God wants to re-train the way in which we hear from Him.

-Bob Sorge
(FDA, pg. 79)

♦ God's method of guiding His people varies with their degree of development.

-J. Oswald Sanders
(POG, pg. 62)

The Helpless Helped

The Lord takes up none but the FORSAKEN,
Makes none healthy but the SICK,
Gives sight to none but the BLIND,
Makes none alive but the DEAD,
Saves none but SINNERS.

-Unknown

Let your conversation be without covetousness; and be content with such things as ye have: for he hath said, I will never leave thee, nor forsake thee (Hebrews 13:5).

♦ The believing sinner's identification with Christ in His death, breaks the power of the indwelling sinful nature. His identification with the Lord Jesus in His resurrection imparts the divine nature.

-Kenneth S. Wuest
(GTL, pg. 82)

♦ Sometimes when our cherished plans are checkmated, it is not denial, only delay for some wise purpose.

-J. Oswald Sanders
(POG, pg. 142)

♦ Man inclines by striving: God inclines by effecting. Neither in that which man attempts, nor that which he by striving achieves goodwards, from the man, but from God, Who gives *both to will and to do of His good pleasure.*

-Herbert Lockyer Sr.
(DP, pg. 583)

♦ Holy mourning is the seed out of which the flower of eternal joy doth grow.

-St. Basil
(DP, pg. 649)

♦ God wants to break us of our self-reliance and produce in us a deep humility and profound dependence upon Him. In a word, it's called brokenness.

-Bob Sorge
(FDA, pg. 117)

♦ The lowest degree of grace is superior to the noblest development of unregenerate nature.

-Charles Spurgeon
(MES, Sept. 30 (E))

♦ Christ's scars remained after his resurrection as a reminder of his still-suffering body. For though he conquered death, his body on earth still suffers, and he can identify with those around the world who bear scars because of their faith in Christ.

Extreme Devotion
(ED, pg. 8)

♦ So many people want to do great things and to be seen doing them, but the one whom God will use is the one who is willing to be told what to do.

-Smith Wigglesworth
(SWD, Nov. 13)

♦ Sometimes God can teach us important spiritual lessons only by letting us have our own way.

-J. Oswald Sanders
(POG, pg. 150)

♦ You have not the making of your own cross, although unbelief is a master carpenter at cross-making; neither are you permitted to choose your own cross, although self-will would fain be lord and master; but your cross is prepared and appointed for you by divine love, and you are cheerfully to accept it; you are to take up the cross as your chosen badge and burden, and not to stand caviling at it.

> -Charles Spurgeon
> (MES, Feb. 23 (E))

♦ We cannot produce from this nature anything acceptable to God. All that can ever come to God is in Christ alone, not in us...that runs directly counter to the whole system of the teaching of humanism-the wonderful thing that man is.

> -T. Austin Sparks

♦ To praise God is the noblest employment of life, and one that glorifies Him.

> -Herbert Lockyer Sr.
> (DP, pg. 611)

♦ God reserves the greatest victories for the vessels that have known the greatest brokenness.

> -Bob Sorge
> (FDA, pg.121)

♦ Selfishness looks first at home, but godliness seeks first the kingdom of God and His righteousness, yet in the long run selfishness is loss and godliness is great gain.

> -Charles Spurgeon
> (MES, Oct. 26 (M))

♦ We read of the love of one disciple manifested to another disciple in a cup of cold water; but Christ hath manifested his love to thee, in pouring out his warmest heart-blood for thy redemption. Oh what a transcendent love is the divine love!

> -John Flavel
> (RR, pg. 180)

♦ As we journey through the wilderness of this world, there will be times when need is not immediately met, but we must not judge the Lord by His delays; but by His covenant-promises. Often "He *waits* that He may be gracious.

> -Herbert Lockyer, Sr.
> (DP, pg. 464)

♦ God is never tightfisted with any of His blessings.
-Smith Wigglesworth
(SWD, (TFT) Mar. 9)

♦ Thus, Divine forgiveness called "the smile of God," binds the forgiven one to Him in a reverential trust and love, commending His grace to others who are yet in their sin. Forgiveness does not lead to lax living, but to a godly fear, and to a life well-pleasing to Him Who is ever ready to forgive.
-Herbert Lockyer Sr.
(DP, pg. 670)

♦ Those who serve God must serve Him in His own way, and in His strength, or He will never accept their service.
-Charles Spurgeon
(MES, Nov. 4 (M))

♦ It seems to me that until God has mowed you down, you can never have longsuffering for others.
-Smith Wigglesworth
(SWD, (TFT) Nov. 16)

Hidden Provision

Servants of God often find that their journey is not as much about what they do for God, but what their circumstances allow God to do in them and for them. As missionaries, Jeannette and I have had to learn what it means to walk by faith. It is like walking towards a barren wilderness. From all experience there is no real expectation to survive it unless God clearly intercedes.

The only way one can walk towards what appears to be his or her demise is to declare as Job, *"Though he slay me, yet will I trust him: but I will maintain mine own ways before him" (Job 13:15)*. In such surrender, there is this awareness in the back of your mind that God does not slay His people, but whatever happens, He does all things well and in the end He will ultimately come through for you whether it is in this life or the next.

The one thing I have learned is that God steps on the scene and provides in most unlikely ways. However, there are times you must cease to look at the circumstances and begin to look around for the answer to your plight. In some cases you must seek high and low with an expectation that God has provided for you in advance to meet your need, but it will not be unveiled to you until you have real need for it.

Pauline Mokebe learned this important lesson. Her husband was away holding revival meetings. There was no food in her home for her or her daughter and there was no money in which to obtain any. She was alone with God, and once again her prayers went forth on the wings of desperation to heaven. After all, she was aware of the many times the Lord had provided in unexpected ways for the basic needs of her family in the past.

After she prayed, she got up from her knees and decided to search everywhere in the house she could think of with the expectation to find the necessary finances. With a prayer on her lips, she began to search in every container and shook any object that may be hiding a hidden treasure. She went into the bedroom and searched through every drawer and methodically through the pockets of her husband's clothes. To her surprise she discovered a certain jacket of her husband's hanging in the closet. She had assumed he had taken it with him. She once again, prayerfully began to search each pocket. To her amazement, she found the right sum of money in one of his pockets that would provide their present needs. Later, her husband would confess he had no idea that there was any money in any of his clothes. (MA, pgs. 64, 65)

God does provide our needs ahead of time. However, such needs may remain hidden until we have need of them. If we are willing to look beyond circumstances and look around in the obscure places, we might discover what God has already planted to bring forth fruit at an expected time of need in our lives.

He is indeed faithful.

But my God shall supply all your need according to his riches in glory by Christ Jesus (Philippians 4:19).

♦ You and I would like to have everything comfortable in religion; and if we had, what should we know about patience?

-John Rusk
(FT, pg. 87)

♦ I choose my battles wisely, I count my opinions as being insignificant, and I lightly hold onto my conclusions so that I can in all sincerely seek the Lord's perspective.

-RJK

♦ You must learn, you must let God teach you, that the only way to get rid of your past is to get a future out of it. God will waste nothing.

-Phillip Brooks

♦ God expects His chosen ones to be both holy and happy. Where holiness is found, happiness is round the corner. Where righteousness is the garment, joy may well be the occupation.

-Herbert Lockyer Sr.
(DP, pg. 682)

♦ He gives grace to His elect because He wills it, to His redeemed because of His covenant, to the called because of His promise, to believers because they seek it, to sinners because they need it. He gives grace abundantly, seasonably, constantly, readily, sovereignly; doubly enhancing the value of the boon by the manner of its bestowal.

-Charles Spurgeon
(MES, Oct. 1 (E))

♦ There is no path to peace or blessing until you confess. Confessing to other people than the ones involved,...is the devil's own snare to keep you in bondage. And the fear of confession is his delusion also.

-Isobel Kuhn
(NAA, pg. 69)

♦ It does not take a cultured or an educated man to fill a position in God's church. What God requires is a yielded consecrated, holy life, and He can make it a flame of fire.

-Smith Wigglesworth
(SWD, (TFT) Mar. 18)

♦ But the iron fetters of Joseph prepared him to wear chains of gold, and made his feet ready to stand in high places. He did not sink under his suffering but came out of his prison to a palace…God often allows His promises to try us, that He may accomplish His own purposes of discipline.

-Herbert Lockyer, Sr.
(DP, pg. 420)

♦ God uses trauma and crisis to enlarge our hearts. Our hearts resist God's stretching processes, and usually it takes something very traumatic to work a permanent enlargement of our hearts.

-Bob Sorge
(FDA, pg.139)

♦ What a comfort it is when undergoing testing times, to know that each one of God's saints is divinely loved by Him. It is a sweet pillow upon which to rest our weary heads and sorely tired hearts.

-Kenneth Wuest
(BNT, pg. 71)

♦ God does not toss His secrets about carelessly. Costly pearls need to be guarded, lest they be stolen and squandered.

-Manfred Haller
(CA, pg. 25)

♦ Jesus Christ is the Son of God. This means He is the sole revealer of God's love, grace, and truth to mankind. He came to earth to set man free by offering Himself as a sacrifice.

-RJK

♦ We will never know the mind of God until we learn to know the voice of God.

-Smith Wigglesworth
(SWD, (TFT) Mar. 24)

♦ Now then you find it is to be a suffering path. Oh, the multiplicity of straits and difficulties that you and I are called to! To describe them is impossible; "But if we suffer with Him, we shall also reign with Him.

-John Rusk

♦ Passionate devotion to the things which are vital delivered Paul from bitterness of soul, from anger and ill will. Disappointments and hardships...may be used for the perfecting of character and for the glory of Christ.

-C. R. Erdman

♦ When our heart kicks against the terrors of the Lord we should see our need of greater humbling before Him, and seek to live more in harmony with His thoughts and less in sympathy with evil.

-Herbert Lockyer, Sr.
(DP, pg. 449)

♦ No it is not by giving us back what He has taken that our God teaches us His deepest lessons, but by patiently waiting beside us till we can say, "I accept the will of my God as good and acceptable and perfect of loss or gain."

-Amy Carmichael

♦ When trials assail us; when afflictions come; when homesickness threatens to overwhelm us, we simply look to Him, and He, our Burden bearer, lifts us up on wings of love, helps us to overcome, heals, comforts us with His blessed presence, and thrills our hearts anew with joy unspeakable and full of glory.

-Dorothy Specter
(SFG, pg. 15)

♦ The first thing we must acknowledge about authority is that those who properly possess it can be clearly identified. Jesus, who actually possessed authority, stood separate from those who patted themselves on the back as they proclaimed the importance of their positions. Jesus never had to make such claims. The main reason is because He never hid behind authority, He walked in it.

-RJK

♦ Heaven is the abode of the enthroned Lord of the universe, who takes an active interest in the temporal as well as the spiritual welfare of those who belong to Him and serve Him.

-F. Ellsworth Powell
(KG, pg.155)

♦ The will of God: nothing more, nothing less, nothing else.

-Unknown
(BB)

♦ **Three** cheers from Jesus:
Be of good <u>cheer</u>, I have overcome the world.
Be of good <u>cheer</u>, your sins are forgiven.
Be of good <u>cheer</u>, it is I, be not afraid.

-Unknown
(BB)

♦ No one can know the true grace of God who has not first known the fear of God.

-A. W. Tozer

♦ Like the Apostle Paul on the road of Damascus before his conversion, we must trust the fact that darkness is sometimes made by the extreme light of God upon the barren places of our souls. The Lord is faithful to reveal the darkness covering the different aspects of our character in order to break forth with His light of truth, salvation, and liberty.

-RJK

God's Pay

Who does God's work will get God's pay,
    However long may be the day.
He does not pay as others pay,
    In gold, or land, or raiment gay,
In goods that perish or decay;
    But God's high wisdom knows the day,
And this is sure, let come what may –
    Who does God's work will get God's pay.

-Author Unknown

And let us not be weary in well doing: for in due season we shall reap, if we faint not (Galatians 6:9).

- It is important to point out that all great people of God had a history with God. In other words, they discovered who He was. They were not content to settle for a few encounters with their Creator, they wanted to know Him in greater ways. They were willing to risk it all to discover the unfolding depths of His character, the incredible heights of His ways, the endless width of His love, the unfolding riches of His grace, and the beauty of His glory.

-RJK

- Christians are not limited editions. We have an unlimited Savior.

-Unknown
(BB)

- Sometimes the Lord calms the storm; sometimes He lets the storm rage and calms the child.

-Unknown
(BB)

- God's kingdom is right side up only when it is upside down.

Extreme Devotion
(ED, pg. 193)

- Jesus said of His words that they were spirit and life. The spirit of His words pointed to the power they have, and the life they brought forth confirmed their authority. It was for this reason that the demons trembled before Him.

-RJK

- If we divorce what Jesus says from Himself, it leads to secret self—indulgence spiritually; the soul is swayed by a form of doctrine that has never been assimilated and the life is twisted away from the center, Jesus Christ Himself.

-Oswald Chambers
(DTD, Dec. 29)

- God's character and nature do not change with humanity's whims, however, we may try to fashion God into another form, but we will ultimately fail.

  Extreme Devotion
  (ED, pg. 172)

- Worship is a way of seeing the world in the light of God.

  -Abraham Joshua Heschel

- The Lord may not have planned that this (circumstance) overtake me, but He has most certainly permitted it. Therefore though it were an attack of an enemy, by the time it reaches me, it has the Lord's permission and therefore all is well. He will make it work together with all life's experiences for good.

  -Unknown

- God is wise to conceal the succours he intends in the several changes of thy life, that so he may draw thy heart into an entire dependence on his faithful promise.

  -William Gurnall
  (CCA, Vol. 1, pg. 96-97)

- Jesus invested in a few men for over three years. He walked with them, supped with them, slept with them, and traveled with them. He served as their patient, anointed teacher and their constant companion, example, and leader. He was a leader in authority, attitude, and conduct. He was as big as the outdoors, yet He was meek and humble. He was powerful, yet obedient and disciplined as a servant of all. He was great, but He became the least among men. He was God, but became man.

  -RJK

The Trump Card

Jeannette was sitting in her motor home after spending a long day in the park attempting to sell her art. She was surrounded by familiar faces because it was not unusual for the same artists to follow a circuit when it came to displaying their art at different community events such as "Art in the Park." Even though she was acquainted with many people, she still did not fit into the crowd.

That particular night, a group of people sought her out. They were excited about a woman who could correctly forecast people's future according to cards. Since Jeannette was a Christian she resisted such a notion, but the people's zeal would not accept her answer. Reluctantly she agreed to go.

When she arrived and was seated, she made an ominous declaration to the fortuneteller. Out of her mouth she declared it would not work for her. The lady apparently accepted Jeannette's challenge to prove her wrong, while brushing her warning aside. Upon shuffling the deck of cards, she told Jeannette to pick a card. Jeannette reached for the cards and picked out a jack. Without any real explanation, the woman put the jack back in the pile and reshuffled the deck and told her to pick another card. The second card she picked turned out to be another jack. After the second jack the woman was becoming somewhat unraveled. She shuffled the deck and told Jeannette to turn over the top card on the deck. Can you guess what the third card was? It was a jack. Without any real explanation as to what the jack meant the woman dismissed the group by telling them it was time to eat.

Jeannette had no idea what a jack symbolized to the occult world, but she later learned that a jack is the one card that cannot be read because it stands for Jesus Christ. If Christ is in our life, He will trump the occult, silence the demonic voices, and unravel any attempts to see beyond what already has been established in our lives by Him. He will do all of this in light of our future inheritance that was secured by His precious redemption.

For ye are bought with a price: therefore glorify God in your body, and in your spirit, which are God's (1 Corinthians 6:20).

THE POWER OF GOD

$\top$

Transforming Power

Evangelist Smith Wigglesworth had noticed a man leaning against a lamppost listening to his preaching. It was obvious he needed the lamppost to keep him upright. Wigglesworth went up to the man and asked him if he was sick. The weak man showed him his hand and Wigglesworth saw that inside his coat he had a silver-handled dagger. The man then confessed that he was on his way to kill his unfaithful wife, but when he heard about the power of the name of Jesus, he could not get away. He was in an utter state of helplessness. Wigglesworth instructed him to kneel down and there the man got saved while people were continuing on with their regular business.

The evangelist actually saw something in the man that he sensed God could use. He took the man home and clothed him in a new suit. The next morning the man gave Wigglesworth a testimony. He told him how God had revealed Jesus to him. He saw how all had been laid upon the precious Son of God.

Wigglesworth lent the man some money and he established a wonderful little home, and in spite of his unfaithful wife living with another man, he invited her back to the home he had prepared for her. Amazingly, she came back to him. Wigglesworth concluded this story in this way, "Where enmity and hatred had been before, the whole situation was transformed by love. God made that man a minister wherever he went. Everywhere there is power in the name of Jesus. God can *save to the uttermost*" (Heb. 7:25). (SWD, pg. 95)

Neither is there salvation in any other: for there is none other name under heaven given among me, whereby we must be saved (Acts 4:12).

♦ It is important to see that Jesus' suffering was a preparation for Him to be offered up as the ultimate sacrifice. Jesus' main reason for coming was not to be regarded in light of His sufferings, but in light of His offering **(John 10:18)**. His cry is not that of a suffering martyr, but as a victorious Redeemer: *"It is finished"* **(John 19:30b)**.

-RJK

♦ Authority is God's reins over the war horse of power.

-Jeannette Haley

♦ It is satanic to feel that God has a special message for you and that you are someone more special than anyone else. Every place that God brings you to in a rising tide of perfection is a place of humility, brokenness of heart, and fullness of surrender, where only God can rule in authority.

-Smith Wigglesworth
(SWD, Nov. 30)

♦ The tragedy is that people today do not tremble nor manifest any solemn awe at the thought of God's majesty as the Sovereign Lord. Failing in reverence for Him, there is no fear of His *autocratic power.

-Herbert Lockyer, Sr.
(DP, pg. 363)

♦ The most staggering thing about Jesus Christ is that He makes human destiny depend not on goodness or badness, not on things done or not done, but on who we say He is.

-Oswald Chambers
(DTD, Mar. 13)

♦ Christ, the polestar, is ever fixed in His place, and all the stars are secure in the right hand of their Lord.

-Charles Spurgeon
(MES, Aug. 6 (M))

♦ Human power is not the stuff of which history is made. For history is not what is displayed at the moment, but what is concealed in the mind of the Lord.

-Abraham J. Heschel
(TP, pg. 219)

♦ God could have chosen to do His work in any fashion He wanted, but He chose to do it (in part) in response to prayer.

-C. S. Lewis
(POG, pg. 74)

♦ God fashions caves for His choice sons: wise parents would do well to permit their children cave experiences within God purposes as well, rather than asserting the instinctive tendency to try to steer them clear of the pain.

-Bob Sorge
(FDA, pg. 74)

♦ The thing for us to do is to claim God's promise and let God take care of the mode of manifestation.

-R. A. Torrey
(PWH, pg. 230)

♦ In a later era Napoleon, we are told, solemnly declared to his Minister of Education: "Do you know, Fontanes, what astonished me most in this world? The inability of force to create anything. In the long run the sword is always beaten by the spirit. (TP, pg. 204)

♦ Amid all the chaos, sin, violence, corruption, and bloodshed characterizing the nations today, it would seem as if Divine rule is inoperative, but in spite of godless and changing kingdoms, God is working out His just purposes with *inexorable justice.

-Herbert Lockyer Sr.
(DP, pg. 353)

♦ The Father is made of none, neither created nor begotten. The Son is of the Father alone, not made, nor created, but begotten. The Holy Spirit is of the Father and the Son: not made nor created, nor begotten, but proceeding.

-Athanasian Creed
(KH. pg. 15)

Prayer: When we consider the fearful mystery of Thy Triune Godhead we lay our hand upon our mouth. Before that burning bush we ask not to understand, but only that we may fitly adore Thee, One God in Persons Three.

-A. W. Tozer
(KH, pg. 17)

♦ Some persons who reject all they cannot explain have denied that God is a Trinity. Subjecting the Most High to their cold, level-eyed scrutiny, they conclude that it is impossible that He could be both One and Three. These forget that their whole life is enshrouded in mystery.

-A. W. Tozer
(KH, pg. 17)

♦ All that Satan has done or is doing or will do is by the permissive will of God, who, since the Lord Jehovah is both omniscient and omnipotent, was certainly never astonished by the outbreak of Satan.

-Donald Grey Barnhouse
(IW, pg. 23)

♦ God is not a hypothesis derived from logical assumptions, but an immediate insight, self-evident as light. He is not something to be sought in the darkness with the light of reason. He is the light.

-Abraham Joshua Heschel

♦ The glory is never so wonderful as when we realize our helplessness, throw down our sword, and surrender our authority to God.

-Smith Wigglesworth
(SWD, Jan. 1)

♦ The A. V., has "The Word was made flesh." To make something is to take something and mold it into a new form, changing its shape. The first form disappears to have something that has a different form take its place.

-Kenneth S. Wuest
(GTL, pg. 29)

♦ Men's curses are impotent, God's blessings are omnipotent.
-Matthew Henry

♦ On earth the Lord's power as readily controls the rage of the wicked as the rage of the sea; His love as easily refreshes the poor with mercy as the earth with showers.
-Charles Spurgeon
(MES, Aug. 12 (M))

♦ God is the climax if He is also the basis. You cannot find Him in the answer if you ignore Him in the question.
-Abraham J. Heschel
(TP, pg. 342)

♦ The reigning Lord has a throne fixed upon the rock of eternal holiness, thus He never departs from straight justice. *"Righteousness* is His immutable attribute, *Judgment* marks His every act."* Blessed to know that absolute power is in the hand of Him Who is not a despot but Who in His rule, cannot err, or act unrighteously.
-Herbert Lockyer Sr.
(DP, pg. 355)

Prayer: I do not seek, O Lord, to penetrate thy depths. I by no means think my intellect equal to them: but I long to understand in some degree thy truth, which my heart believes and loves. For I do not seek to understand that I may believe, but I believe, that I may understand.
-Anselm

♦ The truth is that the Man who walked among us was a demonstration, not of unveiled deity but of perfect humanity. The awful majesty of the Godhead was mercifully sheathed in the soft envelope of human nature to protect mankind.
-A. W. Tozer
(KH, pg. 35)

♦ We may be sure that any questioning of the Word of God is Satanic in its origin. Whether the doubt comes from a group of atheists, from secular educators, or from theologians, its source is always the same. Satan can never win any victory, even a *Pyrrhic one, over the Christian who holds to the Word of God.

-Donald Grey Barnhouse
(IW, pg. 87)

♦ Hard things are always opportunities to gain more glory for the Lord as He manifests His power.

-Smith Wigglesworth
(SWD, Feb. 28)

♦ The sun in its zenith casts no shadow; it is the tropic, or turning of its course, that causes shadow: the very substance of turning is with man but not the least shadow of turning with God.

-John Flavel
(RR, pg. 133)

♦ It may be interrupted. It may be diverted. It may even be temporarily suspended. But God's kingdom is constantly advancing forward. It can never be stopped.

Extreme Devotion
(ED, pg. 211)

Dedication

You never can tell
When you look at a clod,
The things it will do
Till you use it for God.

-Author Unknown

But God hath chosen the foolish things of the world to confound the wise; and God hath chosen the weak things of the world to confound the things which are mighty (1 Corinthians 1:27).

♦ God uses ordinary men by giving His extra ordinary power.

-Unknown
(BB)

♦ The penalty for sin is pronounced against *man*, not against God; therefore it must be paid by *a man*. But no finite man could pay that penalty. Thus, God, in His infinite love and grace, became a man through the virgin birth so that He, as man, could take the judgment we deserved and make it possible for us to be forgiven.
-Dave Hunt

♦ What an unspeakably wonderful day the Day of Pentecost was! There is only one Bethlehem, one Calvary, one Pentecost: these are the landmarks of Time and Eternity, everything and everyone is judge by them.
-Oswald Chambers
(DTD, Jun. 2)

♦ The mightiest ruler must wait his permission before he can place a finger on a child of God.
-Herbert Lockyer, Sr.
(DP, pg. 419)

♦ God is of no importance unless He is of supreme importance.
-Abraham Joshua Heschel

♦ He is unspeakably good, His doctrine is divine, His manner is condescending, His spirit is gentleness itself. No error mingles with His instruction—pure is the golden truth which He brings forth, and all His teachings lead to goodness, sanctifying as well as edifying the disciple.
-Charles Spurgeon
(MES, Jun. 2 (E))

♦ God hath many ways of teaching; he teaches by book, he teaches by His fingers, He teaches by His rod; but His most comfortable and effectual teaching is by the light of His eye.
-Richard Alleine
(DP, pg. 595)

***

In all our Maker's grand designs,
Omnipotence, with wisdom, shines;
His works, through all this wondrous frame,
Declare the glory of His Name.

-Thomas Blacklock
1721-1791
(KH, pg. 64)

O LORD, how great are thy works! and thy thoughts are very deep (Psalm 92:5).

- We deal with the only Being in the universe who has never made a mistake, who has never been astonished, who has never been caught at a disadvantage, who has never been surprised at a superior force or *stratagem.

  -Donald Grey Barnhouse
  (IW, pg. 134)

- There is no other way into the deep things of God except through a broken spirit. There is no other way into the power of God.

  -Smith Wigglesworth
  (SWD, Feb. 16)

- If God is really enthroned in our hearts, we will think and talk about Him, 'for out of the abundance of the heart the mouth speaketh,' said Jesus.

  -F. Ellsworth Powell
  (KG, pg.184)

- What God delights in where His people gather to worship is not beauty of architecture and apparel, but in the moral and spiritual beauty of the worshippers. "Purity is the white linen of the Lord's choristers; righteousness is the comely garment of His priest, and holiness the royal apparel of His servitors."

  -Herbert Lockyer, Sr.
  (DP, pg. 349)

Prayer: Father, in Jesus' name we come before You believing in Your almightiness, that the power of Your hand does move us, chasten us. Build us. Let the Word of God sink into our hearts this day. Make us, O God, worthy of the name we bear, that we may go about as real, holy saints of God. Jesus as if You were on the earth, fill us with Your anointing, Your power, and Your grace. Amen.

-Smith Wigglesworth
(SWD, Dec. 11)

♦ In reference to the Mount Transfiguration, Kenneth Wuest made this statement, "He (Jesus) gave expression to the essence of deity in which He is a co-participant with God the Father and God the Holy Spirit The splendor and majesty of His deity shone through the clay walls of His humanity, and by means of a medium discernible to the physical eyesight of the spectators." (BNT, pg. 82)

***

The majesty of God
　Is seen in His wondrous
　　Love of me—
A mere speckle of sand
　In Abraham's covenant.

His promise of love
　Is seen unfolded
　　Through the ages—
Displayed throughout
　The characters of time.

Arrayed in earthly flesh
　And glorious splendors,
　　Nailed upon the cross

Your redemption
　Paid in full.

Abraham's covenant is
　Drawing near

For all the world
To see—
His glorious majesty!

-Maureen Human

Behold, he cometh with clouds; and every eye shall see him, and they also which pierced him: and all kindreds of the earth shall wail because of him. Even so, Amen (Revelation 1:7).

♦ What does it mean for the Lord to be our Shepherd? We need to keep in mind that we are sheep in need of full time supervision. We have a choice. We can be led by the Shepherd or chased by the dogs.

-Unknown
(BB)

♦ "All that God is He has always been, and all that He has been and is He will ever be." Nothing that God has ever said about Himself will be modified; nothing the inspired prophets and apostles have said about Him will be rescinded. His immutability guarantees this.

-A. W. Tozer
(KH, pg. 50)

♦ If a sparrow cannot fall to the ground without God's notice, is it possible that an empire can rise without His aid?

-Benjamin Franklin
1787 Speech
(DP. pg. 651)

♦ We should never forget that all religion in the world that does not accept fully the person and work of the Lord Jesus is Satanic religion.

-Donald Grey Barnhouse
(IW, pg. 149)

♦ The striking thing about Moses is that it took him forty years to learn human wisdom, forty years to know his helplessness, and forty years to live in the power of God.

-Smith Wigglesworth
(SWD, Mar. 24)

♦ For Christ to be made flesh was more humility than for the angels to be made worms...He stripped Himself of the robes of His glory, and covered Himself with the rags of our humanity.

-Thomas Watson
(PDC, pg. 374)

♦ An incontestable proof, this to me, that those who deny our Lord's divinity never effectually felt his power; if they had, they would not speak so lightly of him; they would scorn to deny his eternal power and Godhead.

-George Whitefield
(GW, pg. 179)

♦ God's throne is "established by justice," and "upheld by mercy."

-Herbert Lockyer, Sr.
(DP, pg. 375)

♦ Our Lord is the Logos of God in the sense that He is the total concept of God, Deity speaking through the Son of God, not in parts of speech as in a sentence composed of words, but in the human life of a divine Person.

-Kenneth S. Wuest
(GN, pg. 51)

***

Soon Thou wilt come—oh, blest anticipation!—
And we shall gaze unhindered on Thy face;
Our longing hope shall have its glad fruition
And in those wounds we shall love's story trace.

Oh cloudless morn of heavenly light and gladness.
When God Himself shall wipe all tears away!
There shall be no more death and no more sadness,
No trace of sin through God's eternal day.

-J. W. H. Nichols

And God shall wipe away all tears from their eyes; and there shall be no more death, neither sorrow, nor crying, neither shall there be any more pain: for the former things are passed away (Revelation 21:4).

♦ We trust to this and that friend, and they greatly deceive and disappoint us. At this we wonder; but God in letting us know that we are hewing out cisterns, broken cisterns, that can hold no water; and as He increases our faith, so He removes these props.
-John Rusk
(FT, pg. 91)

♦ We know nothing like the divine holiness. It stands apart, unique, unapproachable, incomprehensible, and unattainable. The natural man is blind to it. He may fear God's power and admire His wisdom, but His holiness he cannot even imagine.
-A. W. Tozer
(KH, pg. 104)

♦ God the Son in His incarnation led the Father out from behind the curtain of His invisibility into full view.
-Kenneth S. Wuest
(GN, pg. 85)

♦ God is the only real majority that counts in a matter.
-RJK

♦ Every miracle begins with a problem or impossibility.
-Earl Lee

Nothing is Impossible With God

Missionary H. B. Garlock was in a quandary in a couple of ways. A missionary, Esther Sandstorm had died from Malaria at another African missionary station and the others wanted Garlock to conduct her funeral service. However, to get to them he had to cross the Sorrika River, which proved to be formidable at that particular time of the year. He felt the intense burden to do whatever he needed to do because the other missionaries were depending on his presence for spiritual and moral support.

The other challenge was that his new wife had just arrived in Liberia, Africa to join him in his work among the people. The unspoken rule was that a new missionary must not be left alone until he or she had his or her first attack of Malaria. His wife agreed that he must go and attend to the business of the Father. To remedy the matter, another missionary was asked to come and stay with Garlock's wife, Ruth until his return.

Sorrika was usually a stream, but during this particular time of the year it would swell into a raging river, flooding the lowlands. At the river the missionary stood on a piece of high ground to observe the flow and width of the river. Garlock realized that he was facing the worst scenario possible. He wondered how he could reach the other side. This was his last memory concerning his plight.

The next thing he knew, he was walking into the yard of the mission station. Except for perspiration, his clothes were not wet. As far as his carriers, there was no sign of them. Obviously, Garlock had reached the station without them and their assistance.

Garlock later learned from his wife that some of the porters returned back to their mission station that same day saying they could not get across the river, and they did not know what happened to Garlock. This of course caused the new bride great concern, but she knew that she had no other recourse but to go to God and commit the welfare of her new husband to Him.

As Garlock thought about the incident he could only conclude that he was translated like Philip in Acts 8:39-40. God knew the heavy hearts of the missionary and took the matters into His own hands. In the past He had parted the waters for the children of Israel and allowed Peter to walk on the water, but in the case of Garlock, He simply lifted him up and placed him at the gate entrance of the mission. No doubt it proved to be the fastest trip the missionary ever experienced.

However, the return journey proved to be a different story. Against the advice of others, Garlock, along with porters and a sick missionary tried to cross the river. It almost cost the life of a courageous porter and the sick missionary. (BKY, pgs. 63-67)

The question is why did God translate Garlock the first time but allowed him to experience the power of the raging river the next time?

There are a couple of factors that must be considered in such matters. The first factor that must be considered is the sovereignty of God. Just because God does it one way, does not mean He will do it that way again. You cannot predict what God is going to do when it comes to the matters of His kingdom. However, when it comes to miracles, believers must keep in mind that the types of miracles done are in proportion to the need or situation. In other words God would not part the Red Sea for one person, any more than He would cause the children of Israel to walk on water. Translating one man compared to a group of people would not be practical.

The second factor comes down to need. God provides our needs but He will not heed to our wants and luxuries. It is for this reason as believers we need to properly discern what is important to the matters of His kingdom. God clearly met those who were in a valley of deep sorrow over the death of the missionary by translating Garlock, while on the other hand wisdom dictated that those of the second party wait for the river to recede before proceeding back to the other mission station. Even though their intentions were honorable, they almost put God to a foolish test by going against the wise advice of those around them. Although God stepped on the scene and delivered the porter and sick missionary from certain death, the journey proved to be a hard and tumultuous adventure.

But Jesus beheld them, and said unto them, With men this is impossible; but with God all things are possible (Matthew 19:26).

THE POWER OF GOD'S SPIRIT

Our Reward

Regardless of the challenges, we as believers must always continue our journey through the deep canyons of repentance and commitment to God. Deeper and deeper the light of the Holy Spirit will search out every last vestige of selfishness and sin.

The narrow path climbs ever closer to the goal. However, first comes the lonely, scorching trials in the desert. Faith is refined like fine gold in such barren places. The soul is then strengthened for the mountainous ascent to holiness.

At last the mountain is reached. However, the high calling of holiness is at the summit. The way appears to be impossible, and yet the call to holiness persists. Eager but reluctant, we as believers must respond to the call. It will require each of us to look upward. The ongoing work of forgiveness, sanctification, and regeneration enables us to press forward and upward. As each one of us nears the apex of our Christian journey, the Spirit of God, the Living Water, continues to wash away every sin and weight that would hinder our progress into His presence.

A pure heart and submissive spirit gives each of us a sure footing on the narrow path. Faith in God and His Word propels us onward. Praise and worship ushers us into that sweet place of communion. At last! We are in the Holy of Holies. His presence, His glory, His majesty, and His holiness are our reward!

70

Elect according to the foreknowledge of God the Father, through sanctification of the Spirit, unto obedience and sprinkling of the blood of Jesus Christ: Grace unto you, and peace, be multiplied (1 Peter 1:2).

♦ Holiness is the combined force of the fruits of the Spirit.
-Unknown
(BB)

♦ The more we see ourselves from the heavenly perspective, the more we will understand what it means to take flight on the current of the Spirit to reach incredible heights in our Lord.
-RJK

♦ True Christianity is nothing else but the Spirit of Christ, so whether that Spirit appears in the person of Christ Himself or His apostles or followers in any age, it is the same thing; whoever has His Spirit will be hated, despised, and condemned by the world, as He was.
-William Law
(DHL, pgs. 212, 213)

♦ You have a peculiar power in prayer; the Spirit of God gives you joy and gladness; the Scripture is open to you; the promises give you joy and gladness; the Scripture is open to you; the promises are applied; you walk in the light of God countenance; you have peculiar freedom and liberty in devotion, and more closeness of communion with Christ than was your *wont.
-Charles Spurgeon
(MES, Jan. 30 (M))

♦ May the Lord save Pentecost from going to dry rot.
-Smith Wigglesworth
(SWD, (TFT) Aug. 5)

♦ Notice of which sin it is that the Holy Spirit convinces men—the sin of unbelief in Jesus Christ. *"Of sin, because they believe not on me* (John 16:9), says Jesus. Not the sin of stealing, not the sin of drunkenness, not the sin of adultery, not the sin of murder, but the sin of unbelief in Jesus Christ.
-R. A. Torrey
(PWH, pg. 84)

♦ As the Holy Ghost is first a sanctifier, and then a comforter, so Satan (is) first a tempter, then a troubler.

-William Gurnall
(CCA, Vol. 1, pg. 85)

♦ How easily we become full of ourselves. We think our strengths are kingdom assets, and God often views them as kingdom liabilities. Why? Because we tend to depend on our strengths, without even realizing it, instead of the Holy Spirit.

-Bob Sorge
(FDA, pg. 214)

♦ By taking texts out of their context, one can prove almost anything from the Bible. But as we study it reverently and expectantly, the Holy Spirit, who inspired it, will illuminate and authenticate its message to us.

-J. Oswald Sanders
(POG, pg. 67)

♦ Genuine, spiritual mourning for sin is *the work of the Spirit of God*. Repentance is too choice a flower to grow in nature's garden. Pearls grow naturally in oysters, but penitence never shows itself in sinners except divine grace works it in them.

-Charles Spurgeon
(MES, Oct. 13 (M))

♦ Only those who have been quieted by the soothing ministry of the Holy Spirit can look fearlessly into Eternity; and all that it holds for those whose hope was in the Lord, will fully justify such confidence.

-Herbert Lockyer Sr.
(DP, pg. 678)

♦ The baptism with the Holy Spirit is not primarily intended to make believers happy but to make them useful.

-R. A. Torrey
(PWH, pg. 171)

♦ Yet as electric power flows only through a conductor, so the Spirit flows through truth and must find some measure of truth in the mind before He can illuminate the heart. Faith wakes at the voice of truth but responds to no other sound...Theological knowledge is the medium through which the Spirit flows into the human heart, yet there must be humble penitence in the heart before truth can produce faith.

-A. W. Tozer
(KH, pg. 104)

***

The Prompting

A Christian worker in Toronto had the impression of going to the hospital and speaking to an unknown individual. He considered who he knew in the hospital and a certain man came to his mind. When he arrived at the hospital, he located the man, but when he began to talk to him, he realized he was not the one he was to seek out. However, there was another man lying across the aisle in the ward. He was struck with the thought that perhaps he was sent to speak to this individual.

He approached the man who had only a knee injury, but he proved to be receptive to his concern for his spiritual plight for he received Christ as His Savior. Even though this man did not have a serious injury, he did pass into eternity that night. (PWH, pgs. 153-154)

The natural man does not understand the prompting of the Holy Spirit. He sees it as a curiosity or being foolish, while the experience, importance, or significance of it is beyond his understanding.

The truth is nothing gets done in the kingdom of God unless the Holy Spirit does the prompting or bidding in such matters.

Now we have received, not the spirit of the world, but the spirit which is of God; that we might know the things that are freely given to us of God (1 Corinthians 2:12).

♦ It is totally impossible to comprehend spiritual things until you have been given a new spirit in the regeneration that God provides on the basis of the atoning death of Christ.

-Donald Grey Barnhouse
(IW, pg. 42)

♦ God does everything through His Spirit. The Spirit of God connects the heart of heaven with the matters of earth.

-RJK

♦ We may be in a very low ebb of the tide, but it is good to be in a place where the tide can rise. Everything depends on our being filled with the Holy Spirit.

-Smith Wigglesworth
(SWD, Jan. 12)

♦ In proportion therefore as mind and heart are fixed on Christ, we may count on the Spirit's presence and power; but if we make the Holy Ghost Himself the object of our aspirations and worship, some false spirit may counterfeit the true and take us for a prey.

-Sir Robert Anderson
(GN, pg. 108)

♦ The grace we have received of the forgiveness of sins and of joy in the Holy Spirit can only be preserved by daily renewal in fellowship with Jesus Christ Himself. Many Christians backslide because this truth is not clearly taught.

-Andrew Murray
(AP, Jan. 2)

♦ If we think of the Holy Spirit, as so many do, as merely a power or influence, our constant thought will be, "How can I get more of the Holy Spirit?" But if we think of Him in the biblical way as a divine person, our thought will instead be, "How can the Holy Spirit have more of me?"

-R. A. Torrey
(PWH, pg. 8)

♦ If the Holy Spirit be indeed so mighty, let us attempt nothing without Him; let us begin no project, and carry on no enterprise, and conclude no transaction, without imploring His blessing.

-Charles Spurgeon
(MES, Nov. 21 (M))

♦ If there are any *buts* in your attitude toward the Word of truth, there is something unyielded to the Spirit.

-Smith Wigglesworth
(SWD, (TFT) Jul. 25)

♦ In relationship to discerning between Satan's devices and the Holy Spirit's work, William Gurnall made this statement, "The Holy Spirit is Christ's spokesman to commend him to souls, and to woo sinners to embrace the grace of the gospel; and can such words drop from his sacred lips, as should break the match, and sink Christ's esteem in the thoughts of the creature. (CCA, Vol. 1, pg. 88)

♦ In being reborn, there is the impartation of life by the Spirit's power, and the one who receives it is saved. In the baptism with the Holy Spirit, there is the impartation of power, and the one who receives it is fitted for service.

-R. A. Torrey
(PWH, pg. 167)

♦ If you die without the Spirit, you will fall into hell. There can be no doubt of this. Without the Spirit you will never be prepared for heaven.

-Charles Finney
(LRR, pg.115)

♦ While God is willing to help us in areas beyond our mental capacity, *He does not do the things for us!* The Holy Spirit will enlighten our minds when we ask Him to and sincerely desire to do God's will.

-J. Oswald Sanders
(POG, pg. 69)

♦ Though you become greatly sanctified by the Holy Ghost, expect that the great dog of hell will bark at you still. In the haunts of men we expect to be tempted, but even seclusion will not guard us from the same trial

-Charles Spurgeon
(MES, Feb. 20 (E))

♦ What "softies" we Christians are with regard to sin in our lives. How we sometimes cherish it, pamper it, play with it, instead of striking it with the nailed fist of a Holy Spirit inspired hatred of sin and a refusal to allow it to reign as king in our lives.

-Kenneth Wuest
(BNT, pg. 56)

♦ If there is anything unholy, impure, selfish, mean, petty, unkind, harsh, unjust, or in any way evil in act or word or thought or fancy, He is grieved by it. If we will allow those words, *"grieve not the holy Spirit of God,"* to sink into our hearts and become the motto of our lives, they will keep us from many a sin.

-R. A. Torrey
(PWH, pg. 14)

♦ This sanctification of the Spirit brings us into definite alignment with the wonderful hope of the glory of God. Lively hope is movement. It presses forward. Lively hope leaves everything behind. It keeps the vision. Lively hope sees Him coming! And you live in it—this lively hope.

-Smith Wigglesworth
(SWD, May 7)

Walking According to God's Leading

What does it mean to be a missionary? If people consider the mission field, they often have a romantic notion about serving God, especially on the foreign fields. However, many missionaries will admit it is not glamorous or romantic. In most cases, the times of ecstasy is often leveled out by hard work, drudgery, and uncertainty of the unseen and unknown.

E.M. Clarkson gives a clear picture of what it means to be sent forth by the Lord. She points out that like Isaiah, we can avail ourselves when we declare, "Lord, here am I! Send me!" Clarkson makes reference to the fact that the missionary labors are unrewarded.

These individuals find themselves toiling alone, living in oppressive situations where they find themselves unpaid, unloved, unsought, and unknown. They can suffer much in the mission field such as scorn and scoffing, but they will endure all for the sake of their Lord.

These stouthearted souls know the bitterness of loneliness and the torment of longing as they strive to bind the bruised and broken. They weep over the lost as they wearily bear the burden of the world. They have left ambitions, learned to die to the self–will, and count it necessary to be consumed by the life of another. Clarkson ends the writing with these words:

> So send I you—to hearts made hard by hatred,
> To eyes made blind because they will not see;
> To spend tho' it be blood—to spend, and spare not,
> So send I you—to taste of Calvary.

The truth of the matter is following the Lord into the mission field can prove to be unpredictable. You may feel led in one direction and end up being led in a different direction. This happened to a couple by the name of Homer (Hyman) and Dorothy Specter.

It is easy to think that it is a breeze for missionaries to leave all behind to follow the Lord into service. However, Dorothy admitted to her sister-in-law that she had misgivings about going to the mission field, but she really wanted to do God's will. It was only as she prayed about the mission field did God give her a love for the place her and her husband felt called to. With the love of God burning in her heart and compelling her, she felt a desire, a passion to go.

When the Specters were first called to the mission field, they felt led to Africa, but instead found the door opened to Haiti. They had to contend with pagan culture, and voodoo. In her letters to their supporters, Dorothy described the spiritual environment. She stated, "Catholicism, which is prominent, is very corrupt in Haiti. The natives will embrace it readily since it does not require them to give up their evil practices in their voodoo religion. They just add another god to their collection" (SFG, pg. 9)

For over a decade the Specters labored in Haiti. Homer often served as doctor, nurse, midwife, dentist, and had to amputate a toe. Dorothy related in her writings about the many who came to salvation which included those who were enslaved to the demonic world of voodoo. But amid the victories were the regular challenges of life, some included illnesses, homesickness, and raising a family of six children, three born when serving as missionaries. Like most families on the mission field, at a certain age the children of missionaries must be sent home to be educated, resulting in difficult separations.

After twelve years in Haiti, the Specters felt they were being called to Africa. She wrote this in her letter to the supporters, "It seemed incredible that we should even consider changing fields and that the Lord should renew that first call after 19 long years! Yet, the tremendous, challenging need of SENEGAL continued to grip our hearts to such an extent that we were led to "follow through" and once again offered ourselves for service in Africa. (SFG, pg. 112)

Dorothy described the spiritual condition of Senegal in this way, "The spiritual condition of Senegal, one of the most challenging and neglected countries in the world, is like the land—barren, dry, desperately in need of the life-giving water from above, which alone can quench the spiritual thirst of these people." (SFG, pg. 115)

In Haiti, the Specters' contended with voodoo, but in Africa it was the Muslim belief. Dorothy made this statement, "The Mohammedan cult is said to be the most difficult of all religions to penetrate with the Gospel." (SFG, 113)   Yet, the light of the Gospel eventually did penetrate the great darkness in the land.

Dorothy writes about the real secret when it comes to people receiving the gift of life, "Only the Holy Spirit can penetrate the veil of darkness, and reveal Christ to them as the true and living Son of God – their only hope of redemption." (SFG, 125)

This missionary couple opened a mission in a predominantly Muslim village. In the whole section that enveloped over 550,000 people, the Specters could only count the Christians on the fingers of one hand. However, they rejoiced because the harvest field was white, ready to be reaped. They started a church and the first Bible School in Senegal. Dorothy wrote how the Muslim children would sit enthralled and listened eagerly to the lesson story about God. However, when the Muslim priest learned about it, some of the children were punished and forbidden to attend classes again.

Dorothy also wrote about the staggering odds against a Muslim becoming a Christian. She went on to say, "They are multiplied a hundred fold when the Muslim is a woman." (SFG, pg. 123)

In 1970, after six years of ministering in Africa, the Specters were called back to America to minister to the Jewish people. It is pretty amazing to think that a Jewish Christian was working among the Muslims. There were conversions in Africa, and praise God for His faithfulness, other Christians caught the fire and vision for Africa, thereby taking the Specters' place, which allowed this couple to return to America to reach out to the Jews.

The Specters formed a ministry now known as the *Rock of Israel*. They located a building, but in order to secure it they had to raise $39,000.00 in a month's time. All but $12,000.00 of it miraculously came in. Even though it had not come in the day before the deadline, God had given them peace about it. On the day it was due, the final $12, 000.00 came in to reveal God is never late.

The Specters had various outreaches that included holding meetings in their building, giving Bibles, handing out tracts, starting a magazine, radio broadcasts, cassette ministry, and appearing on Christian TV. In one year they distributed over 450,000 pieces of literature. And, even though they were in America, they were attacked: a bomb went off close to their building, only miraculously causing minimal damage.

Dorothy Specter gained her great independence on July 4th, 1978 at the age 54, when she went home to be with the Lord. Hyman went home to be with the Lord at age 78. As we have peered into a small window that represent the Specters in their service to the Lord, it becomes obvious that such individuals may remain unknown by most of Christendom, but their names have been assuredly declared in the courts of heaven and their deeds recorded in the book of heaven. And, something else we must remember, they have left a legacy. The *Rock of Israel* continues under the watchful eyes of the Specters' son, Robert. And, as I thought about the earthquake in Haiti and the persecution taking place in the Muslim country in Africa where they ministered, I wandered how many Christians not only learned how to stand, withstand, and find peace in such trials because someone dared to adhere to their commission to bring the Gospel to their homeland, but how many of these souls would accredit their salvation and testimony to a couple by the name of Specter; a couple who were faithful to a higher calling, a life of consecration, and sacrificial service to the One who is worthy of all consideration and honor?

How then shall they call on him in whom they have not believed? and how shall they believe in him of whom they have not heard? and how shall they hear without a preacher? And how shall they preach, except they be sent? as it is written, How beautiful are the feet of them that preach the gospel for peace, and bring glad tidings of good things (Romans 10:14-15).

♦ It is not enough that one be filled with the Holy Spirit once. We need a new filling for each new emergency of Christian service. The failure to realize this need of constant refillings with the Holy Spirit has led to many a man, who at one time was greatly used by God, being utterly laid aside.

-R. A. Torrey
(PWH, pg. 200)

♦ The very design and object of the Spirit of God is, to tear away from the sinner his last vestige of a hope, while remaining in sin; to annihilate every crag and twig he may cling to.

-Charles Finney
(LRR, pg. 332)

♦ It is therefore not without significance that our understanding the will of God is linked with the ministry of the Spirit, specifically with our "being filled with the Spirit."...The tense of the verb "be filled' in Ephesians 5:18 indicates a continuous action, so we are commanded to keep on being filled with the Spirit—so yielded to Him that He can control, empower, and guide us.

-J. Oswald Sanders
(POG, pgs. 70, 71)

♦ We must live in the fire. We must hate sin; we must love righteousness. We must live with God, for He says we have to be blameless and harmless amid the crooked positions of the world.

-Smith Wigglesworth
(SWD, Jan. 22)

♦ Being "upright" means that such a person is always the right side *up*, always obeying the dictates of His Spirit-enlightened conscience in all his transactions with others.

-Herbert Lockyer, Sr.
(DP, pg. 471)

♦ Put your faith in the Lord Jesus as your personal Saviour, and you will find that God the Father chose you to salvation, God the Holy Spirit brought you to the act of faith, and the Son cleansed you from sin in His precious blood.

-Kenneth Wuest
(BNT, pg. 23)

♦ No amount of preaching, no matter how orthodox it may be, and no amount of mere study of the Word will regenerate unless the Holy Spirit works. It is He and He alone who makes a man a new creature.

-R. A. Torrey
(PWH, pg. 99)

♦ In Ephesians 5, understanding God's will is linked to being filled with the Spirit. He exercises both a constraining ministry and a restraining influence when we are not in line with His will.

-J. Oswald Sanders
(POG, pg. 84)

♦ We must know that the baptism of the Spirit immerses us into an intensity of zeal, into a likeness to Jesus; it makes us into pure liquid metal so hot for God that it travels like oil from vessel to vessel.

-Smith Wigglesworth
(SWD, Aug. 15)

♦ This blind life of the spirit, a life that delights to live in the dim regions of the spirit, refusing to bring the leadings of the Holy Spirit into the national life, gives occasion to supernatural forces that are not of God.

-Oswald Chambers
(DTD, Dec. 5)

♦ From long experience and observation, I am inclined to think that whoever finds redemption in the blood of Jesus — whoever is justified — has the choice of walking in the higher or lower path. I believe the Holy Spirit at that time sets before him 'the more excellent way . . . to aspire after the heights and depths of holiness — the entire image of God. But if he does not accept this offer, he insensibly declines into the lower order of Christians.

-John Wesley

♦ The rush and bustle of carnal activity breathes a spirit of restlessness; the Holy Spirit breathes a deep calm. This is the atmosphere in which we may expect a lasting work of God to grow.

-James O. Fraser
(MR, pg. 155)

♦ So Christians today have a revelation by the Spirit, and many are failing to depend upon Him to interpret the revelation to them, and so go astray.

-R. A. Torrey
(PWH, pg. 141)

♦ The human spirit, when perfectly united with the Holy Spirit, has but one place, and that is death, death, and deeper death. In this place, the human spirit will cease to desire to have its own way, and instead of "my will," the cry of the heart will be, "may Your will, O Lord, be done in me."

-Smith Wigglesworth
(SWD, Jan. 30)

♦ All through our Lord's life on earth, as the Man Christ Jesus, He lived in dependence upon the Holy Spirit. That was part of His humiliation. To be God, and yet to live as man in dependence upon God, that was His normal life on earth.

-Kenneth Wuest
(BNT, pg. 89)

♦ In our spiritual experience, the Holy Spirit, reigning within our hearts, is the Fire consuming our lusts and melting our wills into loving obedience.

-Herbert Lockyer, Sr.
(DP, pg. 356)

♦ The letter of the law was brought by Moses, exceeding glory that Jesus brought to us in the Spirit of life. The glory of Sinai paled before the glory of Pentecost.

-Smith Wigglesworth
(SWD, Mar. 7)

♦ He will not, by his Holy Spirit, be your Divine teacher unless you renounce self, and live in a state of continual consecration to him.

-Charles Finney
(LRR, pg. 430)

♦ Experiences will never lead to God; rather through communion with the Lord, we will be led into experiences with Him by the Holy Spirit.

-RJK

The Needed Discipline of the Negative

We often paint an unrealistic picture of Christianity. We try to attract people to a perfect life by pointing out the positives. However, we fail to define that a perfect life points to a mature life and such a life first requires that a believer comes to a place of spiritual perfection or maturity. Perfection entails a process that includes positive advancements that are first disciplined by negative restraints.

True to human nature we have a tendency to present and prefer the fantasy over the rewarding reality of the things of God. We make all the right claims but we are not willing to subject ourselves to what we consider to be negative. We fail to realize that without the contrast of the negatives, we would never recognize the positives. It takes both factors to produce that which has value and purpose.

J. Oswald Sanders brings this very reality out in his book about discovering the plan of God for one's life. He made this statement, "The negative authority of the Holy Spirit is as much a part of guidance as His positive thrust." (POG, pg. 110)

Sanders then goes on to back up his statement with the following examples, "David Livingstone attempted to go to China, but God redirected him to Africa. Adoniram Judson had India in view as his sphere of service, but the Spirit had chosen Burma. William Carey wanted to serve in Polynesia, but God directed him to India. When we are already in action and need to be directed to the next sphere of service, it is not unreasonable for us to expect somewhat similar (if less dramatic) redirection to the place of God's choice." (POG, pg. 111)

We have a tendency to think we know what is best, but God has in mind what would constitute that which is excellent for us. He has prepared us according to who He made us and the plan He had in mind before we were even conceived in the womb. In some cases it is that which was obscured from our knowledge that would prove to be superior in the end, and other times it is that which proves greater than our very expectation that He had in mind for us. The key is whatever His plan for our life, we can trust that in the end it will prove to be superior to our greatest imagination or expectation.

For I know the thoughts that I think toward you, saith the LORD, thoughts of peace, and not of evil, to give you an expected end (Jeremiah 29:11).

◆ True spirituality consists in a life which is free from law and which is lived, to the minutest detail of individuality, by the power of the Spirit.

-Lewis Sperry Chafer
(POG, pg. 97)

◆ Do not hastily ascribe things to God. Do not easily suppose dreams, voices, impressions, visions, or revelations to be from God. They may be from Him, they may be from the devil. Therefore do not believe every spirit but try the spirits whether they be of God.

-John Wesley
(POG, pg. 98)

◆ You may ask, "why do we need teachers when the Bible says in **1 John** that we need no man to teach us if we have the Holy Ghost?" You need to understand that God gifts people, *through the Holy Spirit*, to teach His Word; but it is only *by* the Holy Spirit that God's Word becomes *living* because of the anointing (of the Holy Spirit). In other words, teachers break the bread of the Word of life to our

84

minds, but it is by the *quickening* of the Holy Spirit that this bread becomes *living* in our *hearts*!

-Jeannette Haley

♦ God fills us with His divine power, and sin is dethroned...You cannot live by faith until you are just and righteous. You cannot live by faith if you are unholy or dishonest.

-Smith Wigglesworth
(SWD, Feb. 3)

♦ The individual as he is born into this world is not a child of God, and in order to become such, he must be born of God by the Holy Spirit.

-Kenneth S. Wuest
(GTL, pg. 54)

♦ Now real holiness principally consists in union to Christ, and being a partaker of His Spirit.

-John Rusk

♦ Today, many Christians have become bystanders to the life Jesus is calling them to. Real commitment and dedication cannot be established in our lives by miracles, but rather by faith in God. We are not called to a life of ongoing prophecies and miracles, but to a life of service and self-sacrifice. Once Jesus is in His rightful position as Lord of our lives, we will begin to experience the abundant life. This life is lived out in the power of the Holy Spirit.

-RJK

♦ The Holy Spirit did not come to exalt you; He came so that you could exalt the Lord.

-Smith Wigglesworth
(SWD, (TFT) Dec. 7)

♦ The sin of your nature, your original sin, is sufficient to sink you into torments, of which there will be no end; therefore, unless you receive the Spirit of Christ, you are reprobates, and you cannot be saved. Nothing short of the blood of Jesus applied to your souls will make you happy to all eternity.

-George Whitefield
(GW, pg. 284)

♦ A person can be technically right and spiritually wrong. That is why we must worship God and live *in spirit and in truth.* Truth without spirit is merciless, harsh, cruel, religious, and legalistic. Spirit without truth has no stability or foundation, and has no way to test anything.

-Jeannette Haley

♦ Do not be satisfied with anything less than the knowledge of a real change in your nature, the knowledge of the indwelling presence and power of the Holy Spirit. Do not be satisfied with a life that is not wholly swallowed up in God.

-Smith Wigglesworth
(SWD, Feb. 1)

♦ With the physical body, man has world-consciousness, with the soul he has self-consciousness, and with the spirit he has God-consciousness.

-Kenneth S. Wuest
(GTL, pg. 148)

♦ Christianity includes morality, as grace does reason; but if we are only mere moralists, if we are not inwardly worked upon, and changed by the powerful operations of the Holy Spirit, and our moral actions proceed from a principle of a new nature, however we may call ourselves Christians, we shall be found naked at the great day...

-George Whitefield
(GW, pg. 268)

♦ God comes in, dwells in, walks in, talks through, and dines with him who opens his being to the Word of God and receives the Spirit who inspired it.

-Smith Wigglesworth
(SWD, Dec. 31)

♦ Our failure in the prayer life is a result of our failure in the Spirit life.

-Andrew Murray
(AP, Feb. 20)

◆ The plan of the church was that everything, even everyday routines, must be sanctified to God, for the church had to be a Holy Spirit church. Beloved, God has never ordained anything less.

-Smith Wigglesworth
(SWD, Jan. 2)

Blinding Obstacles of Circumstances

Evangelist Smith Wigglesworth looked into the face of a young man who had been lame for 18 years of his 26 years of life. He had been placed in a chair by others. It was obvious that the upper part of his body revealed that he was a big man, but the lower part did not appear to belong to the upper torso, for his legs were frail and small.

Wigglesworth asked the young man, "What is the greatest desire of your heart?"

One would think the answer to the question would be obvious. However, Jesus would ask a blind man a similar question, "What would you have me do for you?" It was not that Jesus did not know what a person had need of, but it was a way of revealing the secret desires of the heart. It was also the means in which priorities were exposed to reveal the inner character.

The young man's answer not only showed his heart condition, but his wisdom in knowing what needed to be a priority in his life. "Oh," and he said, "Receive, receive the Holy Spirit." Instantly, the young man became drunk with the Spirit and fell off the chair like a bag of potatoes. As the Spirit went through and over his body like currents and waves of a river, he began to speak in tongues as he wept and praise the Lord. However, to Wigglesworth, his legs remained unchanged.

Wigglesworth admitted that by looking at the appearance of his legs he missed what God wanted to do. It is through such situations that the Lord is able to expose each of our weakness so that He can teach us important lessons. Faith never considers the circumstances of a matter, for it knows that such faith will cease to be and the person will go into unbelief. After all, faith is not based on personal understanding but on the character and ways of our great God. Wigglesworth reiterated this powerful truth by stating, "The man who wants to work the works of God must never look at conditions but at Jesus, in whom everything is complete.

As Wigglesworth considered the young man on the floor, he realized that he could not be moved. He asked the Lord what did he need to do in regard to this young man who appeared to be lying helplessly on the floor. The answer was, "Command him to walk in My name."

The evangelist admitted this is when he missed what God wanted to do as he looked at the condition of the young man. He and the young man's father tried to lift him up to see if his legs had any strength, but together they could not move him. It was then the Lord showed Wigglesworth his mistake and he immediately repented and asked God to forgive him. He also said to the Lord, "Please tell me again."

The longsuffering, merciful, and gracious God said to the evangelist, "Command him in My name to walk." Wigglesworth shouted, "Arise and walk in the name of Jesus."

The question is did the young man with the fail, weak legs get up and walk again. Wigglesworth put it in this text, "No, I declare he never walked. He was lifted up by the power of God in a moment, and he *ran* through the wide open door, out across the road into a field where he ran up and down before coming back to his home. It was indeed a miracle. (SWD, Mar. 14)

If ye then, being evil, know how to give good gifts unto your children: how much more shall your heavenly Father give the Holy Spirit to them that ask him (Luke 11:13)?

THE POWER OF GOD'S WORD

The Enduring Testimony

In America, we have a tendency to take the Word of God for granted. Because of what appears to be a casual attitude towards it, I fear that we are now in a spiritual drought, a drought that involves the Word of God. Even though we have many Bibles, much of the intent of the Word has been compromised or done away with altogether, leaving us with dry, miserable crumbs that have no substance or life in them. Therefore, it is hard to find where the unadulterated Word of God is being preached with authority and in power.

I recently read a testimony that a man gave concerning the Word of God. His insight in it was and remains thought provoking and inspirational. "Never compare this Book with other books. Comparisons are dangerous. Never think or say that this Book contains the Word of God. It *is* the Word of God. It is supernatural in origin, eternal in duration, inexpressible in value, infinite in scope, regenerative in power, infallible in authority, universal in interest, personal in application, inspired in totality. Read it through, Write it down. Pray it in. Work it out. Then pass it on." (SWD, pg. 88)

Behold, the days come, saith the Lord GOD, that I will send a famine in the land, not a famine of bread, nor a thirst for water, but of hearing the words of the LORD (Amos 8:11).

♦ Maturity is the accomplishment of years, and I can only surrender to the will of God as I know what that will is. Hence the fullness of the Spirit is not instantaneous but progressive, as I attain fullness of the Word, which reveals the Will.

-James Elliot
(SOA, pg. 91)

89

♦ Everything depends on our believing God. If we are saved, it is only because God's Word says so. We cannot rest upon our feelings.

-Smith Wigglesworth
(SWD, Jan. 12)

♦ Propaganda is nothing more than twisted truth that hides an unsavory attitude and agenda.

-RJK

♦ The Scripture is the compass by which the rudder of our will is to be steered; it is the field in which Christ, the Pearl of price, is hid; it is a rock of diamonds; it is a sacred "eye salve", it heals their eyes that look upon it; it is a spiritual optic-glass in which the glory of God is resplendent; it is the panacea or "universal medicine" for the soul.

-Thomas Watson
(PDC, pg. 217)

♦ Men do not reject the Bible because it contradicts itself, but because it contradicts them.

-Unknown

♦ The Bible was not written by God for information but for transformation.

-Unknown
(BB)

♦ The Scriptures are the swaddling bands of the holy child Jesus; unfold them and you find your Savior. The *quintessence of the word of God is Christ.

-Charles Spurgeon
(MES, Jun. 10 (E))

♦ In the realm of theology, shallowness is treason.

-Abraham J. Heschel
(TP, pg. 225)

♦ Through the devout reading and study of the Scriptures we learn authoritatively the thoughts and ways of God, and His will for daily living. In the *canonical Scriptures, His basic revelation of Himself and His will is complete, and we are warned against accepting any other professed revelation as authentic and authoritative.

-J. Oswald Sanders
(POG, pg. 66)

♦ The purpose of the theological crisis is not to change your theology (although that will happen) but to change you. Instead of viewing the Christian life through your lens of selected Bible verses (God's **acts**), you will begin to view the kingdom with a fresh appreciation for and understanding of God's **ways**. In the end we discover that His voice does not contradict His written word, even though for a time we couldn't reconcile them. The problem wasn't in His word but in our boxed-in understanding.

-Bob Sorge
(FDA, pg.30)

♦ To preach doctrines in an abstract way, and not in reference to practices is absurd. God always brings in doctrine to regulate practice...All preaching should be doctrinal, and all preaching should be practical.

-Charles Finney
(LRR, pg.189)

♦ What is the mariner without his compass? And what is the Christian without the Bible? This is the unerring chart, the map in which every *shoal its describe, and all the channels from the quicksands of destruction to the haven of salvation mapped and marked by the One who knows all the way.

-Charles H. Spurgeon
(POG, pg. 69)

♦ Adherence to the Word of God is the only way you can ensure an acceptable walk before the Lord. To properly obey His Word, you must first discipline your disposition with humility. You must submit your attitude in meekness to the truth of a matter. You must bring all of your imagination into obedience to Christ, and you must beat all your bodily members into subjection.

-RJK

♦ Love for the Word is the measure of our love for the One it magnifies.

-Herbert Lockyer Sr.
(DP, pg. 577)

♦ The Word of God is not like a boxed chocolate cake mix—all sweet and nice and fluffy—but rather resembles a heavy fruit cake, full of substance and hard sayings that people in our time or day and age prefer to reject.

-Jeannette Haley

♦ O what need have we to study the Scriptures, our hearts, and Satan's wiles, that we may not bid this enemy welcome, and all the while think it is Christ that is our guest!

-William Gurnall
(CCA, Vol. 1, pg. 75)

♦ What do I now owe to the Lord for permitting me to take a part in the translation of His Word? Never did I see such wonders, and wisdom, and love, in the blessed Book, as since I have been obliged to study every expression, and it is a delightful reflection that death cannot deprive us of the pleasure of studying its mysteries.

-Henry Martyn
(DP, pg. 593)

Afflictions Brings Men Home

Though for the present strifes do grieve me sore,
    At last they profit more,
And make me to observe thy Word, which I
    Neglected formerly;
Let me come home rather by weeping cross
    Than still be as a loss.
For health I'd rather take a bitter pill,
    Than eating sweet-meats to be always ill.

-Thomas Whasbourne
Died in 1687

For our light affliction, which is but for a moment, worketh for us a far more exceeding and eternal weight of glory (2 Corinthians 4:17).

♦ In the basements of our great libraries are past editions of the encyclopedias which reveal the shifting changes in man's opinions about science, but always the Word of God stands, unchanged.
-Donald Grey Barnhouse
(IW, pg. 70)

♦ No number of Bibles upon our tables or in our libraries will not save us, but the truth of the Bible written by the Spirit of the living God in our hearts will save us.
-R. A. Torrey
(PWH, pg. 98)

♦ Many modern critics are to the Word of God what blowflies are to the food of men: they cannot do any good, and unless relentlessly driven away they do great harm.
-Charles Spurgeon
(DP, pg. 711)

♦ According to R. A. Torrey, there are two laws of interpretation universally recognized among Bible scholars. These two laws are the law of usage...and the law of context. The law of usage operates in the cases of coming to a proper understanding of a word of phrase. It requires you to go to the Bible, look up the various passages in which the word is used and see how the writer is using it in relationship to the passage it is found in. The law of context is applied when it comes to properly studying the passage. You must look at what goes before it and what comes after it. And even though the word may have various meanings, there is only one meaning that will apply to the word in light of the intent of the full text in which it is being presented. (PWH, pg. 195)

♦ Prophecy is not simply the application of timeless standards to particular human situations, but rather an interpretation of a particular moment in history, a divine understanding of a human situation. Prophecy, then may be described as *exegesis of existence from a divine perspective.*
-Abraham J. Heschel
(TP, pg. xxvii)

♦ Words are the clothing of the thoughts of our mind. Jesus came as the revelation of the mind or thought of God.

-Herbert Lockyer Sr.
(DP, pg. 540)

♦ The Word tells us it is the water that cleanses us, preparing us to be the bride of Christ (*Ephesians 5:26*). For me when I obeyed it in the right spirit, it became a washing machine that created the right action in my life to produce godly character. It was a hammer that knocked a lot of personal notions out of my thinking, an ongoing fire that illuminates and purges what remains of my selfishness, and a sword that penetrates down to my motive, exposing it, while circumcising the intents of my heart (*Jeremiah 23:29; Hebrews 4:12*).

-RJK

♦ If men are to come to reality, they must hack through the accumulation of false doctrines that have come from Satan and build upon the clean rock of the Word of God.

-Donald Grey Barnhouse
(IW, pg. 244)

♦ Men preach science, art, literature, philosophy, sociology, history, economics, experience, etc., and not the simple Word of God as found in the Holy Spirit's Book, the Bible.

-R. A. Torrey
(PWH, pg. 143)

♦ God's Son is placed in power over the power of the Enemy; anybody who deals falsely with the Word of God nullifies the position of authority that Christ has given him over Satan.

-Smith Wigglesworth
(SWD, (TFT) Jun. 7)

♦ We may sit under the wisest teachers and yet remain fools. If, however, we love the Word, and seek to live in it, and by it, wisdom will become ours—a wisdom outweighing the teachings of men if they were all gathered into one vast library. Thus, "it behooves us to follow closely the chart of the Word of God, that we may be able to save the vessel when even the pilot errs.

-Herbert Lockyer Sr.
(DP, pg. 579)

♦ The entire New Testament never so much as mentions that we should make it a matter of daily heedfulness, whereas the religion or devotion that is to govern the ordinary actions of our lives is found in almost every verse of Scripture.

-William Law
(DHL, pg. 11)

♦ He showed us that the surest road to wisdom is not speculation, reasoning, or reading human books, but meditation upon the Word of God.

-Charles Spurgeon
(MES, Jan. 18 (E))

♦ He that sells cheapest shall have most customers, though, at last, best will be best cheap; truth with self-denial (is) a better pennyworth, than error with all its flesh-pleasing.

-William Gurnall
(CCA, Vol. 1, pg. 82)

Making a Left Turn

Through the years I have fed and challenged my soul on the writings of the saints of the past. Many times I have marveled at the fact that you could rightly apply their writings to present day challenges. Granted, when you begin to check out the culture surrounding them it was a bit different but these writers defended the attributes and truth of God and His Word, and contended with the issues of sin, faith, grace, and judgment. As I have read these writings of past years, I can also hear the same urgency and call for God's people to come back into line with the standard that can only be lifted up by His Spirit according to His immutable Word.

The reality is that truth is truth. It marches to a consistent beat. There is no skipping or deviation to the rhythm it pulsates to. Admittedly, I have enjoyed the credence of truth that I often follow in these books. However, occasionally, I find myself tripping over boulders that mark detours. It is almost like going straight but you end up taking a detour as the writer makes a sharp left. These left turns involve pet doctrines or causes.

Each generation must fight a different fight when it comes to theological matters. Granted, non-essential doctrines and heresies may vary with each new generation. It is a known fact that Satan just repackages old lies and adjusts them to the present environment. He also can bring non-essential theological issues to the forefront that have nothing to do with salvation. They simply take Christians on a rabbit trail of foolish debate that often ends in frivolous division.

Every time I find myself taking a left turn in a book, I silently want to yell, "Get back to the original point!" However, I have been guilty of falling into the trap of theological causes. I have debated and argued about non-essential points to prove my own take on a matter. I have even had to alleviate whole chapters out of my books because I got on a tangent. Through it all I have learned that immaturity takes a *zealous* stand in such issues, a guilty conscience takes an *offensive* stand, self-righteousness adopts a *critical* stand, and ignorance a *fearful, angry* stance.

Once I remember that I have caused such detours in the past, I have to stop and know that we can do nothing against the truth. In the end, it will always remain standing. With this thought in mind I begin to plow through the non-essential matters of the book, knowing that I will pick up the rhythm of truth that awaits me on the other side. I know that on the other side of the detours, there are other nuggets to discover, gems to obtain, and treasures to possess.

For we can do nothing against the truth, but for the truth (2 Corinthians 13:8).

♦ The debates as to whether God said something, or whether He meant what He said is always the big "IF" people throw in the equation when discussing the credibility of God's Word. When we get into the debate of the imagined "IFS" in regard to the validity of God's Word, we will always digress into a state of unbelief.

-RJK

♦ Our nation is desperately in need of spiritual awakening. But our emphasis on evangelism apart from doctrine will certainly not do it.

-Warren Wiersbe
(VCK, pg. 117)

♦ I was aware of one of the ways in which the Bible was spelled out: **Basic Instructions Before Leaving Earth.** However, I came across another such spelling: **Blessed Information Bringing Life Eternal.**

-Unknown
(BB)

♦ I want us to examine ourselves in the light of the Word. God has definitely purposed that we should inherit all the Scriptures, but we must meet the requirements necessary to claim them. Remember this, there are any number of things you may quote without possessing the essential reality of them.

-Smith Wigglesworth
(SWD, Jun. 17)

♦ The readiest way to be spiritually rich in heavenly knowledge is to dig in this mine of diamonds, to gather pearls from this heavenly sea. When Jesus Himself sought to enrich others, He wrought in the quarry of Holy Scriptures.

-Charles Spurgeon
(MES, Jan. 18 (E))

***

There is a light that pierces
    Through the darkness—

A sword that cuts through marrow
    And bone—

The truth is laid bare.

Shining through the lens of eye
    The soul is seen—
The heart beats it's steady rhythm

As blood flows through the stream
Of arteries and walls unseen—

The truth is laid bare.

Dry bones lay in the valley
Covered with age and despair—

O Spirit come and fill us
We need your tender care.
Only by your leading can we stand
And breathe in air.

Alive are we when truth is laid bare.

-Maureen Human

For the word of God is quick, and powerful, and sharper than any twoedged sword, piercing even to the dividing asunder of soul and spirit, and of the joints and marrow, and is a discerner of the thoughts and intents of the heart (Hebrews 4:12).

♦ The Bible does not claim to legislate in detail for every matter of conduct that may arise. Instead, clear principles of conduct are enunciated. When correctly applied, these will be found to cover most contingencies—but we must work at searching them out. If God had not made clear guidance available to us, how could He hold us responsible if we failed to do His will?

-J. Oswald Sanders
(POG, pg. 68)

♦ If our consciousness differs from the statements of this Book, which is so plainly God's Book, it is not yet fully Christian, and the thing to do is not to try to pull God's revelation down to the level of our consciousness but to tone our consciousness up to the level of God's Word.

-R. A. Torrey
(PWH, pg. 239)

♦ ...be assured you will find no rest in philosophizing divinity. You may receive this dogma of one great thinker, or that dream of another profound reasoner, but what the chaff is to the wheat, that will these be to the pure word of God.

-Charles Spurgeon
(MES, Sept. 25 (E))

♦ All grace grows as love to the Word of God grows.

-Matthew Henry

♦ We read the works of the historians and the writings of the journalists, we listen to the statement and the commentators, but we are not engaged in the same guess-work that occupies them. We have in the Bible a full-width sample of the cloth that is to come from the machine at a certain time. We do not know when that moment is to be.

-Donald Grey Barnhouse
(IW, pg. 265)

♦ If the Word stays not in the memory, much spiritual nourishment is lost. "Some can better remember a piece of news than a line of scripture; their memories are like those ponds, where frogs live, but fish die.

-Herbert Lockyer Sr.
(DP, pg. 555)

♦ Inactivity must be brought to a place of victory. Inactivity—what wavers, what hesitates, what fears instead of having faith—closes up everything, because it doubts instead of believe in God. What is faith? Faith is the living principle of the Word of God.

-Smith Wigglesworth
(SWD, Feb. 3)

♦ Men, you turn people into sin by preaching a doctrine that contradicts the teaching of the Son of God.

-R. A. Torrey
(RA, pg. 123)

♦ The phrase, "with our eyes," John included in order to combat false doctrine in the first century which was known as Docetism, namely, the teaching that our Lord only had a seeming body, not a truly human one.

-Kenneth S. Wuest
(GTL, pg. 100)

♦ I want us to have something more than the literal word. Words are of no importance unless the believer has the assurance of the abiding of those words. You can quote the words of Scripture without being in the place of victory.

-Smith Wigglesworth
(SWD, Jun. 17)

Who Saved Who?

The bombs were hitting the buildings that had housed the women prisoners during the Japanese occupation of the islands in the East Indies during WWII. All the women had taken refuge in the trenches, but while in the trench, Darlene Deibler had remembered that since her Bible had fallen apart, she had borrowed Mrs. Lee's Bible and she needed to save it from its burning fate.

Darlene ran into the burning barracks, scrambled up the ladder of her bunk and retrieved the Bible. When she came out of the building to witness the ensuring chaos, someone had opened the gate of the compound and people were fleeing across the mote to hide in the rice paddies.

After the bedlam was over with, Darlene was surprised that many prisoners had survived the bombing, bullets, and fires. As the prisoners came back to their burn-out buildings, she heard someone crying that her mattress had been burned. Darlene reminded the woman that all the buildings were burned but they were still alive. However, the crying woman told her she did not leave the mattress in the barracks; rather she had thrown it in the ditch where Darlene had been lying.

It was then that Darlene realized the Lord has used the urgent need to retrieve the Bible from the burning building as a means to get her out of harm's way of a bomb. (ENS, pgs. 165-168)

Men and brethren, children of the stock of Abraham, and whosoever among you feareth God, to you is the word of this salvation sent. (Acts 13:26).

- The discernment of God's truth and the development of character go together.
-Oswald Chambers
(DTD, Oct. 30)

- Religion is the greatest enemy to reality and truth. Religion is man's solution to man's problem by doing things man's way.
-Jeannette Haley

- God wants to bring us into harmony with His will so that we will see that if we do not believe all of the Word of God, something in us is not purely sanctified to accept the fullness of His Word.
-Smith Wigglesworth
(SWD, Jan. 12)

- There is no magical charm about the letter of the word — even God's Word. Apart from the power of God's Spirit, the best instruction is as dead as the dry bones of Ezekiel 37. But with the "breath of God" breathing on it, it could become as powerful as "the exceeding great army" the dry bones became. The power came from the breath of God, not from the dry bones.
-Eileen Fraser Crossman
(MR, pg. 210)

- All heresy is either the Bible plus, or the Bible minus.
-Lewis Sperry Chafer

- Ignorance of the Word of God will kill you!
-Unknown
(BB)

- Not a single thing in the Scriptures clashes with or contradicts the Spirit and makes trouble.
-Smith Wigglesworth
(SWD, Jun. 18)

What is in a Bible?

Jesus states that His Words are spirit and life. In summation, the Holy Spirit will bring life to His Words. The Bible is a diary of God's heart and love towards man. In it God sets forth the greatest aspirations He has for each of us. These aspirations have been signed and delivered through the death and resurrection of Jesus Christ. It is for this reason the Bible is the most priceless book one can possess.

This brings me to another question. How many Bibles do you possess? I have various Bibles, but there are only two Bibles that I prefer when it comes to studying the Word. They are my faithful standbys. One of my preferred Bibles is the first study Bible I received on January 14, 1977. It was a Scofield's Study Bible. It is 36 years old. In the front of it are sayings and poems that I considered to be valuable gems. In the back is the record of reading the Bible through along with study material during the first initial years of my salvation. I noted which Bible I read and what day and year I finished it. Amazingly, I read the Bible through six times, starting from 1977 through 1981.

Other notations in the back of my Bible include some of my favorite Scriptures along with the Romans' Road and bits and pieces of information and a few gems. The Bible's corners are torn, ragged, and curled up from constantly turning the pages. I can tell I spend a great deal of my time in the New Testament. Sadly, the glue of the spine has lost its staying power and as a result pages have torn away from it, but I still will not part with it.

The other Bible that I value is my present Bible. You have to break a Bible in. It is like breaking in a new pair of shoes, but once they are broken in they often become your favorites. After all, they fit quite nicely.

The Scriptures in my Bible have been underlined according to theme. I know where my favorite Scriptures are and how to locate those I am thinking of. That describes a Bible that fits quite nicely.

Because I collect gems, I have asked saints who attend the same church I do, if they have collected or recorded any sayings or information that I could use for my nugget books. Sure enough, a saint by the name of Betty Allen told me that she had sayings recorded in her Bible.

One Sunday in Church she walked up to me with a Bible in her hand. She gingerly handed it to me with a certain look that spoke volumes to me as to how important the Bible was. I assured her I would guard it with my life. It had a big rubber band around it. Even though the actual Bible was sandwiched in between a brown Bible cover, I could tell that she had done much to protect the integrity of it. When I opened the cover I could see that the spine and edges of the Bible had been reinforce with good old duct tape and a label with her name on it.

Amazingly, it was a Scofield Study Bible. It was given to Betty by her mother and it was dated December of 1959. True to her word, she had recorded many nuggets in the front and back of it. Some of the gems have already been recorded in my other books, but there were others that were new and priceless; therefore, they have been recorded throughout this book and I have identified them with the letters "BB", Betty's Bible.

What is in a Bible: the valuable, insightful, and priceless treasures of heaven. What is in the Bible: everything that is dear, precious, and inspirational. What is in the Bible: living wisdom, eternal truths, and the incredible revelation of God Almighty.

All scripture is given by inspiration of God, and is profitable for doctrine, for reproof, for correction, for instruction in righteousness: That the man of God may be perfect, thoroughly furnished unto all good works (2 Timothy 3:16-17).

◆ If you want to go to hell, all you need to do is to disbelieve the Word of God.

-Smith Wigglesworth
(SWD, (TFT) Feb. 9)

◆ Too many Christians have all the doctrine in their heads, but live lives that contradict it.

-Watchman Nee
(WN, May 4)

♦ Scripture itself is the best interpreter of Scripture. To say that the Bible explains itself would not be an overstatement. Knowing the full counsel of God is critical to our understanding of it.

-T. A. McMahon

♦ Men unsound in doctrine complicate the issues. Ah, for a place where Scriptures have not been twisted!

-Jim Elliot
(SOA, pg. 140)

♦ The truths you stand for, you are tried for.

-Smith Wigglesworth
(SWD, (TFT) Jul. 13)

♦ George Horne said that we on earth are subject to a threefold *darkness*—"the darkness of error, the darkness of sorrow, the darkness of death. To dispel these, God visiteth us, by His Word, with a threefold *light*—the light of truth, the light of comfort, and the light of life.

♦ (Said to fellow pastors): Take heed of growing remiss in your work. Take pains while you live...The Scripture still affords new things, to those who search them.

-Matthew Henry
(VCK, pg. 92)

***

Holy Bible, Book Divine,
Precious treasure thou art mine,
Mine to tell me whence I came,
Mine to teach me what I am.

-Unknown
(BB)

For if any be a hearer of the word, and not a doer, he is like unto a man beholding his natural face in a glass: For he beholdeth himself, and goeth his way, and straightway forgetteth what manner of man he was (James 1:23-24).

♦ I understand God by His Word. I cannot understand God by impressions or feelings. I cannot get to know God by sentiments. If I am going to know God, I am going to know Him by His Word.

-Smith Wigglesworth
(SWD, Feb. 16)

♦ His works and words can never fail, for His power supports them, and His providence preserves the record of all He has said and done. All His works are nothing else but the making good of His Word, and not one jot or title shall pass from the law of His mouth, till all be fulfilled.

-Herbert Lockyer, Sr.
(DP, pg. 465)

♦ Every revelation of God is something internal. And it is always personal.

-Manfred Haller
(CA, pg. 27)

♦ If the sinner is attracted by the modernism of the believer's adornment, the fundamentalism of the believer's doctrine will be neutralized.

Kenneth Wuest
(BNT, pg. 109)

♦ The all-important thing is to make Jesus Lord of your life. Men can become lopsided by emphasizing the truth of divine healing. Men can get into error by preaching on water baptism all the time. But we never go wrong in exalting the Lord Jesus Christ, in giving Him the preeminent place and glorifying Him as both Lord and Christ.

-Smith Wigglesworth
(SWD, Oct. 31)

Who Was Jesus Talking To?

While getting her hair cut, my co-laborer in the Gospel, Jeannette quietly sat in the chair in the beauty salon, listening to her beautician and another woman discussing whether Satan existed or not. The beautician stated that she did not think Satan was real. It was upon that statement that Jeannette interjected a simple question into the women's conversation.

She asked the beautician, "If Satan is not real, who was Jesus talking to during the time He was tempted in the wilderness?" The beautician was stunned into silence at which time the woman who had been discussing the matter with her, piped in, "Touché!"

Then was Jesus led up of the Spirit into the wilderness to be tempted of the devil (Matthew 4:1).

♦ The devil's cleverest ruse is to make men believe that he does not exist.

-Baudelaire
(IW, pg. 156)

What Satan Says

The Fallen Angel says, "I am thy heaven, there is no other hope.
The prince of this world declares, "There is no other world."
The Tempter tests with, "There is no judge."
The Accuser of believers tries to convince them that, "There is no pardon."
The Liar summarizes it all by offering a world a free pass without consequences, and lying declares, "There is no reality."
And, the Legion speaks the ultimate blasphemy, "There is nobody."

-Taken from the writings of
De Rougemont
(IW, pg. 157)

But if our gospel be hid, it is hid to them that are lost: In whom the god of this world hath blinded the minds of them which believe not, lest the light of the glorious gospel of Christ, who is the image of God should shine unto them (2 Corinthians 4:3-4).

♦ According to the Bible, sin in its final analysis is not a defect but a defiance, a defiance that means death to the life of God in us.

-Oswald Chambers
(DTD, May 22)

♦ The dangers of legalism are best combated by teaching "the word of His grace, which is able to build you up, and to give you an inheritance among all them which are sanctified."

Isobel Kuhn
(NAA, pg. 165)

♦ Satan wants to rob us of sound doctrine. He entices us to believe in a form of "watered-down" Christianity that allows for worldly compromise. With religious acts and games, Satan lulls us into a spiritual sleep. He affords us the false luxury of believing we are on the correct path, when in fact, we have not even begun to pay the necessary price to know God *(Luke 14:28-33)*.

-RJK

♦ You have the Scriptures, and you have the Holy Spirit. The Holy Spirit has wisdom, and He does not expect you to be foolish. The Holy Spirit has perfect insight into knowledge and wisdom, and truth always gives you balance.

-Smith Wigglesworth
(SWD, Nov. 25)

♦ Smith Wigglesworth stated that the more of God's Word you hide in your heart, the easier it is to live a holy life. Then he identifies the challenge Christians must honestly contend with, "I find nothing in the Bible but holiness, and nothing in the world but worldliness. Therefore, if I live in the world, I will become worldly; on the other hand, if I live in the Bible, I will become holy." (SWD, Mar. 17)

♦ A revealed secret is no longer a secret. Dissected truths are no longer spiritual truths; they are ineffective, lifeless *theorems.

-Manfred Haller
(CA, pg. 17)

♦ ...without the Bible, humanity would be nearly clueless about God; without the Bible, people would be completely deluded about their moral condition; without the Bible, humanity would have no idea what its purpose might be; without the Bible, mankind is lost in a condition of hopelessness and worse.

-T. A. McMahon

♦ We learn God's will, mainly, not by impulses and impressions, but by the prayerful study of the principles of Scripture and by their intelligent application to the case at hand.

-J. Oswald Sanders
(POG, pg. 105)

♦ You cannot sacrifice the truth for your environment without coming into agreement with a wrong spirit.

-Jeannette Haley

♦ It is our privilege to preach the Word, but no single one of us is God's oracle. We cannot utter his words without bringing to them something personal of our own.

-Watchman Nee
(WN, Feb. 15)

♦ Today much of the Church appears to major in disagreements and minor in basic truths of Christianity. We see people making doctrinal statements based on denominational affiliation or schools of thought inspired by men, rather than on the Word of God.

-RJK

♦ Nothing makes you so foolish as to turn aside from the Word of God. If you ever want to be a fool, turn away from God's Word, and you will find yourself in a fool's paradise.

-Smith Wigglesworth
(SWD, (TFT) Nov. 28)

Defying the Waves of Testing

The Bible tells us that the Word of God is eternal. It will survive when other things become lost or consumed during times of testing.

There is a story about missionary, Dr. Alexander Duff. On his first voyage on the ship Lady Holland to India in 1836, the vessel was wrecked amid breakers off the coast of South Africa. In spite of the traumatic experience, each passenger miraculously reached a small island with nothing but their lives.

Later, an object caught a sailor's attention who was walking alone on the beach. He found it to be a quarto copy of Bagster's Bible, and a Scottish Psalm Book with the name of Dr. Duff on them. Although badly shattered, the sailor sought out the missionary at the shelter that housed the passengers and presented the two tattered books to the doctor. Upon receiving the books, the doctor quoted Psalm 107, thanked God and took courage. Of the 800 volumes Dr. Duff had taken with him to establish a library in India, only his Bible and Psalm Book defied the stormy waves of testing and were carried to the shore as a message from God as to His abiding protection on His people, His Word, and His work. (DP, pg. 430)

The grass withereth, the flower fadeth: but the word of our God shall stand for ever (Isaiah 40:8).

♦ According to the wise counsel of the Rabbins, there are three best safeguards against falling into sin. First, there is an ear which hears everything; secondly, there is an eye which see everything; thirdly, that there is a hand which writes everything in the Book of Knowledge which shall be opened at the judgment. (DP, pg. 336)

♦ If Christianity is false, we ought to suppress it; if Christianity is true we are bound to propagate it

-Archbishop Whateley

♦ "A people that does err" literally means, *a people of wanderers in heart*—they were morally astray through ignorance of God's ways. All mortals err, but here it is said that the Israelites erred *in their heart*. They went astray not through ignorance, but through corruption and perversity of heart, which was not right with God. "Lust in the heart, like vapor in the stomach, soon affects the head and clouds the understanding."

-Herbert Lockyer, Sr.
(DP, pg. 344)

♦ Thank God for His Word. Live it. Be moved by it. We will become anemic and helpless without the Word. We are not any good for anything apart from the Word. It is everything. When the heavens and earth are melted away, then we will be as bright as the day because of the Word of God.

-Smith Wigglesworth
(SWD, Dec. 21)

Denying The Authority of the Word

Anytime a person does not believe and obey the Word of God, he or she is showing contempt towards it. Through the years the debate has raged that the Word of God cannot be trusted. Such foolish individuals claim that there are inconsistencies in it.

In his book, *Great Truths To Live By*, Kenneth Wuest, refutes such claims. Admittedly, he points out in his book that for 1500 years until the age of printing, the New Testament manuscripts were copied by hand. He also noted that during that time mistakes did manage to creep into the texts. However, these mistakes were later eliminated by textual critics.

These critics had a vast amount of material in which to work from. These works included the following: 4,000 Greek manuscripts, 8,000 copies of the Latin Vulgate, and 2,000 copies of the New Testament in other languages, along with 14,000 other sources.

It is important to also point out that the Greek manuscripts go back to the third century in an unbroken succession that included the writings and commentaries of the Apostolic and Church Fathers. One of the early Church Fathers, Tertullian, stated that the original manuscripts were still in existence A.D. 200. The conclusion is that in the end the best Greek New Testament texts were brought forth.

According to scholars of his day, Wuest records the results of the critics' efforts to ensure integrity of the New Testament: That 999 words out of every 1000 are the same as those in the original manuscripts. The dispute over the 1000th word is minor and does not affect the historical fact or the intent of Scripture. (GTL, pg. 44)

For I testify unto every man that heareth the words of the prophecy of this book, If any man shall add unto these things, God shall add unto him the plagues that are written in this book: And if any man shall take away from the words of the book of this prophecy, God shall take away his part out of the book of life, and out of the holy city, and from the things which are written in this book (Revelation 22:18-19).

THE POWER OF PRAYER

An African's Prayer

Do prayers to the true God of heaven differ from nation to nation, people to people? I believe that they will vary according to the circumstances, but as far as the spiritual plight of humanity, I believe they are of the same caliber. Granted, the way a person may express him or herself might be based on cultural and language influences, but the inward struggles and challenges would prove to be the same.

A simple, but profound prayer of an African believer at Gendia, on Lake Victoria was recorded in the year 1935 by a missionary. It was only a few years prior to this prayer that these same people were naked savages, steeped in superstition and filthy. As a testimony to God's incredible work, more than 2,000 earnest Christians gathered under a great spreading tree for this service. The following is the beautiful, sincere prayer that was recorded:

"Our Father, we kneel down before Thee, Thou great Creator. Thy power is manifest in the making of all things from nothing. Thy voice is the thunder and Thine eye like the lightning, but Thy character is merciful and Thy heart is kind.

"As now we pass the portal of this day, and enter into this the beginning of another year, hold Thou our hands and walk with us along the way, that road which is narrow but takes us where we want to go— the village of our Lord.

"We thank Thee for our unknown friends in Europe who sent messengers of peace to us who were black in custom as in color, but who now share the hope that is in Jesus, our Saviour.

"Even now we know our own weakness, weak as marrow and frail as eggs. Increase our faith that we may stand as firm as our mountains, and fight the good fight with the power of an earthquake.

"Heal us from our disease. The greatest of them is leprosy, this leprosy of sin eating away the heart, and worse than syphilis, in that it brings blindness, not of the eyes, but of the soul. Thou alone art our doctor, and therefore inoculate us with Thy certain cure, the Holy Spirit, that, circulating in us, may kill the germs of sin.

"Wash us and place the soap at the door of the heart to cleanse everything before entering into it. Keep our minds pure like the drinking water of the Europeans, which has been boiled and filtered.

"How many wonders the white man has created and brought here, but they are all vain and nothing when we think of the miracle of redemption. O Lord, Thy love is higher than the sun, deeper than our great lake (Victoria Nyanza), broader than the horizon, and stronger than death. Because of this love we crave Thy blessing on us, our children, and Thy great work in every land, and we want to be found at last with our characters built up and complete, as a house roofed and finished.

"When the register is marked in heaven, we are anxious to be marked 'Present' at the coming of the Lord, and have our tickets ready and in order. Guide us, therefore, we pray in the days to come, and when the angels garner the fruit of the earth, gather us with them, the Christians of every land, to live with Thee evermore in Thine own kingdom. Amen."

And he spake a parable unto them to this end, that men ought always to pray, and not to faint (Luke 18:1).

♦ The issue of prayer is not prayer; the issue of prayer is God.
-Abraham Joshua Heschel

♦ Keep the altar of private prayer burning. This is the very life of all piety. The sanctuary and family altars borrow their fires here, therefore let this burn well. Secret devotion is the very essence, evidence, and barometer, of vital and experimental religion.

-Charles Spurgeon
(MES, Jul. 15 (M))

♦ The prayer of faith is generally short and always to the point, taking the soul and placing it before God in its real state and true character.

-Herbert Lockyer, Sr.
(DP, pg. 506)

♦ Prayer is not in itself meritorious. It lays God under no obligation nor puts Him in debt to any. He hears prayer because He is good, and for no other reason. Nor is faith meritorious; it is simply confidence in the goodness of God, and the lack of it is not a reflection upon God's holy character.

-A. W. Tozer
(KH, pg. 83)

♦ There are earnest Christians who have just enough prayer to maintain their spiritual position but not enough to grow spiritually.

-Andrew Murray
(AP, Feb. 18)

♦ When we depend upon organizations, we get what organizations can do. When we depend on education, we will get what education can do. When we depend upon psychology, we get what psychology can do. When we depend upon man, we get what man can do. But when we depend upon PRAYER, we get what GOD can do!

-A. C. Dixion

♦ Prayer is an interruption to personal ambition, and no man who is busy has time to pray. What will suffer is the life of God in him, which is nourished not by food but by prayer.

-Oswald Chambers
(DTD, Oct. 27)

♦ In prayer it is better to have a heart without words than words without a heart.

-Unknown
(BB)

♦ You cannot have holy prayers and divine petitions without a holiness of life suitable to them; and you cannot have a holy and divine life without prayers.

-William Law
(DHL, pg. 10)

♦ When God does something to you, all you can do is submit and pray and wait for God to fulfill His purposes.

-Bob Sorge
(FDA, pg. 51)

♦ Prayer is the state of the heart. The spirit of prayer is a state of continual desire and anxiety of mind for the salvation of sinners.

-Charles Finney
(LRR, pg. 27-28)

♦ A surrendered will implies that we are as willing to have our plans vetoed as to have them confirmed by our heavenly Guide. This attitude is not always reached overnight. Sometimes it will come only after many prayers and much soul-travail. But divine obligations must always take precedence over personal preferences.

J. Oswald Sanders
(POG, pg. 60)

♦ It is always best to get blessings into our house in the legitimate way, by the door of prayer; then they are blessings indeed, and not temptations.

-Charles Spurgeon
(MES, Sept. 19 (E))

♦ How we need to pray daily for a holy collectedness of spirit and for Divine watch upon our lips.

-Herbert Lockyer Sr.
(DP, pg. 510)

***

O make me, Lord, thy statutes learn!
    Keep in thy ways my feet,
Then shall my lips divinely burn;
    Then shall my songs be sweet.

Each sin I cast away shall make
    My soul more strong to soar;
Each deed of holiness shall wake
    A strain divine the more

My voice shall more delight thine ear,
    The more I wait on thee;
Thy service begin my song more near
    The angelic harmony.

-T. H. Gill
Published in 1881
(DP, pg. 611)

Wait on the LORD: be of good courage, and he shall strengthen thine heart: wait, I say, on the LORD (Psalm 27:14).

♦ In the allegory of the ancients, "*Hope* was left at the bottom of the basket, as the sweetener of human life, but God in far richer *mercy* gives prayer as the balm of human trial.

♦ Prayer is not convincing heaven of my agenda but of submitting to heaven's agenda. Prayer has no advance agenda. The purpose of prayer is to hear the heart purposes of God, lend intercession toward that purpose, and make oneself available to the Master's purposes.

-Bob Sorge
(FDA, pg. 107)

♦ To pray effectually, you must pray with submission to the will of God. Do not confound submission with indifference. No two things are more unlike.

-Charles Finney
(LRR, pg. 51)

♦ Prayer and guidance are to be regarded as Siamese twins. They cannot exist apart.

-J. Oswald Sanders
(POG, pg. 66)

♦ Prayer is the safest method of replying to words of hatred.
-Charles Spurgeon
(MES, Jan. 15 (E))

♦ Prayer that is not an effort of the will is unrecognized by God.
-Oswald Chambers
(DTD, Nov. 20)

♦ Let us not pray for a light burden, but rather for a strong back.
-Unknown

♦ When we pray for God's perspective on persecution, we find the courage to be obedient at all costs.
Extreme Devotion
(ED, pg. 1)

♦ Christians around the world agree prayer is essential to see God move on our behalf, win the lost world to Christ and build God's kingdom. Yet studies show pastors spend about 12 minutes in prayer a day, and the average believer spends only eight minutes.
-K. P. Yohannan

♦ In relationship to how prayer works in the kingdom of God, China missionary James O. Fraser said this, "Desire, however deep, does nothing in itself, any more than steam pressure in a boiler is of use, unless it is allowed to drive machinery." (MR, pg. 117) Fraser understood prayer drives all matters in the kingdom of God. As believers we would be surprised to see how much our desires have led us to spiritual dead ends. However, prayer is like hurricane force winds. It can drive a matter right through any hindrance or obstacle to see the impossible accomplished.

***

And the LORD came, and stood, and called as at other times, Samuel, Samuel. Then Samuel answered, Speak; for thy servant heareth (1 Samuel 3:10).

♦ Prayer is the nearest approach to God, and the highest enjoyment of Him, that we are capable of in this life. It is the noblest exercise of the souls, the most exalted use of our best faculties and the highest imitation of the blessed inhabitants of heaven.

-William Law
(DHL, pg. 149)

♦ When the answers to our prayers are delayed, and our circumstances reach emergency proportions, God uses the crisis to break us open, to empty us of everything that is not of Him, and to soften the soil of our hearts with tears.

-Bob Sorge
(FDA, pg. 117)

♦ When Christians are united, and praying as they ought, God opens the windows of heaven, and pours out his blessings till there is not room to receive them.

-Charles Finney
(LRR, pg. 119)

♦ Prayer plumes the wings of God's young eaglets, that they may learn to mount above the clouds. Prayer girds the loins of God's warriors, and sends them forth to combat with their sinews braced and their muscles firm.

-Charles Spurgeon
(MES, Oct. 11 (M))

♦ Our prayer and God's mercy are like two buckets in a well; while the one ascends, the other descends.

-Herbert Lockyer Sr.
(DP, pg. 731)

♦ Prayer is our first defense against spiritual warfare, yet often our last resort.

-Extreme Devotion
(ED, pg. 47)

♦ Prayer alters a man on the inside, alters his mind and his attitude.
-Oswald Chambers
(DTD, Jan. 14)

♦ It has been well said, "Your kneeling keeps you in good standing."
-Unknown

♦ In prayer we must expect difficulties which can be conquered only by determined perseverance.
-Andrew Murray
(AP, Mar. 6)

♦ It is frightening to consider that we have our prayers answered but be impoverished for it. As George Veach once shared with me, "We can insist on something to our own hurt."
-Bob Sorge
(FDA, pg. 184)

♦ I often used to pray, "Lord, have compassion on a lost world," At last He said to me, "I have had compassion; it is now for you to have compassion. I gave my heart, give yours."
-A. J. Gordon

♦ Prayerful waiting ensures that your prayers are lifted up by the wings of quiet confidence to be taken to the throne room of God.
-RJK

♦ The man in a storm prays to God, not for safety from danger; but for deliverance from fear.
-Unknown
(BB)

***

Not all can Go; not all can Give
To speed the message on its way,
But young or old, or rich or poor,
Or strong or weak – we all can Pray: --

More Heavenly Gems

Pray that the gold-filled hand may Give
    To arm the others for the fray;
That those who hear the call may Go,
    And pray – that other hearts may Pray!

-Annie Johnson Flint
(1866-1932)

Then saith he unto his disciples, The harvest truly is plenteous, but the labourers are few: Pray ye therefore the Lord of the harvest, that he will send forth labourers into his harvest (Matthew 9:37-38).

♦ Prayer at its highest is a two-way conversation—and for me the most import part is listening to God's replies.

-Frank C. Laubach

♦ Prayer needs sacrifice of comfort, of time of self. Sacrifice is the secret of powerful prayer.

-Andrew Murray
(AP, Jul. 21)

♦ But the hypocrites in heart treasure up wrath; they cry not when God binds them. See this difference in Saul and David; Saul goes to the witch of Endor, but David always cried to the Lord.

-John Rusk
(FT, pg. 60)

♦ A prayer is none the less but all the more a prayer because veins of praise run through it.

-Herbert Lockyer, Sr.
(DP, pg. 287)

♦ I shall work as if everything depended on me; I shall pray as if everything depended on God.

-Maxim of St. Augustine
Fifth-century thinker

♦ Did you ever try getting on your knees to help you to get on your feet?

-Unknown

♦ P.U.S.H. Pray until something happens.

-Unknown
(BB)

♦ One of the first lessons we learn in the Ministry of the Interior is to talk things out before God in soliloquy—tell God what you know He knows in order that you may get to know as He does.

-Oswald Chambers
(DTD, Mar. 7)

♦ If a Christian does not pray, he becomes a worrier. If he does pray, he becomes a warrior.

-Unknown

♦ Prayer is the never-failing resort of the Christian in any case, in every plight.

-Charles Spurgeon
(MES, Nov. 3 (E))

♦ Too often, we tumble into the presence of the Almighty with no clear idea of what we want to speak to Him about.

-Herbert Lockyer Sr.
(DP, pg. 731)

♦ Prayer, to be effectual, must be offered from right motives. Prayer should not be selfish, but dictated by supreme regard for the glory of God.

-Charles Finney
(LRR, pg. 53)

Simple Request, Glorious Results

His new cell mate, Aaron Moiseyevich was a Jew. Mikhail Khorev was in a Russian prison for his faith in Jesus Christ and initially suspected that Moiseyevich was of Jewish descent. It was a miracle Khorev was allowed to keep his small New Testament during his incarceration. He had cherished such a privilege by keeping a spiritual regimentation up by reading it and praying. In fact, he became known as a "holy man."

When Moisyevich asked Khorev what was he reading, he told him the New Testament. However, his answer made Moisyevich recoil. Khorev offered to read about Abraham and Moses in Hebrews 11, but the Jew would have none of it and told him that he must not read it out loud

After being in the cell for a week the two men developed a friendship. One Sunday Khorev asked Moisyevich permission to read the New Testament out loud for ten minutes as a means to receive comfort. The Jew gave him permission.

Khorev turned to the Sermon on the Mount. He read chapter 5 and chapter 6 as Moisyevich listened, but when he got to chapter 7 where it says, ask, seek, and knock, and related it to a son asking for bread and fish, it was at that point the Jew interrupted with a command to stop, startling Khorev. He wanted to know what it would mean to ask for something, and God would actually grant the request. The Jew went on to say, "Your God will answer your prayers...Whatever you ask?"

Khorev nodded, and assured him that God answer prayers for He has answered many of his prayers. It was then that Moisyevich snorted and asked why God had not delivered him out of prison? Khorev related that he could have gotten out of prison the night they arrested him, but it required him to deny his faith and he refused to deny what he knew was true. He was an evangelist that traveled to the different underground churches in Russia to encourage them in their faith. Khorev related his life to the Jew and even though he had a wife and three sons waiting for him at home, he told him that he was not praying to go home but to continue God's work in prison.

The Jew thought about their conversation for several moments, saying, "For everyone that asketh, receiveth. Is that what it really says?"

The godly man nodded his head and replied, "Yes."

Moisyevich laughed and with a challenging look stated, "Then I will tell you what to ask. Ask your God to send some apples. In the two years I have been in prison, not once have I tasted an apple."

After Khorev considered the request, Moisyevich once again challenged him to ask for an apple. Khorev agreed to do so. That is when Moisyevich commanded him to pray out loud. He wanted to hear him ask for apples.

Like Daniel of old, Khorev in his regular fashion kneeled on the floor beside his cot and said this prayer, "Lord God of Abraham, Isaac, and Jacob, I am glad you have always been attentive to the needs of your people. You kept your people in the wilderness when they left Egypt, and gave them manna from heaven to eat. When they asked for meat, you sent them quail. You heard every prayer from the hearts of those who were truly seeking you."

Khorev stated that he knew God would hear the desire of one of the descendants of Abraham, and that he was asking for apples. Since nothing was impossible for God and He heard the prayers of those who sincerely seek Him, he had the assurance that God would hear the request and grant it.

As Khorev was about to finish his request, Moisyevich added a P.S. to it. The Jew wanted Antovnov apples. These are native to Russia and are similar to Granny Smiths apple. Khorev added the P.S. and ended his prayer.

Two weeks later, the cell door opened and without explanation, a man entered the cell and thumped a box of apples on the cot. Moisyevich was stunned and Khorev rejoiced to his answered prayers. And within the assortment of apples, there were several that were Antonov. (SPP, pgs.138-138)

We often valued prayer in light of great miracles but in so many cases the answered prayers that touch us the most are those that are personal. In my years of serving God, the answered prayers to the personal, secret desires of the heart have not only proved His love and faithfulness to me, but that He is aware of all that I have need of. He can part the Red Sea, but He will also bring that specific request that in the scheme of things may be small and petty, but will prove to be just as miraculous as parting great rivers.

Be careful for nothing; but in every thing by prayer and supplication with thanksgiving let your requests be made known unto God (Philippians 4:6).

THE POWER OF THE MESSAGE
OF THE CROSS

The Unmistakable Command

The command to God's servant is simple enough. It is a command, "to go." For one to go, it means they are moving forward, to some goal or purpose. Such individuals are not aimless for they have been commanded to go. They are not lost for they have a definite road map as to their purpose and destination.

Jesus told those who want to be His followers that they must "Go, preach the Gospel and make disciples of all nations." It was pointed out that His disciples went forth with something more powerful than the rod of Moses that parted the Red sea. They went forth with the scepter of the Gospel, that can break in pieces the ungodliness of the world.

Herbert Lockyer Sr. made this statement in reference to the power of the Gospel: "The rod of the Cross, which to men seemed the very emblem of shame and weakness, was, in truth, the power of God unto salvation. By the Cross, Christ rules in the midst of His enemies, making rebels willingly submissive and disposing the antagonistic to obey Him. He makes 'the rebel a priest and a king.'" (DP, pg. 456)

And he said unto them, Go ye into all the world, and preach the gospel to every creature. He that believeth and is baptized shall be saved; but he that believeth not shall be damned (Mark 16:15).

♦ When there is no battle for the Gospel it rusts and it finds no cause and no occasion to show its vigor and power. Therefore, nothing

125

better can befall the Gospel than that the world should fight it with force and cunning.

-Martin Luther

♦ Your occupation is what you do for a living,
Your work is what you do to live.
Your work is believing the Gospel of Jesus Christ.

-Unknown
(BB)

♦ He empties Himself of self, setting aside His desire to be worshipped, the legitimate desire of deity, in order to come to earth, take upon Himself the outward expression of a bondslave, and go to the Cross for guilty sinners, paying the penalty for their sins, satisfying the just demands of God's law...

-Kenneth S. Wuest
(GTL, pg. 33)

♦ What we may perceive as obstacles to evangelization are merely opportunities in disguise.

Extreme Devotion
(ED, pg. 197)

♦ The Cross is the greatest leveler in the universe. It brings every one of us to zero.

-Watchman Nee
(WN, Feb. 4)

♦ All our victories are won before we go into the fight.

-Smith Wigglesworth
(SWD, (TFT) Jan. 12)

***

Perhaps the way is wary oft,
Thy feet grow tired and lame;
I wearied when I reached the well,
I suffered just the same:

And when I bore the heavy cross
I fainted 'neath the load;

And so I've promised rest to all
Who walk the weary road.

-S.C.U.

For consider him that endured such contradiction of sinners against himself, lest ye be wearied and faint in your minds (Hebrews 13:3).

♦ All the mysteries of the Gospel are proofs of God's desire to make His love triumph over sin and disorder from all nature.

-Andrew Murray
(AP, Aug. 13)

♦ Those who feel the vital power of the gospel, and know the might of the Holy Ghost as he opens, applies, and seals the Lord's Word, would sooner be torn to pieces than be rent away from the gospel of their salvation.

-Unknown

♦ We are to preach the death, burial, and resurrection of Christ for our sin during the good times and bad times, easy times and hard times, in the flat lands and the mountain, along the highways and from the rooftops.

-Marvin Rosenthal

♦ Today in pulpits across America a "new brand" of the gospel has been foisted on congregations. It is "Jesus loves you!"...Yielded Christians are holy Christians. Today in America, believers and the lost world around us think of God only as a God of love. They have forgotten that God hates sin.

-E. A. Johnston
(NTB, pg. 38)

♦ All too often, Christians assemble in social or domestic gatherings and utterly forget God, and His Word and ways. They talk about themselves and other folks, about the weather and the world in general, but not a word about their Lord and the Gospel of His Salvation—these things that **are,** or **should** be, the most important things in all the universe to them and their loved ones.

-F. Ellsworth Powell
(KG, pg. 184)

Carrying the Torch

I have always enjoyed reading about missionaries. Whether it is books about their lives or their personal diaries, I become so encouraged by the reality that most of them were ordinary people. Granted, some had abilities like missionary James O. Fraser. He could play Mozart like a concert pianist, but served in China where there were very few pianos to play. Although he faithfully served the Lisu tribespeople of Yunnan province for decades, he died from malignant cerebral malaria.

There was Eric Liddell. Most recognize his name because of the movie, "Chariots of Fire." He had the ability to run like the wind and as a result won a gold medal at the Olympics. However, Liddell picked up the torch of the Christian's commission to preach the Gospel to every nation. He carried the torch to Asia where he died in a Japanese detention camp from a brain tumor.

We know the five martyrs, James Elliot, Nate Saint, Roger Youderian, Ed McCully, and Pete Fleming who allowed their lives to be poured out in the jungles of Ecuador, South America so the seed of a new church could be brought forth and nurtured. But, there are so many other martyrs who have left a cloud of witness all over the world. There were Stan Dale and Phil Masters. They were murdered by cannibals in Indonesia, formerly known as Netherlands New Guinea. There were also Martin Burnham in the Philippines, Chet Bitterman in Colombia, South America, John and Betty Stam in China, and Veronica Bowers and her infant daughter, Charity were killed in an airplane by a Peruvian Air Force A-37 fighter while Veronica and her husband were serving as missionaries in Peru.

These are just a few examples, but it is clear that in so many cases where the Gospel of Jesus Christ was advanced, it first started with the blood of the martyrs watering the seed which was planted through their sacrificial endeavors. Although their accomplishments are rarely known to the world, heaven has a record of these dear saint's names and sacrifices. Even though they would claim that such sacrifices were their reasonable service, their lives and examples serve as a powerful witness to those who follow in their footsteps.

Those called to any mission field must continually consecrate their lives for one purpose, and that is to offer them up as a drink offering for the glory of God. Such lives might burn brightly for a short time, but fall into the ground of death. For example, there was William Borden who died at 25 in Egypt, along with Robert Murray McCheyne and David Brainerd who passed from this world at age 30; missionary to India, Henry Martyn at age 31, and Bible Teacher and expounder Oswald Chambers died in Cairo, Egypt at age 43.

These people along with many other servants of the Most High God died carrying the torch that was lit by the Holy Spirit. They were simply running the race and just before they enter through the door of glory, they found themselves lifting the torch high for others to see in hopes that those who sense they were being called to mission work, would pick up the torch and continue the race.

Today much of the world is caught up with lineage, but I have often wondered about my spiritual lineage. Would it lead me back to the Apostle Paul, or perhaps I would find Barnabas in it. Only heaven will reveal the scope of my spiritual lineage, but meanwhile, I choose to remember that someone picked up the torch and it has been passed down from generation to generation. For almost four decades I have been running with this torch, and my hope is that when I leave this world, it will continue to burn brightly in a dark and dying world as others pick it up and run with it.

So he departed thence, and found Elisha the son of Shaphat, who was plowing with twelve yoke of oxen before him, and he with the twelfth: and Elijah passed by him, and cast his mantle upon him (1 Kings 19:19).

♦ The Gospel is G – O – S – P – E – L
    G od's
    O nly
    S on
    P aid
    E very
    L iability!

-James A. Stewart

♦ It is one thing to bear the cross; it is another thing to die on it.

-James O. Fraser
(MR, pg. 163)

♦ There is a great need today. People are hungry for truth. People are thirsting, wanting to know God better. There are thousands *'in the valley of decision"* (Joel 3:14), wanting someone to take them right into the depths of God.

-Smith Wigglesworth
(SWD, Dec. 11)

♦ If we had a religion comprised of absurd superstitions that had no regard to the perfection of our nature, people might be glad to have some part of their lives excused from it. However, the religion of the Gospel is only the refinement and exaltation of our best faculties. It requires a life of the highest reason.

-William Law
(DHL, pg. 51)

"GO"

Hear your commission, O Church
   of the Master;
Friends and disciples of Jesus
   take heed.
How are ye doing the work of the
   Father?
How are ye caring for hunger
   and need?

Go—to the sheep that are scattered
   and fainting,
Having no shepherds, and tell them
   to come;
Go to the highways and tell every
   creature
Still the feast waiteth and yet there
   is room.

Go—the time shortens, the night
   Is approaching,
Harvests are whit'ning and reapers
   are few.

Somewhere, perhaps, in the darkness
   are dying
Souls that might enter the kingdom
   with you.

Go—Church of Christ, for He
   goeth before you,
And all the way that ye take He
   doth know.
On the bright morrow He'll say,
   "Come ye blessed";
But till the dawning the message
   is, "Go!"

-Annie Johnson Flint
(1866-1932)

And he said unto them, Go ye into all the world, and preach the gospel to every creature (Mark 16:15).

♦ The gospel needs to be declared far more than it needs to be defended.

-Unknown

♦ I have but one candle of life to burn, and would rather burn it out where people are dying in darkness than in a land which is flooded with lights.

-Selected

♦ Many fair beginnings have ended very bad, fair in appearance; many have been called to lose their lives for Jesus; and if the real love of God is not in us, we never can lose our lives for Him. Talking is one thing, and doing is another.

-John Rusk

♦ There is a mighty "go" in the word "gospel".

-Unknown

♦ There is nothing more death dealing than the gospel without the Spirit's power.

-R. A. Torrey
(PWH, pg. 199)

♦ The Cross of Calvary is the sufficient answer. "The cross assures of God's intention. Creation assures us of the sufficiency of His wisdom and skill."

J. Oswald Sanders
(POG, pg. 34)

♦ "Here am I; send me!" WE TOO OFTEN FORGET WHAT FOLLOWS: and He said unto me, "Go!"

-Unknown

What Determines Success?

A. J. Gordon relates a story about a Moravian missionary named George Smith. He was called to Africa to do mission work. He was there a short time before being driven from the country, and even though his labor was great his hard work only produced one convert, a poor woman. From all appearance his effort was a complete failure. He died a short time later. However, it was obvious that he had spent time on his knees praying for Africa before his death.

A company of men eventually stumbled onto the place where he had prayed and found a copy of the Scriptures he had left. They also met the poor woman who was his convert.

A century later George Smith's mission counted more than 13,000 living converts that had sprung up from his "so-called" failure.

Failure, not hardly! It is not the man that possesses the power to bring forth the Living Church of God. He is only responsible to plant the seeds. The power of salvation is found in the Gospel. God knows how to nurture that one seed of the Gospel that falls on the ground of one tender heart and multiply it beyond anyone's imagination.

Verily, verily, I say unto you, Except a corn of wheat fall into the ground and die, it abideth alone: but if it die, it bringeth forth much fruit (John 12:24).

♦ In reference to an agnostic's response to the Gospel, R. A. Torrey said this, "His agnosticism is not his misfortune; it is his sin. The first and most solemn obligation resting on the creature is to know and worship and serve the Creator. (RA, pg. 270)

♦ Some see evangelism as a means to change individuals so the world will believe. Others strive to change the world in order for people to believe. However evangelism is viewed, the message of God is able to change lives.

-RJK

♦ Preach nothing DOWN but the devil, and nothing UP but Jesus Christ.

-Unknown

♦ There appears to be no scriptural reason why we should expect a clearer call to service overseas than at home, since the difference is only geographical. We need no special call to spread the gospel; rather we should expect a special call to exempt us from doing so.

-J. Oswald Sanders
(POG, pg. 118)

***

My God, shall sin its power maintain
   And in my soul defiant live!
   "Tis not enough that Thou forgive,
The cross must rise and self be slain.

O God of love, thy power disclose:
   Tis not enough that Christ should rise,
   I, too, must seek the brightening skies,
And rise from death, as Christ arose.

-Greek Hymn
(KH, pg. 31)

For if we have been planted together in the likeness of his death, we shall be also in the likeness of his resurrection (Romans 6:5).

♦ The gospel message embodies three distinct elements: an announcement, a command, and a call. It announces the good news of redemption accomplished in mercy; it commands all men everywhere to repent and it calls all men to surrender to the terms of grace by believing on Jesus Christ as Lord and Savior.

-A. W. Tozer
(KH, pg. 112)

♦ We need to pray that God will teach the people to believe that when Christ is preached to them, they are seeing as in a mirror the glory of the Lord and may be changed into the same image by the Spirit of the Lord.

-Andrew Murray
(AP, May 21)

♦ To us who believe, the Cross of Christ is central; central to all time because it is central to the whole work of God.

-Watchman Nee
(WN, May 26)

♦ The gospel is too profound for the lazy public; too positive for discursive thinkers. We have no right to preach unless we present the gospel; we have not to advocate a cause or a creed or an experience but to present the gospel, and we cannot do that unless we have a personal testimony based on the gospel. That is why so many preach what is merely the outcome of a higher form of culture. . . . Our obligation to the gospel is to preach it.

-Oswald Chambers
Approved Unto God

♦ Each church should be a miniature Bible Institute, a training station from which saints go out to spread the gospel.

-Kenneth S. Wuest
(GN, pg. 37)

An Unusual Evangelist

In *Romans 10:14*, the Apostle Paul asked how can one believe unless he or she hears the Gospel? The truth is hearts must be prepared to receive; therefore, the light of the Gospel must part the darkness of the mind before one can see the hope of salvation.

The commission of the evangelist is simple. It is to go. When there is no evangelist, who will declare the message to those who are under judgment and wrath? For the rich man in hell, he actually asked Abraham to send Lazarus to his five brothers to tell them of the pending judgment in front of them, but Abraham reminded him they have the prophets and if they do not believe their words, then how will they believe one sent from the dead.

Obviously, the people we are talking about are not those blinded by their own self-righteousness, but blinded by their ignorance. They have no written or verbal witness of God's great provision of Jesus Christ. Who will become their evangelist? After all, the Word promises the Gospel will be preached throughout the world. God does not lie. He will keep every promise.

In her book, *Nests Above the Abyss,* missionary Isobel Kuhn, shared an interesting story about how God used a very unlikely evangelist to prepare a backward people known as Lisu in the great mountain canyon in West China for the Gospel. The evangelist the Lord used actually caused certain individuals to seek out the truth about the Son of God. He used a demon.

These remote people were steeped in the demonic world of the occult. Certain individuals of the villages would come together to encourage demon possession. In the case of this village, one man and two women would come together and allow themselves to be possessed so the demons could speak through them.

On one occasion the message caused great disruptions. Although what came forth was laced with a couple of lies, the truth remained in the minds of those who heard it. This was the message that was reported as coming out of the man. "Worship God." the demon shrieked, "He has a Son named Jesus and two daughters. They live in the stratosphere above the clouds. Cast out your demon altars. God will give you eternal life. He will raise the dead and the old shall be made young." After the message the two women possessed turn upon the man, and scolded his devil, using this new name, Jesus.

Even though the three vessels had been used in such an unusual way, they could not remember the message. However, there were those who would not forget. They had been instructed by the demon to only worship Jesus. But, who was this Jesus? Where could they look to now fill the spiritual vacuum that had been left by the message?

Once again the demons attempted to fill the void. The man's demon actually instructed them to not worship demons and to repent of sins. Once again the two devils in the woman cursed him and for three years his familiar spirit did not come upon him.

However the concept of worshipping Jesus opened these people up to receive revelation. They were told to rest on the seventh day and to quit drinking wine, smoking opium, and committing adultery. They were to refrain from stealing and giving false witness and they were to honor parents, something strange to their culture. In essence, they were to be honorable people. However, even that which is meant for good can be taken into the extremes and abused by religious rigidness and foolishness, causing grave damage to those who are vulnerable and ignorant.

It was the extremes of the oppressive demonic influence that caused one man, later named Mark, along with a friend to dare to venture and find those who could speak of and teach them about Jesus. Their first attempt to find one who would teach them about the Son of God was hit with a wall of fear and ignorance, driving them back into their worlds of confusion and uncertainty.

As Mark realized that his people were being enslaved by these demons, he and his friend set out once again. The second time, God rewarded their diligent search. They actually discovered books written about God and Jesus in their own language. From there they had to find a teacher who would teach them to read. However, no teacher was available to come to the village and teach them. They were all committed elsewhere.

It was Mark who stayed behind to learn how to read so he could share the life-changing message with his people. It proved to be a battle for Mark to actually accomplish such a task. Satan affronted him in different ways, but eventually he learned how to read and learned of the true Jesus who is the Son of God; and, that it is He alone who gives eternal life and in that life is the light that can break through any demonic stronghold.

This incident happened in 1923. Fifteen years later, missionary Isobel Kuhn would travel to this remote village and confirm the events of this story. She in term would record it in one of her missionary books. (NAA, chapt. 6)

> And there was in their synagogue a man with an unclean spirit; and he cried out, Saying, Let us alone; what have we to do with thee, thou Jesus of Nazareth? Art thou come to destroy us? I know thee who thou art, the Holy One of God (Mark 1: 23-24).

♦ In other words, our focus as born-again believers isn't to practice rituals from the cultures we were born into. We are born again, into a brand new culture—God's culture. The one "culture" that God has bestowed on all mankind is the Gospel; it is the one heritage passed on to us by God, yet we are destroying it today.

-Nanci Des Gerlaise

♦ Evangelicals tend to present the gospel exclusively as a remedy for personal sin and procurement of an eternal home in heaven. They generally neglect to proclaim it as God's means of bringing peace to this troubled planet, as did the angels at the birth of Christ and as did the early Church.

-Dave Hunt

♦ G. Michael Cocoris in his book about evangelism divided Christians into four groups. He noted that John distinguished three of them in **1 John 2:12-14**. They are the babes who are noisy and defenseless, the children who are noisy and busy, the young men who have energy and ambition, and the fathers who have much wisdom.

♦ The things that hedge us in, the things that handicap us, the tests that we go through and the temptations that assail us, are all divinely appointed wood cutters used by God to hew out a path for our preaching of the Gospel.

-Kenneth S. Wuest
(GN, pg. 103)

♦ The gospel of a broken heart begins the ministry of bleeding hearts.

-John Henry Jowett

♦ Everyone has a work to do for God in this world, but if God wants you in the ministry or in missionary work, then He will not suffer you to guess, to speculate, to conjecture. He will come and tell you so Himself.

-Selwyn Hughes
(POG, pg. 126)

♦ It is enough to make humanity weep to see the fog and darkness that have been thrown around the plain directions of the Gospel, till many generations have been emptied into hell.

-Charles Finney
(LRR, pg. 380)

♦ I am a Roman, saith Paul, I appeal to Caesar. I am a Christian, say, I appeal to Christ's law. And what is the law of the gospel concerning this? Heart-sorrow is gospel sorrow; they were pricked in their heart',...'Believe on the Lord Jesus.' Now a prick to the heart is more than a wound to the conscience. The heart is the seat of life.

-William Gurnall
(CCA, Vol. 1, pg. 91)

They Are All Dead Gods!

In today's world, we are given an impression there are many ways to God. Whether we take on a religious pose or major in good deeds, many feel that they are influencing the just balances of the unseen God. Without knowing it, such individuals are simply adjusting the concept of God to their ideas of goodness, justice, righteousness, holiness, and salvation. In the end, these misguided souls end up worshipping idols, lifeless gods who cannot hear, care, or save.

However, the Bible is clear there is only one God. He is Creator of all and ultimately will be judge over all. He is not only real, but He will not be adjusted to mere man's ideas. He will shake any faulty understanding and foundation under a person. If he or she is not grounded on the Rock of ages, Jesus Christ and His message of redemption, his or her foundation, false gods, and pagan altars will all collapse as the storms of life reveal that they are void of any sustaining substance.

This shaking happened to a Hindu Priest in India. One evening he came home to learn that his pregnant wife had become very ill and died. She was declared so by four different medical professionals. In compliance to the Hindu custom, the body of the dead woman was placed outside of the house on a stone slab and covered with a sheet.

Rest eluded the grief-stricken priest that night. The early hour of the morning found him turning to the only source of power he knew. He cried out to the gods and goddesses that he worshipped, but to his utter dismay, there was no answer. It was at that time he decided in his heart to go back to the temple the next day and announce to all the people, "Don't worship the idols any longer. They are all dead gods!"

Then the words of an Indian Christian evangelist suddenly came to him. The evangelist had preached the Gospel in his town several months prior. The Hindu Priest opposed his preaching with threats of death, as he ordered him out of town. However, the evangelist's parting words were coming back to him, "There is nothing too hard for my Jesus. I will pray for you."

The priest suddenly cried out in the stillness of the night, "Jesus, if You are real, then show Yourself to me!"

Immediately, Jesus stood in the midst before him, highlighted by a bright light. He said to the priest, "I love you and I died for you."

The priest pinched himself in unbelief and then he posed this test, "If what I see and hear is real, then repeat what you just said to me." Again, the voice spoke quietly, "I love you and I died for you."

It was then the priest began to weep and confess his sins. A deep peace came into his heart. He said tenderly, "Jesus, I will love and serve You the rest of my life." And, he also added this to his declaration as if presenting a postscript, "And Lord, if my wife were alive she would serve You, too, but alas, she is gone!"

At the time the priest added this postscript, his wife's body had been lying on the stone slab for almost twelve hours. He went over to the body and pulled back the sheet to gaze upon his wife's face and to gently stroke her hair. Abruptly, he felt her body move and she opened her eyes. The first words out of her mouth were, "Husband, who is this Jesus?"

She shared how a man, named Jesus came to her in a dream. She was about to fall off a steep cliff, when He spoke to her from behind, saying, "Daughter, don't do it; I can help you." The man took her by the hand and led her to a place of safety. As He was parting, she asked Him who He was. His reply was, "I am Jesus."

You can imagine how everyone was astonished that this woman lived. Not only did she live but she gave birth to a healthy, beautiful baby girl. This former priest and his wife not only turned from dead gods to commit all to the only true God of heaven, but the man also became a pastor of a church. (ISL, pgs. 56-58)

Jesus said unto her, I am the resurrection, and the life; he that believeth in me, though he were dead, yet shall he live (John 11:25).

THE POWER OF HIS LIFE

Seeing Jesus

It is the goal of radical Muslims to proselytize the whole world whether by force or death. We know how dangerous it is for Christians in Muslim controlled countries. The torture, abuse, and death that believers experience at the hands of these fanatics are indescribable. However, the light of Jesus is penetrating the great darkness of this belief system, and these blinded people are beginning to see Jesus, not only in the lives of believers, but in a personal way.

There are many stories of Muslims actually seeing Jesus and coming to salvation. There is a story about a girl by the name of Shahnaz that was featured in, "The Voice of the Martyrs" periodical. When she became a Christian, her father thought it was a passing fancy. Upon realizing that she was serious, her parents devised a plan to arrange a marriage with her former boyfriend. However, when that did not work, Shahnaz's father resorted to beating her with his belt.

As her father was beating her, he screamed that he could legally kill her because she was an apostate. Shahnaz called out to the Lord to help her, for she did not want to deny her faith. Suddenly the beating changed. Instead of her father beating her, he began to hit himself with his own belt. His voice had even changed.

Her father declared that he was a bad person and stated, "I am so dirty. I am so stupid. I am fighting with God!" He began to call out for forgiveness from God, and finally he passed out and fell to the floor.

Shahnaz's mother thought she had killed her father. An ambulance was called, but the now conscious father told them he didn't need one. He wrapped his arms around his daughter and began to apologize. He asked her to forgive him and then he said, "Ask your Jesus to forgive me. Now I realize who I am fighting against."

Shahnaz's father told her that while beating her, God opened his eyes and he saw a vision of Jesus with his left arm wrapped around Shahnaz and his right arm motioning for Ebi to stop swinging the belt. Jesus then told him, "Don't beat her. She belongs to me."

Her father became a Christian and today he hosts a church meeting in his home.

And he is the propitiation for our sins; and not for ours only, but also for the sins of the whole world (1 John 2:2).

♦ <u>Joy</u> is the flag that flies over the palace when the <u>King</u> is in residence.
-Unknown
(BB)

♦ To hold on the plow while wiping our tears—that is Christianity.
-Watchman Nee
(WN, Apr. 29)

♦ The question of true service to God does not begin with who we are, but with who God is.
-RJK

♦ Christians try to live the Christian life without Christ.
-Jeannette Haley

♦ Are you satisfied with anything short of a conscious knowledge of your union and interest in Christ? Then woe unto you. If you profess to be a Christian, yet find full satisfaction in worldly pleasures and pursuits, your profession is false.
-Charles Spurgeon
(MES, Jun. 25 (E))

♦ It is useless speaking about fearing the Lord unless we are prepared to walk in His ways. *Fear of the Lord* is the internal principle, but unless there is a corresponding expression in the outward life, the existence of the inner principle is to be doubted.

-Herbert Lockyer Sr.
(DP, pg. 658)

***

For Mercy has a human heart,
Pity a human face,
And Love, the human form divine,
And Peace, the human dress.

-William Blake
1752-1827
(DP, pg. 696)

For in him dwelleth all the fullness of the Godhead bodily (Colossians 2:9).

♦ The battle between the Lord and Satan in the soul of man cannot be over the possession of the soul. The battle is within the soul of the redeemed as to whether he will honor and glorify God or whether he will live to his own ends.

-Donald Grey Barnhouse
(IW, pg. 139)

♦ Here lies the whole secret of a real Christian life, a life of liberty and joy and power and fullness. To have the Holy Spirit as one's ever-present friend and to be conscious of this fact and to surrender one's life in all its departments entirely to His control—this is true Christian living.

-R. A. Torrey
(PWH, pg. 22)

♦ The graces of the Christian character must not resemble the rainbow in its transitory beauty, but, on the contrary, must be stablished, settled, abiding.

-Charles Spurgeon
(MES, Jul. 11 (M))

Prayer: Lord, let me find my life in Thee, and not in the mire of this world's favour or gain.

-Charles Spurgeon
(MES, Dec. 27 (M)

♦ The Christian life is the outliving of the indwelling Christ.

-Unknown

♦ God intends each soul in Pentecost to be a live wire—not a monument, but a movement.

-Smith Wigglesworth
(SWD, (TFT) Feb. 8)

♦ Christianity implies deliverance from this world, and whoever claims to be a Christian, claims also to live contrary to every thing and every passion that is peculiar to this evil world.

-William Law
(DHL, pg. 207)

♦ The character of a righteous man is not spasmodic, he is not generous by fits and starts, nor upright in a few points only; his life is the result of principle, his actions flow from settled convictions, and therefore his integrity is maintained when others fail.

-Herbert Lockyer, Sr.
(DP, pg. 474)

♦ A life, in which the love of the world is predominant, is incompatible with that dignified and edifying piety, which should be the distinguishing characteristic of the sacred Ministry.

-Charles Bridges
(1849)

***

Over and over,
    Yes, deeper and deeper,
My heart is pierced through
    With life's sorrowing cry;

144

But the tears of the sower;
    And the songs of the reaper,
Shall mingle together
    In joy by-and-by!

-Selected

He that goeth forth and weepeth, bearing precious seed, shall doubtless come again with rejoicing, bringing his sheaves with him (Psalm 126:6).

♦ A little thing is a little thing, but faithfulness in a little thing is a great thing.

-Hudson Taylor

♦ The mind grows by what it takes in, and the heart grows by what it gives out.

-Unknown

♦ As we have said before, Christ did not come to straighten out the natural, but to "cross" it out.

-E. A. Johnston
(NTB, pgs. 25-26)

♦ We are not built for mountains and dawns and artistic affinities; they are for moments of inspiration, that is all. We are built for the valley, for ordinary stuff of life, and this is where we have to prove our *mettle.

-Oswald Chambers
(DTD, Jan. 1)

♦ In speaking of Christian suffering, Kenneth Wuest differentiates between persecution or trials and testings. Persecution is a result of a Christ-like life while trials and testing produce a refined Christ-like life. He goes on to say this about such sufferings, "It burns out the dross, makes for humility, purifies, and increases our faith and enriches our lives. And like the goldsmith of old, God keeps us in the smelting furnace until He can see the reflection of the face of the Lord Jesus in our lives." (BNT, pg. 73)

♦ The spiritual responsibility of the believer is to "fear" and "walk" and his practical responsibility is to "work" and to enjoy the sustenance and happiness it provides. He is not to be so heavenly-minded as to be of no earthly use.

-Herbert Lockyer Sr.
(DP, pg. 659)

***

Let Him lead thee blindfold onwards,
  Love needs not to know;
Children whom the Father leadeth
  Ask not where they go.
Though the path be all unknown,
Over moors and mountains lone.

-Gerhard Tersteegen
1697-1769
(KH, pg. 63)

The LORD is my shepherd; I shall not want. He maketh me lie down in green pastures; he leadeth me beside still waters (Psalm 23:1-2).

♦ In Christ on the cross of Calvary, making an atoning sacrifice for sin, bearing the curse of the broken law in; our place, we have Christ *for* us. But by the power of the Holy Spirit bestowed upon us by the risen Christ, we have Christ *in* us. Herein lies the secret of a Christlike life.

-R. A. Torrey
(PWH, pg. 117)

♦ "A fire goes before Him" (Ps. 97:3). When Jesus visits us, His face is always preceded by His fire. He knows we won't be prepared for His face until we've been purified by His fire.

-Bob Sorge
(FDA, pg.15)

♦ Do not think that you must reform, and make yourself better before you can come to Christ, but understand distinctly, the coming to Christ, alone, can make you better.

-Charles Finney
(LRR, pg. 427)

♦ We have only to sit more continually at the cross foot to be less troubled with our doubts and woes. We have but to see His sorrows, and our sorrow we shall be ashamed to mention. We have but to gaze into His wounds and heal our own. If we would live aright it must be by the contemplation of His death; if we would rise to dignity, it must be by considering His humiliation and His sorrow.

-Charles Spurgeon
(MES, Jul. 22 (E))

♦ God wants daring followers who will be strong in Him and dare to do exploits. How will we reach this place of faith? Let go of your own thoughts, and take the thoughts of God, the Word of God. If you build yourself on imaginations, you will go wrong. You have the Word of God, and it is enough.

-Smith Wigglesworth
(SWD, Dec. 31)

♦ Great devotion and holiness are not to be left to any particular sort of people, but they are to be the common spirit of all who desire to live up to the terms of common Christianity.

-William Law
(DHL, pg. 226)

♦ Now contentment is one of the flowers of heaven, and if we would have it, it must be cultivated; it will not grow in us by nature; it is the new nature alone that can produce it, and even then we must be specially careful and watchful that we maintain and cultivate the grace which God has sown in us.

-Charles Spurgeon
(MES, Feb. 16 (M))

***

Tightly clasped
my little hand in yours,
walking silently along the
cobbled streets.

Passing by the gates
of iron,

147

More Heavenly Gems

amidst the gardens of green—
a nunnery.

Walls of brick and
quiet loneliness
surround the serenity.

Waiting, waiting,
time stands still
forever it seems

Darkness, despair
everywhere.

Brown eyes
look for the butterfly
to start new dreams.
Doors wide open
into arms that
once were shut
new life beginning.

My heart sings with joy
as older I am
with softness
that replaces hardness.
His voice
calls me beloved.

It was His mercy
and grace that gave
me new life—oh,
to be alive!

Renewed in mind,
new creature am I.

-Maureen Human

My beloved spake, and said unto me, Rise up, my love, my fair one, and come away (Song of Solomon 2:10).

♦ A true Christian life is not one governed by a long set of rules outside of us, but rather one led by a living and ever-present person within us.

-R. A. Torrey
(PWH, pg. 125)

♦ Mercy provided a deliverance, and the same mercy and power gave the people the courage to make use of the offered means of escape, and they marched dry shod through the heart of the sea. "Mercy cleared the road, mercy cheered the host, mercy led them down, and mercy brought them up again."

-Herbert Lockyer Sr.
(DP, pg. 699-670)

♦ High spirits criticize and object, but lowly minds glean and receive benefit. A humble heart is a great help towards profitably hearing the gospel. The engrafted soul-saving word is not received except with meekness.

-Charles Spurgeon
(MES, Aug. 2 (E))

♦ Brokenness is the place of blessing. Broken personalities letting the fragrance of Christ out; broken purposes meaning power; broken plans meaning life; broken periods meaning glory. The corn of wheat breaks when it has let itself go to the ground and the embryo is free.

-Miss Frances Brook

♦ The Christian is not only to be different, he is to glory in this difference. He is to be different from other people as the Lord Jesus Christ was clearly different from the world in which He lived. The Christian is a separate, unique, outstanding kind of individual; there is to be in him something which marks him out, and which is to be obvious and clearly recognized. Let every man, then, examine himself.

-D. Martyn Lloyd-Jones

♦ True Christianity aims at having the character of Christ formed in us.

-Andrew Murray
(AP, Oct. 10)

149

♦ The more we die; the more He lives! The more we empty, the more He fills!

-Unknown

♦ Grace is a universal principle. At the first moment of thy spiritual life, suffering grace was infused as well as a spraying grace.

-William Gurnall
(CCA, Vol. 1, pg. 96)

♦ A test of a people is how it behaves toward the old. It is easy to love children. Even tyrants and dictators make a point of being fond of children. But the affection and care for the old, the incurable, the helpless are the true gold mines of a culture.

-Abraham Joshua Heschel

***

A noble life is not a blaze
    Of sudden glory won.
But just an adding up of days
    In which good work is done.

-Written in Isobel Kuhn autograph book
By her grandmother
(NAA, pg. 184)

In all things shewing thyself a pattern of good works: in doctrine shewing uncorruptness, gravity, sincerity (Titus 2:7).

♦ Our love to God is but the reflex beam of his love to us, and we know there can be no reflex without a direct beam.

-John Flavel
(RR, pg. 183)

♦ All Christians are cisterns having living water IN THEM; but few have the spiritual maturity that makes them fountains GIVING FORTH to others.

-G. Woods

♦ All real beauty of character, all real Christlikeness in us is the Holy Spirit's work; it is His fruit. He produces it. He bears it; we do not. It is well to notice that these graces are not said to be the *fruits* of the Spirit but the *fruit.*

-R. A. Torrey
(PWH, pg. 121)

♦ Sickness may befall, but the Lord will give grace; poverty may happen to us, but grace will surely be afforded; death must come but grace will light a candle at the darkest hour.

-Charles Spurgeon
(MES, Oct. 1 (E))

♦ In the eternity before this universe was created, the Divine Sculptor had it in His heart to make some images of His Son, the Lord Jesus, not carved out of granite, but moulded from living personalities.

Kenneth Wuest
(BNT, pg. 101)

♦ I longed for resignation to His will and mortification to all things here below.

-David Brainerd
(LDD, pg. 148)

Coming To Terms with Life

What is life,
 if there is no high calling?
What is an accomplishment,
 if there is no excellent honor to obtain?
What is success,
 if there is no real lasting purpose?
What good is there being in the limelight,
 if it quickly recedes into nothingness?
What merit is there to wear badges and medals,
 if their luster fades with time?
What benefit is there in acquiring accolades
 when they leave you empty?
What honor is it to possess memories of what was,
 but have an empty heart?

151

I have experienced much of the world's accomplishments
    but none of these things added to who I was.
I have earned the accolades and the glitter of the world,
    but none of these could put a song in my heart.
When the fading things of the world
    fell into a ruinous heap before a rugged cross, hope found me.
When the nail-pierced hands of Jesus pierced my heart,
    life began to take form as eternity came into view.
It was only when I committed all to God,
    that the songs of heaven filled my heart
Now my life has purpose, my ways satisfying,
    my focus clear, and my heart lifted up by heaven's harmony.

-RJK

The LORD is my strength and song, and he is become my salvation: he is my God, and I will prepare him an habitation; my father's God, and I will exalt him (Exodus 15:2).

♦ There is an atheistical stupid patience, and there is a godly patience. Satan numbs the conscience of the one, and no wonder he complains not, that feels not; but the Spirit of Christ sweetly calms the others, not by taking away the sense of pain, but by overcoming it with the sense of his love.

-William Gurnall
(CCA, Vol. 1, pg. 60)

♦ Life is a powerful testimony, more powerful than clever words.

Isobel Kuhn
(NAA, pg. 170)

♦ Now it is easy to slide into a profession of Christ Jesus, but to endure to the end in reality is another thing.

-John Rusk
(FT, pg. 21)

♦ We make a living by what we get, but we make a life by what we give.

-Unknown

152

♦ Christian life is not to be lived in the realm of the power of natural endowment. Christian life is to be lived in the realm of the Spirit, and Christian work is to be done in the power of the Spirit.

-R. A. Torrey
(PWH, pg. 159)

♦ Numberless marks does man bear in his soul, that he is fallen and estranged from God; but nothing gives a greater proof thereof, than that backwardness which everyone finds within himself, to the duty of praise and thanksgiving.

-George Whitefield
(GW, pg. 37)

♦ The measure of our wielding Divine power is determined by the measure of our yielding to God's will.

-Unknown

♦ A "bit of love" is the only bit that will bridle the tongue.

-Fred Beck

***

He liveth long who liveth well!
    All other life is short and vain;
He liveth longest who can tell
    Of living most for heavenly gain.
He liveth long who liveth well!
    All else is being flung away;
He liveth longest who can tell
    Of true things truly done each day.

-Horatius Bonar
(1808-1889)

For what is a man profited, if he shall gain the whole world, and lose his own soul? or what shall a man give in exchange of his soul (Matthew 16:26)?

♦ The highest mission on earth is submission.

-Unknown

♦ Every worthwhile accomplishment, big or little, has its stages of drudgery and triumph: a beginning, a struggle, and a victory.

-Unknown

♦ Christian suffering is the Crucible into which God places us, and in which He keeps us until He can see a reflection of the face of Jesus Christ in our lives.

Kenneth Wuest
(BNT, pg. 80)

♦ A good conscience before God is the best armor against fate.

-Unknown

♦ A mission is not so much a place as it is an attitude—one's approach towards life.

-Extreme Devotion
(ED, pg. 43)

♦ The test of elemental honesty is the way man behaves himself in grief and in joy.

-Oswald Chambers
(DTD, Jan. 23)

♦ Works do not justify the man, but the justified man works.

-Unknown

♦ If you love God, you must have an experimental knowledge of Him (not only in the Law, for this will never of itself bring you to love God) no; but you must experimentally know Him as a covenant God in Christ Jesus.

-John Rusk

♦ The Devil loves it when you worry. It takes our mind off of God...Worry steals. It sickens. It stagnates. It defeats. It deflates. It destructs...When we place Him first and foremost in our lives, worry drops away!

-E. A. Johnston
(NTB, pg. 49, 50)

♦ Love refuseth nothing that love sends. It is not the weight or worth of the gift, but 'the desire of a man is his kindness.

-William Gurnall
(CCA, Vol. 1, pg. 89)

Challenging the Acceptable

Peter's denial of knowing Jesus on the night before His crucifixion is well known. Previously before his denial of knowing Jesus, Peter had zealously declared his willingness to die for Him. However, the love that obviously compelled Peter to make such a declaration was unsustainable when tested in the crucible of uncertainty and confusion.

We also know how Jesus gave Peter three opportunities to reaffirm his devotion in *John 21:14-19*. However, in studying the usage of the word, "love" as spoken by Jesus was different then the "love" declared by Peter.

Kennett Wuest brings this out in his books on word studies in the Greek language. The word Jesus was using for love was "agapan", while the word for Peter's type of love is "philein" "Philein" is a love associated with pleasure and fondness. "Agapan" is a love that denotes preciousness or great value. Therefore, "philein" has to do with that which brings pleasure to self, while "agapan" has to do with prizing something above self, the type of love that caused Jesus to embrace the cross.

When Jesus was asking Peter if He loved Him with a complete devotion, Peter was offering Him a love of that which came from a heart emotion. Jesus was asking for a love that would completely surrender in obedience, while Peter offered Him a love of personal attachment.

We know that Peter's love proved to be fickle when tested. However, the love of God is enduring and proves it will withstand even when it came to the cross.

When Jesus was asking Peter if he loved Him enough to feed His lambs, sheep, and flock, Peter was offering Him a love of sentiment, fondness, and affection that may be acceptable when times are good, but will often prove to be inferior when it comes to finishing the course.

Peter did not know then what we do know. "Philien" is acceptable and capable of zeal that can take on a noble pose, but to fulfill his godly commission, he would have to possess "agapan". It was in the upper room that Peter would receive the reality of heavenly devotion. He would be endued with power from above in the form of the baptism of the Holy Spirit.

The Apostle Paul made this statement in *Romans 5:5*, *"And hope maketh not ashamed; because the love of God is shed abroad in our hearts by the Holy Ghost which is given unto us."* The Holy Spirit is the One who shed abroad in our hearts "agapan." This love not only puts a value on its point of attraction and fondest, but it will prove sacrificial and enduring. And, it has the enduring quality to help saints like Peter to finish the course, as he ever abides in what he would prize, Jesus. He would also be ever dying (to mere fondness), while ever living for that day such love would be consummated in the presence and majesty of Jesus Christ. (BNT, pgs. 190-122)

And from Jesus Christ, who is the faithful witness, and the first begotten of the dead, and the prince of the kings of the earth. Unto him that loved us, and washed us from our sins in his own blood (Revelation 1:5).

♦ Whenever self comes into the ascendant, the life of the Son of God in us is perverted and twisted, there are irritations, and His life suffers. Growth in grace stops the moment we get huffed.
-Oswald Chambers
(DTD, Oct. 19)

♦ If we exhibit the love that was in God towards Christ, and in Christ to us, the world will be obliged to confess that our Christianity is genuine.
-Andrew Murray
(AP, Jan. 15)

♦ Character is what we make, disposition is what we are born with; and when we are born again, we are given a new disposition.
-Oswald Chambers
(DTD, Jan. 25)

♦ ...as the sufferings of Christ abound in us, so our consolation by Christ. God lays in suitably to what men lay on mercilessly; Christ would not draw the poor* timorous disciples out of Jerusalem unto hard encounters, until first he had endowed them with power from on high.

-John Flavel
(RR, pg. 93)

♦ Every grace in our heart has got a corruption to oppose it; this every believer will find out sooner or later; and yet all this is very needful, and they work together for our good.

-John Rusk

♦ The fanatic sees the real only and ignores the actual; the materialist looks at the actual only and ignores the real. The only sane Being who ever trod this earth was Jesus Christ, because in Him the actual and the real were one.

-Oswald Chambers
(DTD, Aug. 13)

♦ It has been said behind every great man, is a good woman. One man who could agree with such a statement was Martin Luther. He lovingly called his wife, Katherine, "Kitty, my rib." His wife brought a certain amount of balance to his life. Although there had been challenging adjustments that had to be made to ensure a healthy marriage, Luther admitted they were for his betterment. It is for this reason he rightfully called, "marriage a school for character."

Do What You Can

It is not unusual for people to look at their limitations and circumstances and ask, "What can I do, what can I offer?" Most people feel inept and uncertain. They realistically know they cannot move mountains, but they never think about what they can do. Giving into the, I CAN'T, rather than looking around to see what I CAN, is why many people miss the opportunity to DO something that would prove to be beneficial.

Evangelist D. L. Moody related a story about an Atlantic passenger who was confined to bed due to being deathly seasick. While lying in bed, he heard the cry of "Man overboard!"

The sick man began to pray for the man for he felt there was nothing more he could do in his state. Then he thought, "At least I can put my lantern in the porthole," which he did.

The man was rescued and the next day recounted the story of his ordeal. "I was going down in the darkness for the last time when someone put a light in a porthole. It shone on my hand and a sailor in a life boat grabbed it and pulled me in."

The Apostle Paul stated that God's strength can become apparent in our weakness. It was for this reason he learned to rejoice in them.

And he said unto me, My grace is sufficient for thee: for my strength is made perfect in weakness. Most gladly therefore will I rather glory in my infirmities, that the power of Christ may rest upon me (2 Corinthians 12:9).

♦ There is no such thing as spiritual victory if it is not in the present tense. We often say, "I am looking forward to this, that or the other." Have we any right to be dissatisfied with our present condition, which God has ordained for us so that we hanker after something in the future.

-James O. Fraser
(MR, pg. 29)

♦ How do you spell joy?
Jesus – first
Others – second
You – last

-Unknown
(BB)

Prayer: Lord, keep me radiantly and joyously Thine.
-Oswald Chambers

♦ <u>Charity</u> enough to see some good in your neighbor, <u>faith</u> enough to make real the things of God, and <u>hope</u> enough to remove all fears concerning the future.

-Unknown
(BB)

♦ It takes time to grow into Christ. We must strike our roots down deep in the soil of the Word and be strengthened by long, long experience. It is a slow process, and it is right that it should be so; God does not want us to be spiritual mushrooms.

-Andrew Murray

♦ You are not ready to <u>live</u> until you are ready to <u>die</u>.

-Unknown
(BB)

♦ <u>Grace</u> is God's unmerited favor towards man. <u>Mercy</u> is God's extension of grace. <u>Peace</u> is when mercy is obtained, thereby, peace of mind is obtained.

-Unknown
(BB)

♦ Life is not a 50 yard dash, it's a marathon. The rewards are not to the fast, but to the steadfast!

-Unknown
(BB)

Prayer: Grant thy blessing upon bitter things, to brighten and quicken me, more and more, and not to depress and make me more lifeless.

-Christmas Evans

♦ That is, if the believer participates in the same nature that God possesses, he must show in his life that he loves the things that God loves, righteousness, and hates the things that God hates, namely, sin. If this evidence is not found in the life of the individual, that shows that that person is only a professing Christian, not a possessing one.

-Kenneth S. Wuest
(GTL, pg. 104)

159

♦ Only what we have let go in committal to him becomes in fact really ours.

-Watchman Nee
(WN, Jan. 13)

♦ The cross of Jesus Christ stands unique and alone. His cross is not our cross. Our cross is that we manifest before the world the fact that we are sanctified to do nothing but the will of God.

-Oswald Chambers
(DTD, Apr. 7)

♦ Meekness is necessary for people in power; a man that is passionate is dangerous.

-George Whitefield
(GW, pg. 329)

***

Thy way, not mine O Lord,
However dark it be,
Lead me by Thine own hand;
Choose out the path for me.

Smooth let it be, or rough,
It will be still the best;
Winding or straight, it leads
Right onwards to Thy rest. I dare not choose my lots,
I would not if I might;
Choose Thou for me my God,
So shall I walk aright.

-Horatius Bonar
1808-1888
(POG, pg. 152)

For this God is our God for ever and ever: he will be our guide even unto death (Psalm 48:14).

♦ Only glass can reflect God's light without distortion. For sand to become glass, it must be processed by fire. Revelation exposes us to the light and fire of God.

-Manfred Haller
(CA, pg. 26)

♦ A believer who is keeping his or her relationship with God in proper focus will find ministry is more of an avenue of preparation for God's greatness to be manifested, rather than the ultimate goal of Christian living.

-RJK

♦ Our chief concern should be to learn how to behave toward them in a Christian manner, for, unless we make good heed to ourselves, we shall embitter our spirits and act unbecoming as the followers of (the) Lord.

-George Whitefield
(GW, pg. 205)

Prayer: Lord, give me firmness without hardness, steadfastness without dogmatism, love without weakness.

-Jim Elliot
(SOA, pg. 110)

♦ If humility were put up as an ideal it would serve only to increase pride. Humility is not an ideal, it is the unconscious result of the life being rightly related to God and centered in Him.

-Oswald Chambers
(DTD, Nov. 14)

Our Foundation

In his book, *"The Fiery Trial,"* John Rusk speaks about how the temptations of Satan are a fire to test our devotion and purge us of hypocrisy. He assured those who are not built on the right foundation that when the wind blows against their house that it will bury the family. He goes on to describe the utter defeat that will occur in such a person's life;

If it has thundered and lightened, terror will fill him or her,

If the person has to cross the water, he or she will drown.

If under bondage, the individual will find oneself as belonging to Hagar's family, never made free by the Son of God.

If a person falls by a besetting sin, he or she will be led captive by Satan at his will.

If the person slips into the same sin over and over, he or she will be a servant of corruption.

If enmity has arisen under sore trials, then the person will hate Zion, God and His cause.

If covetousness has worked itself up, the individual will become like Ananias and Sapphira.

If a worldly spirit is fallen into, a person will never be separated from this world.

Rusk goes on to say, "A man must be well fixed or established indeed to stand fast here." (pg. 18)

And every one that heareth these sayings of mine, and doeth them not, shall be likened unto a foolish man, which built his house upon the sand: And the rain descended, and the floods came, and the winds blew, and beat upon that house; and it fell: and great was the fall of it (Matthew 5:26-27).

THE POWER OF HOPE AND INTERVENTION

✝

The Liberty of Truth

The two missionaries were weary after sharing the Gospel with a village in Korea. The people in the village had never heard the good news of salvation. When the light of the Gospel begin to penetrate their hopeless darkness, the whole population gathered to hear what these men had to say. As a result, the meeting had continued until a late hour.

After the missionaries settled in for the night the people remained, murmuring. The missionaries could not find any rest due to the people being in a state of discussion. One of the missionaries went back to the people and asked why they did not return home.

The head man of the village gave this answer. "How can we sleep? You have told us that the Supreme Power is not an evil spirit trying to injure us, but a loving God who gave His only begotten Son for our salvation; and that if we will turn away from our sins and trust Him, we may have deliverance from fear, guidance in our perplexities, comfort in our sorrow. How can we sleep, after receiving a message such as this?"

Upon hearing the response, the missionaries forgot their weariness and sat down with those poor people and communed with them until the morning dawned.

-The Gospel Banner

For the Son of man is not come to destroy men's lives, but to save them (Luke 9:56a).

♦ A person's hope is only as good as the object of his or her hope.

-Pastor Rob Greenslade

♦ When at night you cannot sleep, talk to the <u>Shepherd</u> and stop counting <u>sheep</u>!

-Unknown

(BB)

♦ He never loses sight of the treasure which He has placed in our earthen vessels. Sometimes we cannot see the light, but God always sees the light, and that is much better than our seeing it.

-Charles Spurgeon

(MES, Jan. 5 (E))

♦ Let us shake off "dull sloth" on the one hand and feverishness on the other. A gourd may spring up in a night, but not an oak. The current may be flowing deep and strong in spite of ripples and counter-currents on the surface. And even when it receives a temporary setback from the incoming tide of evil, we may yet learn to say — as Jeremiah once said under the most distressing circumstances — "It is good that a man should hope and quietly wait for the salvation of the Lord."

-James O. Fraser

(MP, pg. 156)

♦ The care of God is engaged by promise for the moderation and mitigation of your afflictions, that they may not exceed your abilities to bear them.

-John Flavel

(RR, pg. 169)

♦ My soul longs to feel itself more of a pilgrim and stranger here below; that nothing may divert me from pressing through the lonely desert, till I arrive at my Father's house.

-David Brainerd

(LDD, pg. 162)

♦ God had one Son without sin; but He has no son without temptation.

-Charles Spurgeon
(MES, Feb. 9 (E))

***

I am sheltered by the Most High God—
Safe and secure in His arms do I rest,
Knowing that all things will come to pass,
And good will outlast that which
  darkened my past.

As a shepherd takes care of His sheep,
So my Lord has us dwell in pastures green,
Laying besides the still watering stream.

"Come," He says, "into the fold, where
Treasures are of silver and gold.
Do not wander off into the distant,
There is plenty to have and more besides.
Fill up upon the living water and the Bread.
Life is ahead!

-Maureen Human

The LORD is thy keeper: the LORD is thy shade upon the right hand (Psalm 121:5).

♦ God will supply, BUT WE MUST APPLY!

-Unknown

♦ God will never lead us into any course that does not fit the character and teaching of Christ.

-J. Oswald Sanders
(POG, pg. 105)

♦ We touch men most when we most touch God!

-Unknown

♦ He (Satan) hunts the Christian by the scent of his own feet, and if once he doth but smell which way thy heart inclines, he knows how

165

to take the hint; if but one door be unbolted, one work unmanned, one grace off its carriage, here is advantage enough.
-William Gurnall
(CCA, Vol. 1, pg. 65)

♦ God makes no mistakes: the STOPS of a good man are ordered by the Lord as well as his STEPS!
-Unknown

♦ The saints are not, by nature, wells, or streams, they are but cisterns into which the living water flows; they are empty vessels into which God pours His salvation.
-Charles Spurgeon
(MES, Nov. 8 (M))

♦ Man sleeps; a sentinel *may* slumber on his post by inattention, by long-continued wakefulness, or by weariness, a pilot *may* slumber at the helm; even a mother *may* fall asleep by the side of a sick child; but God is never exhausted, is never weary, is never inattentive.
-Albert Barnes
(DP, pgs. 625-626)

♦ The cure for inquietude is to be found in a hope which begins as a struggling ray, but expands into the *forever* of Eternity.
-F. B. Meyer

♦ Soul-emancipation is the noblest form of liberation, and calls for the highest praise; he who is delivered from the dungeons of despair is sure to magnify the name of the Lord.
-Herbert Lockyer Sr.
(DP, pg. 741)

***

Madame Prosni was in a precarious position. A civil war had ensued in France in 1627-8. The land and the people were under siege. Famine was becoming rampant and Madame Prosni had four children that were also in dire straits. She had sought help from a callous sister-in-law who had turned a deaf ear to her need. But, the gracious woman had something else to fall back on, her faith in the merciful God of heaven.

Even though Prosni had resolved to meet death with patience, she was determined in her faith that eventually God would work out the matter. As she reached the door in dejection due to the callousness of her relative, her children met her at the door dancing with joy. Unbeknown to her, a stranger had knocked at the door of their home and thrown in a sack of wheat through the door and quickly departed. The heavenly gift maintained her family until the stronghold of famine was broken.

He raiseth up the poor out of the dust, and lifteth the needy out of the dunghill (Psalm 113:7).

♦ Jesus Christ is no security against storms, but He is a perfect security in storms. He never promised an easy passage, only a safe landing.

-Unknown
(BB)

♦ God sets the Christian at work, and then meets him in it.
-William Gurnall
(CCA, Vol. 1, pg. 67)

Prayer: Breathe upon me the power of Your Resurrection, Life, and presence. In the name of Jesus, Amen.

-Andrew Murray

♦ Men have testified that they have learned more of God and of the Lord Jesus Christ in an hour in a meeting during a revival than they had learned in a lifetime of Bible study and reading theology.
Dr. Lloyd-Jones

***

The angels from their home on high
    Look down on us with pitying eye,
That where were but pasting guests,
    We build such strong and solid nests;
167

While where we hope to dwell for *aye,
    We scarce take heed one stone to lay.

-Unknown

Doth the eagle mount up at thy command, and make her nest on high? She dwelleth and abideth on the rock, upon the crag of the rock, and the strong place. (Job 39: 27-28).

♦ But with every man and woman...there is the power of sin within ourselves, which is more than we can master in our own strength. We need a hiding-place from the power of sin within.

-R. A. Torrey
(RA, pg. 67)

♦ Death as not an obstacle or a punishment, merely a doorway into the eternal presence of God.

-Extreme Devotion
(ED, pg. 45)

♦ Christ sends none away empty but those who are full of themselves.

-Unknown

♦ What wealth can equal that of the love of God? What riches can rival a contented heart? It matters nothing that the roof is thatched, and the floor is of cold stone; the heart which is cheered with the favor of Heaven is "rich to all intents of Bliss."

-Charles Spurgeon

Prayer: Help me to wait silently, and patiently upon Thee, for the fulfillment of these things, and not become enraged, angry, and speak unadvisedly with my lips, like Moses, the servant of the Lord. Sustain my heart from sinking, to wait for fresh strength from Zion.

-Christmas Evans

The Practical in the
Midst of the Impossible

Although isolated in a small cell, serving as a prisoner in a Japanese concentration camp, and facing death for being falsely accused of being an American spy, missionary Darlene Deibler's only desire was to eat a banana. She had witnessed another prisoner receiving a bunch of bananas from some unknown source outside of the barbed wire that enclosed the compound.

Darlene had come to Celebes, one of the many islands within the New Guinea region, as a bride of a missionary in 1938. She knew adventure waited her, but she had no idea how crooked and twisted the path would take her. She would leave Celebes in September 1945, a widow and a witness of the horrors of war.

Now isolated from others, separated from her husband, and suffering the affects of sickness, malnutrition, the uncertainty of the future, and the constant grind of the unmerciful camp, she only had one arm to lean on, the everlasting arms of Jesus. She grappled with what seemed a simple enough desire, but from all appearances it seemed to be impossible. She craved bananas and there was only God who could hear her prayers and silence her great craving. Darlene dropped on the floor of the cell and asked the Lord for just one banana.

As she considered how God could get her one banana, the impossibility of such a task grew in her mind. Admittedly, she knew that she needed to link her impotence to God's omnipotence.

Darlene had been gravely sick in the small cell and had not yet regained her strength. Fearful of the repercussions that came when a prisoner failed to bow before the Japanese officers, she was asking God for the strength to stand and bow. However, the familiar face of the camp commander came through the cell door, and recognized her plight. It was after that visit that the prison guard laid at her feet bananas, 92 in all.

Darlene had only asked for one banana, but God provided an abundance of them. These bananas not only helped her regain her strength, but saw her through until she was moved from the small cell.

In fact, the day she was relocated back into the main camp, she ate her last (black) banana. (ENS, pgs. 148-150)

We often do not know what to ask for, for we do not know what we have need of to endure what we are facing or about to encounter. However, God knows and He put it in Darlene's heart to crave a banana so in turn she would ask Him for it. He not only wanted to show her that He could bring forth the practical in the midst of the impossible, but that He could abundantly provide to meet any future needs.

And he that searcheth the hearts knoweth what is the mind of the Spirit, because he maketh intercession for the saints according to the will of God (Romans 8:27).

♦ He will cause every refuge to fail, and then He will appear, "when there is no eye to pity and no hand to help." You may try lawful means, and it is right you should; But He will not let you succeed, till He has humbled you again and again; and in this way, you will be led to watch His hand.

-John Rusk
(FT, pg. 59)

♦ Hope is like the sun, which as we journey towards it, casts the shadow of our burden behind us.

-Herbert Lockyer, Sr.
(DP, pg. 167)

♦ Misery should always place itself right in the face of mercy.

-Charles Spurgeon
(MES, Feb. 14 (E))

♦ Hope is what happens when we see God changing us...Hope is your natural response when you see the character of Jesus developing in yourself.

-Bob Sorge
(FDA, pg. 60)

♦ To the modern historian, history is not the understanding of events, but rather the understanding of man's experience of events. What concerns the prophet is the human event as a divine experience. History to us is the record of human experience; to the prophet it is a record of God's experience.

-Abraham J. Heschel
(TP, pg. 219)

♦ ...springs represent *hopes*, or *affections*, or *thoughts*. Of this we are confident—all the silver springs of grace, and the golden springs of glory are in Him, Who is the hidden source of calm repose, and Who, in want, is our plentiful supply.

-Herbert Lockyer, Sr.
(DP, pg. 292)

♦ Some are called to the field of gold nuggets. Some are called to the field of great needs.

-Unknown

Prophetical Intervention

In the book, *Memories of Miracles in Africa,* the author, Carol Zurcher records a testimony of an elderly woman by the name of Mrs. Frankford. She lived in Steinberg, Cape Town, South Africa.

After prayer meeting, Mrs. Frankford was walking through a pitch-dark area on her way home. She suddenly found herself in the midst of gangsters, waving their knives at her. Through tears, she related how God gave her courage and the boldness to testify to these young men. She urged them to come to God instead of giving way to their wicked ways. She warned them that they would hurt someone and end up in jail. Silently, the gangsters disbursed, leaving her standing alone. She thanked God for His abiding protection on her.

The next morning she was sweeping her porch when a young man walked by. He greeted her and as he came closer, he thanked her for preaching to his gang the night before. He admitted they were on their way to kill his girlfriend and drop her body at a planned place.

However, after their encounter with Mrs. Frankford, his gang dissolved and the members went their separate ways. (pgs. 50, 51)

Finally, my brethren, be strong in the Lord, and in the power of his might (Ephesians 5:10).

♦ To do good wins fame in Heaven, but to do good to *yourself* is the prudent thing among men of the world.

-Herbert Lockyer, Sr.
(DP, pg. 197)

♦ Believers are his jewels, his peculiar people, his special portion, or treasure in this world, and as such he prizes and esteems them above all the people of the earth, and accordingly exerciseth his special care in all the dangers they are here exposed to. Special love engageth peculiar care.

-John Flavel
(RR, pg. 158)

♦ You shall see the sinner's hope perish, for he trust his native strength; you shall see the proud Pharisee's confidence totter, for he builds his hope upon the sand; you shall see even your own schemes blasted and withered, but you yourself shall find that your place of defense shall be the munition of rocks.

-Charles Spurgeon
(MES, Feb. 29 (M))

Revival!

I have read books on revival. Revival means to revive that which is dead or comatose. We know when a person is born again of the Spirit, they have been revived with the resurrection power that comes with eternal life.

However, when the church begins to call upon God to intervene and bring revival, it means that the church is in a comatose state which prevents it from being an effective, powerful witness in the world.

What does revival entail and what would it look like? As I have witnessed and read about revival there is a consistent pattern to what will be addressed to ensure real revival. Missionary James O. Fraser outlined the manifestations of revival. He pointed out that such manifestations were according to Scripture. (MR, pgs. 238, 239) This is his outline along with some of my summation of each point.

1. *Conviction of Sin*: Sins are no longer winked at because the Spirit of holiness will throw a searchlight on hearts producing repentance, confession of sin, and the putting away of such sin.
2. *Revelation of Jesus*: People come out with a greater sense of Jesus and the many gifts that come with His redemption and realize the need to prepare for His coming.
3. *Understanding Truth*: The blinders upon their hearts are taken away so that their souls can be gripped by the truth and their minds transformed by the Spirit.
4. *Outpouring of Love*: Because of the Spirit, the love of God will be shed abroad in their hearts. The Bible is clear the true disciples of Jesus are known because they have love for one another. Such love will result in forgiveness and reconciliation.
5. *Anointing of Power*: Now the Holy Spirit can be poured out in greater measure in our lives to ensure anointing and power to walk out the life in us and become true witnesses.

For thus saith the high and lofty One that inhabiteth eternity, whose name is Holy; I dwell in the high and holy place, with him also that is of a contrite and humble spirit, to revive the spirit of the humble, and to revive the heart of the contrite ones (Isaiah 57:15).

THE POWER OF FAITH
AND OBEDIENCE

The Plumb Line of the Fence

The Lord showed me there are four different responses to the walk of faith. Jesus Christ's command to all disciples is, *"Follow Me."* All Christians are called to be disciples, but there are those who want to control when and how they follow Jesus. Following Jesus requires consecration which takes love, commitment, and faith. For this reason many well-meaning Christians fall to the wayside, take detours, or cease to hear His call. It is in everyday living that our walk of faith is put to the test. Falling to the wayside, taking detours, and failure to hear Jesus' voice does not happen suddenly, but day by day, decision by decision.

In helping me to understand these four responses, the Lord showed me a fence. On one side of the fence was the world. On the other side was a mountain with a narrow path whose route and destination could not be seen. Surrounding the fence were four distinct groups of people. The *first* group represented the world. This worldly group was distinctly on the worldly side of the fence. The *second* group of people stood on the fence, talking about the pros and cons of the two sides. In essence, they were trying to strike a balance between the world and Christianity. The *third* group was on the other side of the fence from the world, but held onto the fence and simply faced the path that led up the mountainside in a mode of wishful thinking. These individuals were aware of their need to let go of the fence in order to have a life in God, but fear prevented them. The *fourth* group of people were individuals who were beginning to embark

174

upon the unknown path. They were few, but God has always stated that He has a remnant of people who will follow Him to His ultimate glory.

And if it seem evil unto you to serve the LORD, choose you this day whom ye will serve; whether the gods which your fathers served that were on the other side of the flood, or the gods of the Amorites, in whose land ye dwell; but as for me and my house, we will serve the LORD (Joshua 24:15).

♦ Faith is a verb, it requires action.

-Unknown
(BB)

♦ Religion is obedience to God, the voluntary submission of the soul to the will of God.

-Charles Finney
(LRR, pg. 393)

♦ Don't dig up in unbelief what you have sown in faith.

-J. Oswald Sanders
(POG, pg. 139)

♦ But Faith listens neither to Presumption, nor to Despair, nor to Cowardice, nor to *Precipitancy, but it hears God say, "Stand still," and immovable as a rock it stands.

-Charles Spurgeon
(MES, Jul. 24 (M))

♦ Believing is an act of the heart for it is with the heart that man believes, and the tongue should be in harmony with the heart. "The tongue should always be the heart's interpreter, and the heart should always be the tongue's suggester; what is spoken with the tongue should be first stamped upon the heart and wrought from it"

-Herbert Lockyer Sr.
(DP, pg. 509)

Prayer: Lord, may my love for you so overwhelm me because you are so magnificent in every way that I will proclaim to the world your incomparable greatness and be **valiant for the faith,** even if it leads to persecution or martyrdom.

-Marvin Rosenthal

♦ Faith is an organ of knowledge, and love an organ of experience. God came to us in the incarnation; in atonement He reconciled us to Himself, and by faith and love we enter and lay hold of Him.

-A. W. Tozer
(KH, pg. 9)

♦ Ordinarily the human eye cannot see the spiritual forces that are arrayed in the invisible realm. The eye of faith can look into the Word of God and know the truth of the power of the Lord we serve, and can be sure that nothing can ever touch us unless it has passed through the will of God.

-Donald Grey Barnhouse
(IW, pg. 134)

♦ Each time you come to the word in study, in hearing a sermon, or in reading a religious book there ought to be a definite act of humility. You must deny your own wisdom and yield yourself in faith to the divine teacher.

-Andrew Murray
(PWH, pg. 142)

♦ It has come home to me very forcibly of late that it matters little what the work is in which we are engaged so long as God has put it into our hands.

-James O. Fraser
(MR, pg.28)

♦ (God) wants to bring us into that blessed place of faith, changing us into a real substance of faith, until we are so like-minded that whatever we ask, we believe we receive, and our joy becomes full because we believe.

-Smith Wigglesworth
(SWD, Jan. 19)

♦ When push comes to shove, are most believers incurably faithful to Christ or merely running a mild fever? Persecution is one sure way to discover the truth.

Extreme Devotion
(ED, pg. 143)

♦ When it comes to the faith walk, the most subtle sin is the one of omission: the failure to do what is right. We often excuse wrong attitudes in order to justify away honorable conduct.

-RJK

♦ Justification before man requires faith and works—Justification before God requires only faith.

-Unknown
(BB)

♦ The only design of doctrine is to produce practice, and it does not seem to be understood by the church, that *true faith* "works by love and purifies the heart," that heresy in *practice*, is proof conclusive of heresy in sentiment.

-Charles Finney
(LRR, pg. 383)

♦ Faith is a most precious grace, "It works by love"—mixes with the Word preached—overcomes the world—is attended with the Spirit's witness—it makes Christ precious—there is joy and peace in believing—it puts on Christ' righteousness—applies the atonement, and triumphs in the glorious victories of His death.

-John Rusk

♦ You will never find true faith unattended by true godliness; on the other hand, you will never discover a truly holy life which has not for its root a living faith upon the righteousness of Christ. Woe unto those who seek after the one without the other!

-Charles Spurgeon
(MES, Sept. 18 (M))

♦ Perfect obedience, such as we cannot render here, will constitute a large proportion of heavenly happiness to all Eternity.

-Herbert Lockyer Sr.
(DP, pgs. 571-572)

♦ Those who have only read but have not lived the book of Job cannot imagine the stress on a struggling human heart which held powerless by His power, is still require to trust the love it cannot see and to pray for the friends who have not been friends at all.

-Jeannie Schantz
(FDA, pg. 23)

♦ Job's life exemplifies that there is a dimension of faith in the power of God that opens to those who persevere through the fiery test of God's delays.

-Bob Sorge
(FDA, pg.40)

♦ Unbelief is actually perverted faith, for it puts its trust not in the living God but in dying men. The unbeliever denies the self-sufficiency of God and usurps attributes that are not His. This dual sin dishonors God and ultimately destroys the soul of the man.

-A. W. Tozer
(KH, pg. 35)

Faith of a Child

The Bible is clear that unless we have a faith as a child to be converted to the simple ways of God, we cannot be saved. The beauty of a child's faith is that they not only believes what he or she has been told, but the child will respond in simple obedience.

This is best illustrated by a story that was told by a parent to her child's Sunday School teacher. Apparently after leaning in Sunday School about Jesus washing the feet of his disciples, the child went home and put it into action. He not only washed the feet of both his parents, but he washed the feet of his dog and cat.

So many times as an adult, I wished I did not see the logical need to debate a Biblical truth or responsibility. I wished I would receive it like a child and lived it out as an obedient, trustworthy servant of God.

And said, Verily I say unto you, Except ye be converted, and become as little children, ye shall not enter into the kingdom of heaven (Matthew 18:3).

♦ Every trial is to bring you to a greater position in God. The trial that tries your faith will take you on to the place where you will know that the faith of God will be forthcoming in the next test.

-Smith Wigglesworth
(SWD, May 23)

♦ Unbelief shudders at the Jordan which still rolls between us and the goodly land, but let us rest assured that we have already experience more ills than death at its worst can cause us.

-Charles Spurgeon
(MES, Jan. 1 (M))

♦ In this generation there is an ever increasing number of people who seek signs, wonders, and prophecy as a means of direction and "faith building" in their lives. On the contrary, we need to diligently seek out *God* for who He is and should be in our lives. Unfeigned faith believes that no matter what happens it is for the glory of God and for our spiritual benefit.

-RJK

♦ A life in Christ' abiding presence must of necessity be a life of unceasing faith.

-Andrew Murray
(AP, Apr. 13)

♦ But faith is that trust or confidence in God, and in Christ, that commits the whole soul to him in all his relations to us. It is a voluntary trust in his person, his *veracity, his word.

-Charles Finney
(LRR, pg. 351)

♦ We read of weak grace, little faith; how can this then be a trial of our armour whether of God or not? I answer, the weakness of grace is in respect of stronger grace, but that weak grace is strong and mighty in comparison of counterfeit grace.

-William Gurnall
(CCA, Vol. 1, pg. 57)

***

Unless I had believed,
I had fainted long ago,
So buffeted by whelming seas,
With treach'rous undertow;
I dare not think what might have been
Unless I had believed.

Unless I had believed,
I could not have won the fight,
Too many and too fierce my foes
To have withstood their might;
They would have torn me, limb from limb,
Unless I had believed.

Now that I have believed,
Are my feet upon the Rock,
My soul established, strong, secure,
To brave the earthquake shock?
What tragic loss, what black despair!—
Unless I had believed.

-T.O. Chisholm
1866-1960

And they said, Believe on the Lord Jesus Christ, and thou shalt be saved, and thy house (Acts 16:31).

♦ The testimony of faith is that, no matter how things look in this fallen world, all God's acts are wrought in perfect wisdom. The incarnation of the Eternal Son in human flesh was one of God's mighty deeds, and we may be sure that this awesome deed was done with a perfection possible only to the Infinite.

-A. W. Tozer
(KH, pg. 62)

♦ Obligation to perform duty never rests on the condition, that we shall first have the influence of the Spirit, but on the powers of moral agency. We, as moral agents, have the power to obey God, and are perfectly bound to obey, and the reason we do not is, that we are unwilling. The influences of the Spirit are wholly a matter of grace.

-Charles Finney
(LRR, pg.101)

♦ Many seek the Lord's guidance, but in their hearts they have no intention of following it if it does not please them.

J. Oswald Sanders
(POG, pg. 60)

♦ True faith doesn't have a contingency plan. Faith only does one thing: it only believes.

-Bob Sorge
(FDA, pg.89)

♦ Faith is an inward operation of the divine power that dwells in the contrite heart and can lay hold of things not seen. Faith is a divine act; faith is God in the soul. God operates by His Son and transforms the natural in the supernatural.

-Smith Wigglesworth
(SWD, Feb. 3)

♦ For necessity is the foundation for miracles. To escape the one is to miss the other. Great difficulties are meant only to force us out of ourselves into reliance on him. When there is no way forward or back, then God is able.

-Watchman Nee
(WN, Jan. 22)

♦ For where reason ends, faith begins. And, however infidels may style themselves reasoners, of all men they are the most unreasonable; for is it not contrary to all reason to measure an infinite by a finite understanding, or think to find out the mysteries of godliness to perfection.

-George Whitefield
(GW, pg. 18)

♦ WILLING to obey Christ is to be a Christian. When a individual actually *chooses* to obey God, he is a Christian.

-Charles Finney
(LRR, pg. 349)

♦ The golden rule for understanding in spiritual matters is not intellect, but obedience.

-Oswald Chambers
(DTD, Sept. 20)

♦ Obedience without knowledge is blind, and knowledge without obedience is lame.

-Thomas Watson
(PDC, pg. 277)

♦ Faith untried may be true faith, but it is sure to be little faith, and it is likely to remain dwarfish so long as it is without trials.

-Charles Spurgeon
(MES, Nov. 12 (M))

♦ The greatness of God rouses fear within us, but His goodness encourages us not to be afraid of Him. To fear and not be afraid—that is the paradox of faith.

-A. W. Tozer
(KH, pg. 84)

♦ Growth in grace, or in the favor of God, is conditioned upon growth in implicit confidence in Him.

-Charles Finney
(LRR, pg. 431)

♦ In the life of faith, humility has a far deeper place than we think. It is not only one among other virtues, but it is the first and chief need of the soul. It leads us to know the absolute and entire inability in ourselves to do any good.

-Andrew Murray
(AP, Aug. 9)

♦ Faith is always understood as in indispensable condition of prevailing prayer.

-Charles Finney
(LRR, pg.297)

♦ During the crisis period of waiting, when everything screams at you, "You must do something **now**!", it takes great faith to keep your expectation of God alone. Will this caliber of faith be found among the saints at Christ's return?

-Bob Sorge
(FDA, pg.95)

♦ Unbelief is the great dethroning place; faith is the great rising place.

-Smith Wigglesworth
(SWD, (TFT) Jul. 7)

♦ Most people fall into the following categories when it comes to sharing their faith: go-go, slow-go, and no-go.

Extreme Devotion
(ED, pg. 185)

♦ My greatest temptation is the temptation to be ordinary. Just an ordinary Christian with an ordinary faith, and ordinary power, loving others in an ordinary fashion. By *corollary, my heart's deepest desire and earnest prayer is to be EXTRAORDINARY—to vacate the ruts of mediocrity and have extraordinary faith, extraordinary power, and love others with an extraordinary love.

-A. L. Gillespie
Missionary to Japan

♦ We are said to be in Christ by faith. But faith is no easy thing, and therefore very many trials attend it. You read of the trial of faith; it is tried with conscience, Law, sin, Satan, the ungodly hypocrite, cross providences, and by the Lord Himself. But yet faith will work through all trials, because it is of Divine origin.

-John Rusk

♦ Do not fail to claim your holy position—the commanding position of faith—so that you will overcome the power of the Devil. The best time you have is when you are in the most difficult position.

-Smith Wigglesworth
(SWD, Jan. 8)

♦ The more we grow in our relationship with the Lord in our faith walk, the more surefooted we will become on our journey through the present age of uncertainty.

-RJK

♦ Ministers are charged with preaching heresy, because they presume to teach that faith is an exercise, and not a principle, and that sin is an act, and not a part of the constitution of man.

-Charles Finney
(LRR, pg. 359)

♦ Modesty may demur at so rash a thought, but audacious faith dares to believe the Word and claim friendship with God. We do God more honor by believing what He has said about Himself and having the courage to come boldly to the throne of grace than by hiding in self-conscious humility among the trees of the garden.

-A. W. Tozer
(KH, pg. 100)

♦ Forgiveness does not depend on the offender's asking for it first. It is an act of obedience, as well as an act of faith.

Extreme Devotion
(ED, pg. 106)

♦ So often, as today, I have been unwilling to shed my own blood, so to speak, and have trusted in Christ alone — arm-chair trust, which has failed.

-James O. Fraser

♦ You need a fixed heart and a made up mind to possess obedience.

-Unknown
(BB)

The Matter of Dependency

The biggest challenge for Christians is to learn complete dependency on God. It is our natural tendency to look to our wits or to others to solve the matters surrounding personal needs being met to continue the work of the Lord's kingdom. However, in such matters, we never have to learn what it means to come to a complete dependency on Him.

As a missionary this has been an ongoing test for me. At first I looked to my wit to find ways of supplying personal needs in our ministry work, only to run into one dead end after another. Then, I looked to others only to find disillusionment, and finally I was forced to look to God. I was to discover in such times the faithfulness of God to meet me in every need, challenge, and situation. It was God who provided my needs and further the work of His kingdom. It was God who showed me that He indeed does all things well. Granted, He has used faithful servants to support us, but He was the One who put it on their hearts to do so and provided them with the means to be faithful in such support. He has used circumstances to teach me that He is great at multiplication as long as I provide the fish and bread according to the measure of faith that had already been placed in my heart. It took a while for me to come to places of complete trust for a matter to be resolved.

A couple of years ago I remember dealing with a man from Africa over the issue of true dependency on God. Since we have a ministry that has a website, it is not unusual to receive solicitation from ministers and ministries in such places as India and Africa. Some have written to receive material, others cell phones, and there are those who ask for money. The problem is you do not know who to trust. Those who receive material often are cons who sell it to desperate Christians. Those who want cell phones will end up taking advantage of the whole situation, and those who want money sometimes are trying to acquire it for their personal benefit. Regardless of status, the great god of greed is everywhere and functions under many disguises even in the poorest of countries. There is no end to how this god exploits those who are poor.

An African minister contacted us that he needed help. Even though we were aware of the fact that we were one in many ministries he contacted, we followed our protocol by offering him a free discipleship course. He in turned informed us he did not need material, he needed money. Admittedly, this did not sit well with me. I realize that people in Africa consider every America rich. It is true according to their standards we might be quite rich, but in America we have a different standard. And, according to the American standard we would not qualify as being financially rich.

I felt the need to write this man. In a way, I wanted to challenge him. To me the most priceless work you can offer anyone is that which adheres to Scriptural teaching and instruction. In essence, I wanted to know how money would further the kingdom of God. When I challenged him he placated me, but he never explained in what way he was going to use the money.

Again I challenged him. This time I warned him that the time is coming when Christians in America would not be able to help him, and who would he look to, to provide for the work of the ministry. You could tell my second e-mail to the man not only rattled him but he turned around and accused me of speaking too much; therefore, I must have a demon.

The truth of the matter is that when man develops a dependency on the flesh, he is building on shifting sand and his ultimate endeavors will not be sustained. It is well known that man cannot sustain the real work of God's kingdom. Although America has been blessed in the past by God, it does not make Christians in America the solution. Yet, how many Christians in foreign countries are counting on Christians in America to support them in their work? How many of these Christians have learned to look to God to totally move the mountains from in front of them.

Missionary James O. Fraser realized that he needed to make the Lisu of China self-supporting. He did not want them to depend on any financial support from England or other places. He perceived that foreign money and control would establish a weak church. He knew that these poor people had to learn straightaway that they must give to the Lord out of the depths of their poverty, and that their sacrifice would have to support their own chapels and evangelists. (MR, pg. 193)

If you know the history of the Lisu people, you would know that they became self-supporting and after the various rebellions and uprisings, they remained standing as a living, viable church in China. Their years of experiencing the fiery test of their faith, simply established them in their devotion to the Lord. They indeed had learned to be dependent on God and not some foreign missionary organization.

Thus saith the LORD; Cursed be the man that trusteth in man, and maketh flesh his arm, and whose heart departeth from the LORD (Jeremiah 17:5).

♦ Sinners often imagine they are seeking *Jesus Christ*, and seeking *religion*, but this is a mistake. No person ever sought religion, and yet remained irreligious. What is religion? It is obeying God. Seeking religion is seeking to obey God.

-Charles Finney
(LRR, pg.319)

♦ Affliction turns up the heat on our faith, Peter says, so that our faith will come through the fire purified and strengthened.

-Bob Sorge
(FDA, pg.103)

♦ Three things work together. The first is faith. Faith can always bring the second thing—fact—and fact can always bring the third thing—joy.

-Smith Wigglesworth
(SWD, (TFT) Jan. 20)

♦ There are two parts to the Gospel: Believing it and Behaving it!

-Unknown

♦ Faith in God is not "blind faith"; rather, it is sincere confidence that chooses to trust God's sovereignty.

-RJK

♦ Faith is a grace that sometimes shines brightest in the dark night of desertion.

-Thomas Watson
(PDC, pg. 276)

♦ A faith that does not lead to confession will never lead to Heaven. There will be no sneaks and cowards in Heaven.

-R. A. Torrey
(RA, pg. 248)

♦ Disobedience is only warranted when we are forced to decide between loyalty to Christ and loyalty to the governing laws.

-Extreme Devotion
(ED, pg. 254)

♦ Over-strained faith is not pure faith, there is a mixture of the carnal element in it. There is no strain in the 'rest of faith.' It asks for definite blessing as God may lead; it does not hold back through carnal timidity, nor press ahead too far through carnal eagerness.

-James O. Fraser
(MR, pg. 99)

♦ Oh, there is faith, but Jesus wants to bring us all into a place in line with God where we cease to be, and His faith takes over. God must have the right of way, of thought and of purpose. God must have control.

-Smith Wigglesworth
(SWD, Jan. 18)

The Contrast

The opposite of godly faith is fear that rides on the waves of fleshly sentiment and/or demonic oppression. I came upon these two definitions that show how true faith and unhealthy fear are poles apart from each other. Consider the contrast on the following page.

Faith

Fantastic
Adventure
In
Trusting
Him

Fear

False
Evidence
Appearing
Real

-Unknown
(BB)

> The LORD is on my side; I will not fear: what can man do unto me (Psalm 118:6)?

♦ Divine favor, as revealed in the Bible, are repentance and abandonment of all known sin, and faith in our Lord Jesus Christ.
-Charles Finney
(LRR, pg. 429)

♦ Faith is an act; faith is a leap; faith jumps in; faith claims. Faith has an author, and faith's author is Jesus.
-Smith Wigglesworth
(SWD, (TFT) Mar. 4)

♦ The less faith, always the more impatience; and the more ability to believe, the more patience to wait.
-John Flavel
(RR, pg. 220)

♦ How is it that we cannot live that life of unbroken fellowship with Christ which the Scripture promises? Simply because of our unbelief.
-Andrew Murray
(AP, Apr. 9)

♦ Various things have been invented by men to remove sin; but faith in the atonement of Christ is the only way. This is sanctification.
-John Rusk

♦ We have learned that suffering is not the worst thing in the world—disobedience to God is the worst.
Vietnamese Christian Pastor
(ED, pg. 7)

♦ Fainting, dear believer, is more apt to occur in the valleys of daily drudgery than on the pinnacles of public performance. The real test of our faith will always be in the dark valleys where we cannot perceive God's presence. It is there we question our calling, our capabilities, and our commitment.
-Jeannette Haley

♦ Faith is the tongue that begs for pardon. Faith is the hand that receives it; it is the eye that sees it; but it is not the price to buy it.

-Robert Traill
(PDC, pg. 292)

♦ Risks are all about choice.

Extreme Devotion
(ED, pg. 97)

♦ Any direction given to sinners that does not require them *immediately* to obey God, is an indulgence to sin. It is in effect, giving them liberty to continue in sin against God.

-Charles Finney
(LRR, pg. 362)

♦ However, the Master does not want us to reason things out, for carnal reasoning will always land us in a bog of unbelief. He wants us simply to obey.

-Smith Wigglesworth
(SWD, Mar. 1)

Capturing the Promises

But the soul must be greatly humbled before he can choose such pain, because it is so very opposite to the flesh. Flesh says, "let me see how I am going on;" but faith trusts a naked promise:

"Almighty faith the promise sees,
And trusts to Christ alone;
Laughs at impossibilities
And says, It shall be done."

-John Rusk
(FT, pg. 91)

That ye be not slothful, but followers of them who through faith and patience inherit the promises (Hebrews 6:12).

♦ NEVER TO WAIT WHERE GOD HAS POINTED OUT YOUR DUTY. We profess to have given up the waiting system, let us carry it through and be consistent.

-Charles Finney
(LRR, pg. 372)

♦ We would rather appropriate a promise than obey a command or heed a warning.

-J. Oswald Sanders
(POG, pg. 149)

♦ People observe our faith at arm's length to determine what God is all about. They watch with keen interest, when we experience a crisis.

Extreme Devotion
(ED, pg. 153)

♦ Faith is the eye that sees Him, the hand that clings to Him, the receiving power that appropriates Him.

-Woodbridge

♦ Faith is more than an attitude of the mind, faith is the complete, passionate, earnest trust of our whole nature in the Gospel of God's grace as it is presented in the Life and Death and Resurrection of our Lord Jesus Christ.

-Oswald Chambers
(DTD, Jul. 18)

♦ If I am obedient, He will appear to me and the humdrum road will shine with miracles of grace.

-John Henry Jowett

♦ Bernard gives us this description of a good ear—"Which willingly hears what is taught, wisely understands what it heareth, and obediently practices what it understandeth.

♦ Work, but trust God, not your works.

-Unknown

♦ Nothing in the past is equal to the present, and nothing in the present can equal the things of tomorrow. Tomorrow should be so filled with holy expectations that we will be living flames for Him.

-Smith Wigglesworth
(SWD, Jan. 1)

♦ Maturity in Christ is measured by how much we've come to depend on Him. The greater the dependency, the greater the maturity.

-Bob Sorge
(FDA, pg. 132)

♦ This is the reason why some people will pray for sanctification, and practice sin, evidently supposing that sanctification is something that *precedes* obedience...But sanctification *is obedience,* and, as a progressive thing, consists in obeying God more and more perfectly and perpetually.

-Charles Finney
(LRR, pg. 396)

♦ Faith is the title deed (substance) of things hoped for...It is God's guarantee in advance that we already possess the things asked for.

-Kenneth Wuest
(BNT, pgs. 18, 19)

♦ Simple faith in God's promise and the way of atonement has always degenerated into a complicated system of human works, with man going his own way in the mistaken belief that his ways and God's will somehow merge in the far distance future.

-N. W. Hutchings

Consecration

Where will faith and obedience lead a follower of Christ? The answer is simple: it will lead to a life of consecration. What does consecration look like? The best way to describe such a life is that it becomes available so that God can direct, broken so that God can make a person a pliable vessel in His hand, and ready to be an open vessel where the life of Christ flows into, overflows, and spills out to others.

The consecrated life leads to spiritual victory. However, to consider it from a worldly perspective, it looks like an utter waste of time, energy, and resources. It looks like a failure because the perspective goal is not always reached.

A consecrated life could be witnessed in the life of a man named William Whiting Borden. Have you heard of him? I have read about him a couple of times. Each time I read about his life, I have come away with a sense of a person that with everything in him, he consecrated all to the Lord. His example is incredible.

Borden was born into a family whose heritage went back to character, achievement, and courage. His relatives fought beside Duke William of Normandy at the Battle of Hastings. They helped establish Hartford, Connecticut. His mother was a descendant of Governor William Bradford, who came over with the Mayflower and helped establish the Plymouth Colony. Borden not only was born into a family of heritage and history, but his family was financially established due to his father's silver adventures in Colorado.

However, it was his mother, a devoted Christian, who had the greater influence on his character and pursuits. Borden's spiritual adventure began at age seven. He was at a meeting where Dr. R. A. Torrey challenged believers to completely consecrate their lives to Jesus. He was one of them that accepted that challenge. Even though he was only seven, he understood the principle of consecration. From that point on, he fixed his heart on living his life for Christ.

Even though Borden was from a wealthy family, he became a serious steward of how he handled money. A humble servant at heart he would never lord his financial status over others. Subsequently, after his father's death in 1906, and before his own spiritual pursuits, he gave away $70,000.00 to various Christian causes. At age 16, he sailed around the world. On the ship, he encountered many missionaries which cemented what he felt was his call: that of being a missionary. He also had Bible Study every day on the ship to maintain his spiritual well-being.

While sailing the oceans of the world, Borden was moved by what he saw in Japan and China. He began to put his eyes on China. Later, due to hearing missionary, Dr. Samuel Zwemer exhortations about Muslims at a conference, it would be directed towards Muslims who were numbered 15 million in North West China. However, before he could fulfill his calling as a missionary to China, he kept his commitment to his family and attended Yale University. In spite of the worldly ways of the university life, he remained separated from it. He kept his eyes on the ultimate goal. Whatever his hand found to do to further the kingdom of God, he did so. He founded the Yale Hope Mission where he often witnessed to others. He served as a delegate to the Student Volunteer Movement and the historic Edinburgh Missionary Conference.

He graduated from Yale in 1909 and entered Princeton Seminary the same year. He was named a trustee of the Moody Bible Institute, and became a member of the North American Council of the China Inland Mission. He graduated from seminary in 1912 and on September 9, was ordain at The Moody Church in Chicago.

Between his ordination and December 17 and the culmination of his missionary pursuit, he was involved in furthering the cause of world missions by speaking in various colleges, no doubt challenging the strength and minds of the upcoming generation to consider impacting the matters which concerned eternity. On December 17, 1912, he sailed for Egypt where he planned to study to get a grasp of the Muslim religion, to fulfill his calling to the Muslims in China. In fact, there were more Muslims in Northwest China than in Persia, Egypt, and the whole of Arabia. There he again threw himself in the cause of Gospel. He avail himself to help reach the lost which included distributing literature.

When I read the first paragraph of the chapter about Borden in the book, it caused me to pause and practically trip over the reality of this man's life. Eighteen years after he dedicated himself to the Lord in the seventh year of life, this statement was written about him, "he died in Egypt preparing to go to China as a missionary." Does this not cause you to pause or maybe even trip a bit? It is true during the Easter season of 1913, at age 25, Borden became ill with cerebral meningitis and died on April 9th.

The world would look at the life of William Borden who knew that his life did not consist of "the abundance of things that a man possesses, but in the abundance of things which possesses the man," and no doubt would declare it a terrible waste. However, heaven sees it different. Borden never wasted years trying to figure out what his calling was. He never allowed the false glitter of this world to take his eyes off of the glory of the next. He never wasted energy, for he was found to be faithful to the cause of Christ. He never got sidetrack from what was important to the heart of God; therefore, he proved to be faithful. He never lost sight of his commitment and devotion towards God. He gave it all up; therefore, what was required of him was no lost on his part for he ultimately gained what was important to him. (VCK, pgs. 27-33)

Even though it appeared that the flame Borden had for the Muslims in China was doused, Dr. Zwemer and Borden's mother would not let his vision die. In Borden's mother's home, Zwemer led earnest men and women in prayer to send young men to the Muslims in northwest China. A young man by the name of George Harris was present. He shared that the very same night that Zwemer and Borden's mother had prayed for missionaries to pick up the torch of her son, and that in his personal prayer time the Lord asked him if he was willing to go anywhere. His reply was one of affirmation. In his mind he imagined "anywhere" to be in Kano, Nigeria, but to his surprise what flashed across his mind was a meeting that took place with three men from China who had spoke to him about Muslims in northwest China. When he got up from his knees, he knew where he was being called. A fellow student asked him where he was planning to go in the mission field. Harris reply was simple, "Just a few minutes ago...the Lord called me to the Muslims in China." Harris gave thirty years of his life to the Muslims of China. ((POG, pgs. 124-126)

William Borden lived a consecrated life, sold out for the purpose and glory of God. Even though he could not carry the torch to China, his death could not put out the flame of his torch. It would burn brightly and his torch would be handed to another.

Oswald Chambers' prophetic description of his personal Christian walk could also be easily applied to Borden, "I feel I shall be buried for a time, hidden away in obscurity; then suddenly I shall flame out, do my work, and be gone."

Borden said it best when he wrote this prayer in his notebook, "Lord Jesus, I take hands off, as far as my life is concerned. I put Thee on the throne in my heart. Change, cleanse, use me as Thou shalt choose. I take the full power of Thy Holy Spirit. I thank Thee." He then added this revealing sentence, "May I never know a tithe of the result until Morning."

True to his statement, he had no idea the tithe his consecration left until he faced the One who rewards faithful service. It is hard to say how many lives he touched in his time on earth. However, we can conclude that in the end, Borden's life did not represent a misstep of what could have been; rather, it represented the steps of consecration: that of faith and obedience that ultimately led him up to and through the earthy portal of death into the glory and majesty of the loving arms of his Lord, Savior, and God.

I beseech you therefore, brethren, by the mercies of God, that ye present your bodies a living sacrifice, holy, acceptable unto God, which is your reasonable service (Romans 12:1).

THE POWERFUL WITNESS
OF CREATION

✝

The Subject of Birds

The Bible uses the examples of birds to give us a valuable picture of where we might be in our spiritual state. For example, in the *Song of Solomon,* the Shulamite girl was described as having eyes like that of doves. It is said that the doves have singled vision, thereby described the girl's singular focus when it came to the one she was betrothed to.

Jesus used the sparrow to assure people that if God is aware of a sparrow falling to the ground, He is also aware of their needs. So many times we feel insignificant in the scheme of things, but God puts tremendous value on His creation. He not only feeds and clothes His creation but He is aware of the life and death of each creature. We need to remind ourselves sometimes that we are part of God's creation, which makes Him our responsible Creator. As Creator, He knows how to bring the best out of us.

In *Psalm 102:7*, David compared himself to a sparrow alone on a house top, watching. This man knew that no matter how insignificant he may seem, no matter how alone he was, God was aware of him. He also compared himself with other birds.

In Herbert Lockyer, Sr. devotional commentary on Psalms, it is pointed out that David also compared himself to an owl in *Psalm 102:6* and an eagle in *Psalms 103:5,* as well as a pelican of the wilderness in *Psalms 102:6*. The owl is a slow bird and points to scorn and being dim-eyed while the eagle is a swift bird and implies sovereignty and being sharp-sighted. David understood what it was to be lonely in his grief like an owl, but he also knew what it meant to fly high with comfort because of his relationship to God. Lockyer goes on to say, "It is interesting to observe that in Christian Art, the *Pelican*, as a symbol of Christ, which is influenced by the comparison to the pelican in the wilderness. (pg. 384)

Are not two sparrows sold for a farthing? And one of them shall not fall on the ground without your Father (Matthew 10:29).

♦ Preparation, delay, and growth, are characteristics of God's working both in history and nature.
> -James O. Fraser
> (MR, pg. 154)

♦ God created the earth for beasts to inhabit, the sea for fishes, the air for fowls, and heaven for angels and stars so that men hath no place to dwell and abide in but God alone.
> -Giovanni Pico
> 14th Century Italian writer

♦ The Lord always deserves to be praised for what He is in Himself, for His works of creation and providence, for His goodness towards His creatures, and especially for the transcendent act of redemption, and all the marvelous blessing flowing therefrom.
> -Charles Spurgeon
> (MES, Jul. 31 (E))

♦ History eloquently testifies that States and Kingdoms, standing out in the world like mountains are utterly dissolved when God decrees their end. Systems as ancient and firmly rooted as the hills, pass away when the Creator which inanimate nature knows and worships after its own fashion, looks upon them.
> -Herbert Lockyer Sr.
> (DP, pg. 356)

♦ This world after all our science and sciences, is still a miracle; wonderful, inscrutable, magical and more, to whosoever will *think* of it.
> -A. W. Tozer
> (KH, pg. 18)

♦ Creation is as the mother, and Providence the nurse which preserveth all the works of God. God is not like man; for man, when he hath made a work, cannot maintain it: he buildeth a ship, and cannot save it from shipwreck; he builds a house, but cannot keep it from ultimate decay. It is otherwise with God Who is Conserver, as well as Creator.

-William Cowper
(DP, pg. 574)

♦ Studying science is studying the works of God. And studying theology is studying God.

-Charles Finney
(LRR, pg.208)

♦ The supreme question is not, "Who made the world?" but rather, "Who transcends the world?" The biblical answer is, "He Who created heaven and earth transcends the world."

-Abraham J. Heschel
(TP, pg. 341)

***

A *chequer board of light and shade?
And we the pieces *deftly laid?
Moved and removed without a word to say
By the same hand that board and pieces made?

No pieces we in any fateful game,
Nor free to shift on Destiny the blame,
Each soul doeth tend its own immortal flame,
Fans it to heaven, or smothers it in shame.

-John Oxenham
1852-1941
(POG, pg. 13)

And five of them were wise, and five were foolish. They that were foolish took their lamps, and took no oil with them (Matthew 25:2-3).

♦ My prayer goes up to the great Lord of sea and land, that He will make the storm a calm, and bring you to your desired haven!

-Charles Spurgeon
(MES, Sept. 7 (E))

♦ The world resembleth a divinity school, and Christ, as the Scripture telleth, is our doctor, instructing us by his *works*, and by his *words*.
-Plutarch
1st Century Greek Philosopher
(DP, pg. 67)

♦ God is self-existent, while all created things necessarily originated somewhere at some time. Aside from God, nothing is self-caused. By our effort to discover the origin of things we confess our belief that everything was made by Someone who was made of none.
-A. W. Tozer
(KH, pg. 25)

♦ It goes without saying that the heaven of God's throne is the center of all things, but the material universe, in the sovereign plan of God, was created as a vast theater to declare the glory of God.
-Donald Grey Barnhouse
(IW, pg. 45)

♦ We found a card that explained what some of the different plants represented. Here is what the card revealed: Bellfower represents gratitude, carnation affection, rosemary remembrance, sage admiration, and dahlia loving thoughts.

♦ Stones are not broken, except by an earnest use of the hammer; and the stonebreaker must go down on his knees.
-Charles Spurgeon
(MES, Feb. 21 (E))

The Exquisite Hand of the Creator

In her book, *Stones of Fire,* missionary and author, Isobel Kuhn relates how God takes the lives of people and molds and shapes them into precious stones. This became apparent to her when she served on the mission field in China. She showed in her book how the Gospel, the Word, His Spirit, and His ways is what God uses to create the passion, the fire that will bring forth a precious stone. She brings this more so to the light by relating a comment made by Dr. Campbell Morgan, "What a strange bringing together of contradictions! 'Stones of Fire'. A stone is the last embodiment of principle—hard and cold. Fire is the essence of passion—warm and energizing. Put the two together, and we have stones—principle; fire—passion; principle shot through with passion, passion held by principle."

Kuhn summation was, "That is the description of a human stone of fire." (pg. 14)

Dr. Kanz, a gem expert to Tiffany & Co. gives us this valuable insight, "Any valuable gem must first be trimmed, cleared, or sawed into suitable shape and size, then cut into the desired form and finally polished."

Kuhn explains how much of our western view is that God wants us happy. It is true He delights to see us happy, but He has a greater purpose in mind for us.

She brought this purpose out by using the analogy of an opal. This gem is usually cut with a smooth surface, but the fire-opal is frequently faceted, which brings out the distinction of it beauty in light and color. An instrument called a "dop" which allows the *lapidary to rub the opal against it until the facet is produced. This work takes great skill by the one working on the stone.

To the naked eye, such a gem blends in with what looks part of the barren landscape. Ellice Hopkins brings this perspective when those with untrained eyes first see an opal, "You are only conscious of the cracks and desert dust, but so He makes His precious opal. We must be broken in ourselves before we can give back the lovely hues of His light and the lamp in the temple can burn in us and never go out"

It was from the example of an opal that Kuhn related how God works in our lives. It takes trials and pressures along with adjustments in relationships and circumstances to bring forth the beauty of our lives. God is an expert at all that He does. Kuhn said it best when she made this statement, "...do not forget the Master lapidary as He bends with skill and love and care over them (His gems). (Emphasis added.) (pgs. 62-63)

Being confident of this very thing, that he which hath begun a good work in you will perform it until the day of Jesus Christ (Philippians 1:6).

♦ Gemstones are not produced in a day. Time is a vital factor in their formation. They are wrought by long process in the fires of earth, and their beauties are displayed by skillful cutting...Grace is free; but only a high price buys precious stones.

-Watchman Nee
(WN, Dec. 17)

♦ Only God can make people right. Only melted gold is minted. Only moistened clay accepts the mold. Only softened wax receives the seal. Only broken, contrite hearts receive the mark as the Potter turns us on His wheel.

-Smith Wigglesworth
(SWD, May 1)

♦ When you're being broken by God, you don't understand what's happening to you. No amount of promise claiming changes anything because God isn't about to relent until the breaking is complete. He is the Potter, and he knows just what it takes to break down each vessel so that it can be reshaped and remade according to His desire purpose.

-Bob Sorge
(FDA, pg. 118)

♦ Only as we melt is God able to mold.

-Unknown

♦ As one pours jelly into a mold, the liquid may swirl around, but it will seek its own level and fit the form of the mold. Day by day history is being poured into the mold of God. The world sees the swirling succession of events, but the mold is invisible to their eyes; and they cannot understand how the churning circumstances will settle down.

-Donald Grey Barnhouse
(IW, pg. 261)

♦ All my jewels were fashioned by heavenly art. I find in God all that I want; but I find in myself nothing but sin and misery. "He only is my rock and my salvation."

-Charles Spurgeon
(MES, Feb. 26 (M))

♦ The Lord Most high: is the Omnipotent, Omniscient, and Omnipresent One and there is none among men, like unto Him. All created beings with all their excellencies are but nothing and vanity in comparison with Him who is "an infinite ocean of perfection, without either brink or bottom."

-Herbert Lockyer Sr.
(DP, pg 180)

♦ Our concepts of measurement embrace mountains and men, atoms and stars, gravity, energy, numbers, speed, but never God.

-A. W. Tozer
(KH, pg. 45)

♦ Deep places beget deep devotions. Depths of earnestness are stirred by depths of tribulation. Diamonds sparkle most amid the darkness.

-Charles Spurgeon
(DP, pg. 669)

♦ Every day the marvels of science and human ingenuity leave us breathless, but unfortunately the advancement of science has not been matched by the progress of morality.

-J. Oswald Sanders
(POG, pg. 18)

♦ When it comes to the type of trials that can beset us, Chrysostom made this statement, "God acts like a *lutenist, who will not let the strings of his lute be too slack, lest it mar the music, nor suffer them to be too hard stretched or screwed up, lest they break." (DP. pg. 643)

♦ They who navigate little streams and shallow creeks, know but little of the God of tempests; but they who "do business in great waters," these see His "wonders in the deep." Among the huge Atlantic-waves of bereavement, poverty, temptation, and reproach, we learn the power of Jehovah, because we feel the littleness of man.

-Charles Spurgeon
(MES, Jul. 19 (M))

♦ Looked upon as worthless refuse, corrupt and loathsome, sinners are marvelously transformed by the condescending Savior into new creatures.

-Herbert Lockyer Sr.
(DP, pg 481)

Prayer: I Thank Thee, Lord, that Thou has given me this joy in Thy creation; in the works of Thy hands. I have proclaimed the glory of Thy works as my finite mind was capable of grasping Thy infinity. If I have sought after mine own honor, forgive me.

-Kepler

♦ Wonder rather than doubt is the root of all knowledge.

-Abraham Joshua Heschel

♦ An outlook through the peephole at the vast mysteries of the universe should only confirm our belief in the certainty of its Creator. I cannot understand a scientist who does not acknowledge the presence of a superior rationality behind the existence of the universe.

-Werner von Braun
German space scientist

♦ There are stars enough in heaven to shine in both hemispheres; and there are saints enough in the world, some to shine in heaven, and some to preserve the church on earth.

-John Flavel
(RR, pg. 41)

♦ Heaven is the abode of Glories impossible for mortal man to describe, and of utterance that human lips cannot repeat.

-F. Ellsworth Powell
(KG, pg.131)

♦ Although God is not seen, His works are called His robes or garments, and as garments both conceal and reveal a man, so do the works of God act in this double way. He is worthy of *honor* for the skill seen in His creations, and of *majesty* for He ever fashions His works according to His sovereignty.

-Herbert Lockyer, Sr.
(DP, pg. 404)

The Center of the Earth?

In his book, *Knothole Glimpses of Glory,* author F. Ellsworth Powell, talked about the uniqueness of the globe we live in. Earth is only one of the nine known planets in our solar system. It weighs some 6,000,000,000,000,000,000,000,000 tons and shoots along century after century, in its vast 600,000,000 mile track around the sun at the amazing speed of 67,000 miles, never missing a beat. (KG, pg. 227)

I have pondered whether the center of the earth has truly been marked in some way. In *Isaiah 40:12* we are told that the very dust of the earth is measured. It also has been proven that God is the Master Mathematician of the universe, and His Word bears this out. Therefore, is there something that marks the center of the earth?

The prophet Jeremiah made mention of the signs and wonders that had been set in the land of Egypt (*Jeremiah 32:19-20*). *Isaiah 19:19-21* talks about an altar to the Lord that would not only sit in the midst of the land of Egypt, but it would serve as a pillar at the border. What signs and wonders were set forth in Egypt, what altar and pillar could be found there, and do such matters have anything to do with the center of the earth? In his book, *Great Pyramid: Proof of God,* author George Riffert, stated that the Great Pyramid in Egypt stands in the exact center of the landmass of the world, thereby, implying to some it qualifies as the foundational stone of Earth. Riffert also related how by multiplying its total weight by 1,000 trillion that we would arrive at a figure equal to the weight of the earth. It was pointed out that the mean ocean and land level of Earth is 455 feet above the Great Pyramid's baseline, and it is in this exact height where the top course of its masonry ends.

N. W. Hutchings elaborates on the incredible mathematical relationship the Great Pyramid has with the earth in his book, *The*

Great Pyramid Prophecy in Stone. Hutchings shares how some believe that the builder of the Great Pyramid was Enoch. He was the one in the Bible who walked with God and was no more for he was translated. As a result, the Great Pyramid would have had to be built before the flood and survived its great destruction. The historian, Josephus concurred that the pyramid was built before the flood by the sons of Seth, of whom Enoch was a member.

It is estimated that the Great Pyramid was built between 2900 B.C. and 2800 B.C., and when it comes to the flood two different years have been accredited to it: 2349 B.C. or 2343 B.C. If the dates are right, it would mean that the Great Pyramid was built 500 years before the flood. Amazingly, there are scientific clues that point to it being built before the great flood of Noah as a means to serve as a witness that not only speaks of the past but clearly points to the future. Perhaps an Arab proverb describes the enduring witness of the pyramids, "Man fears time, yet time fears the Pyramids."

In his book, Hutching also relates how the Great Pyramid serves as the shadow of the Gospel. We know Abel left a sacrifice that serve as an excellent witness of the sacrifice to come, the offering of Isaac served as a prefigure of the Son of God, and Moses refuse to sin, to avoid bringing a reproach of Christ, knowing that greater riches than Egypt awaited him (*Hebrews 11:4, 17-19, 24-26*).

Hutching not only made reference to the book written by George Riffert, but other individuals who took on the task of measuring the different aspects of the pyramid and recording their findings. Here is a summary of the some of their findings, as well as the spiritual implications.

- It was erected on a solid rock foundation and sealed with 144,000 limestone blocks that were polished and sealed with an astounding glue. We know according to *Revelation 7* in the last of the end days that 144,000 Jews from the different tribes will be sealed to declare forth the foundational truths of redemption and salvation secured in Jesus Christ.
- The measurements used as far as the solid rock that served as the pyramid baseline was the Hebrew cubit, which is 25.025 in length. The length of each baseline is 365.2422 cubits, the exact number of days in the solar year. Our calendar is 365

days, but every fourth year we add an extra day to allow for the fractional day.

- When the angle of the slopes of the sides of the pyramid is such that they meet at an apex with a predetermined height of 232.52 cubits. When twice the length of the base is divided by this number, we get the number 3.14159, or *pi,* the relationship for the diameter of a circle to its circumference. This shows that the designer had a knowledge of geometry, 2500 years prior to Greek geometry. This brings us to another important aspect of the Great Pyramid. The perimeter of the base of the pyramid is equal to the circumference of a circle whose diameter is twice the height of the pyramid. Their solution to the problem of how to square the circle is that for every ten feet up the slope, one rises nine feet in altitude, and by multiplying the altitude of the pyramid by ten raised to the ninth power; one arrives at a figure of 91,840,000, which is the distance of the earth from the sun in miles.

- The exact sum of the diagonals of the base of the Great Pyramid totals 25,826.54 inches, and it takes the sun 25,826 years to make its journey through the twelve signs of the zodiac.

- For the stars to complete a cycle and return to the exact position at any one period of time requires a time period of 25,827 years. When the diagonals of the pyramid's base, in pyramid inches, are rounded off, they come out to 25,827 inches.

- The sides of the pyramid, measure from corner sockets are 9,140 British inches. It was calculated that the inward curve of the baselines of each of the sides at the exact middle were a depth of three feet. This curve corresponded to the exact curvature of the earth. For years they thought the earth was flat, and if you stand and consider the pyramid at a distance, it likewise looks straight or flat, but it is an illusion.

The Shadow of the Gospel:

- The Great Pyramid with its empty coffer and missing capstone speaks of the cornerstone that was missing and eventually rejected, but was established in Christ. The empty grave reminds us of resurrection power, symbolizing the resurrection and immortal life that comes to every believer through faith, while the lesser pyramids speak of the futility of man's attempt to attain immortality through his own works.

- The Great Pyramid is also related to the spiritual building spoken in Scripture where Christ is the chief Cornerstone, but the spiritual building is the Church, the Body of Christ.
- Even though there are idolatrous signs around it, there are no signs of Egypt's idolatry within. It is obvious that inward the Great Pyramid stands without spot, blemish, or wrinkle which points to the sinless Lamb of God.
- There is a subterranean chamber that is sunk down in the depths of the earth. The passage way that leads to it descends 370 feet, which 275 of it descends through a solid rock base. It is believed that this chamber represents hell.
- However, the Great Pyramid speaks of hope for Christians of not descending into hell, for the king's chamber stands between the Grand Gallery and the subterranean chamber, and below the King's chamber is the Queen's chamber.
- The Queen's chamber was prepared after the King's chamber. Christ is now preparing a place for His Body. Upon completion, He will come for His bride to be united with Him forever.

In that day shall there be an altar to the LORD in the midst of the land of Egypt, and a pillar at the border thereof to the LORD. And it shall be for a sign and for a witness unto the LORD of hosts in the land of Egypt: for they shall cry unto the LORD because of the oppressors, and he shall send them a saviour, and a great one, and he shall deliver them (Isaiah 19:19-20).

THE POWERFUL WITNESS
OF JUDGMENT

How Will You Meet Jesus?

After his born again experience, Julius Massey, exchanged his law books with the greatest book of all, the Bible. Instead of practicing law, he became a pastor and served in that position until his death in 1978.

Massey had one desire and that was to have a vision of Christ. He would often ask for this vision in his prayer times. One night he was awaken by someone gently tapping the side of his mattress. He knew as he looked at the shoulder length auburn hair and the dazzling white garment of the man that came to stand at the foot of his bed that it was Jesus.

The Lord's face was beautiful, but it appeared to possess two diametrically opposite looks. One look was the look of a Savior, kind and compassionate. However the other appearance was that of the King, a stern, majestic look that spoke of judgment.

Massey was speechless before the Son of God. The Lord only stood before him for ten seconds before disappearing. Massey then said to himself, "Jesus is the Savior of some and the judge of others." It was then he more fully understood the Scripture that says the wicked will pray for rocks to fall on them to hide them from the face of Him who sits on the throne. (ISL, pgs. 133-134)

There is so much in this life that can take our attention off of what is important, but in the end, what will count is this: in what capacity will each of us meet Jesus? Will He recognize us as part of the redeemed, washed in His blood, sealed by His Spirit, or will He address us as a King who will deem us traitors and enemies of both Him and His kingdom?

And said to the mountains and rocks, Fall on us, and hide us from the face of him that sitteth on the throne, and from the wrath of the Lamb: For the great day of his wrath is come; and who shall be able to stand (Revelation 6:16-17).

◆ This earth is the only HELL the Christian will ever know—and the only HEAVEN the non-Christian will ever know.

-Unknown
(BB)

◆ Christians can never sin cheaply; they pay a heavy price for iniquity. Transgression destroys peace of mind, obscures fellowship with Jesus, hinders prayer, brings darkness over the soul; therefore be not the serf and bondman of sin.

-Charles Spurgeon
(MES, May 30 (E))

◆ Those who seek to defame and destroy the righteous are "worse than cannibals," for they only eat men after they are dead, but slanderers eat them up alive.

-Herbert Lockyer Sr.
(DP, pg. 619)

Prayer: Father in heaven, I come to you only on the merits of the precious blood of your Son shed for me on the cross. Nothing I have ever done can prepare me for facing you on the judgment throne. I commend my spirit into your hands in the name of my Saviour, Jesus Christ.

-Mikhail Khorev
(SPP, pg. 216)

◆ It is impossible to keep our moral practices sound and our inward attitudes right while our idea of God is erroneous or inadequate.

-A. W. Tozer
(KH, pg. viii)

♦ The earth will be the scene of the final triumph of Christ and His Church and the scene of Satan's final defeat. It is the dust of this earth which shall season Satan's diet for ever and ever.
-Donald Grey Barnhouse
(IW, pg. 27)

♦ Justice is scarce, injustice exceedingly common.
-Abraham J. Heschel
(TP, pg. 261)

♦ It ill behooves us to sport while our eternal destiny hangs on a thread.
-Charles Spurgeon
(MES, Sept. 26 (E))

♦ Hugo Cardinalis said that there are three sorts of blasphemers of the godly—Devils, Heretics, and Slanderers. The *devil* must be answered by the internal word of humility—The *heretic* by the eternal word of wisdom—The *slanderer* by the active word of a good life. (DP, pg. 551)

♦ Hell is a place of no pleasure because there is no love there. Heaven is full of music because it is the place where the pleasures of holy love abound.
-A. W. Tozer
(KH, pg. 101)

♦ It's possible to remain loyal in our love for the Lord but still miss His highest purposes for our life.
-Bob Sorge
(FDA, pg.133)

♦ Nothing is more deadly than self-righteousness, or more hopeful than contrition.
-Charles Spurgeon
(MES, Sept. 29 (M))

♦ *Soon ripe, soon rotten,* and the prosperity of the wicked is transient and their destruction is speedy. They may be up on *housetops,* but the very height of their position hastens their progress and hurries their doom. The wicked who afflict God's children are weak, rootless beings who come and go, and whose evil carries the seed of dissolution within itself.

Old Proverb
(DP, pg. 665)

♦ It's not light pleasure steamers skirting the coast we need, but battleships to launch out into the deep.

-D. E. Hoste

♦ How dare anyone think that a world ripening for judgment can be rescued by Christians working together in political/ social activism with followers of all religions, and with humanists and atheists! Scripture says repeatedly that nothing but the personal and physical return of Christ to this earth can put an end to its wickedness and suffering.

-Dave Hunt

♦ But what it means to perish in all the eternal outworkings of a depraved character, what it means to perish in that endless vista that lies ahead of us, no human language can describe, no human fancy can conceive.

-R. A. Torrey
(RA, pg. 157)

♦ *Flood* and *waves* are emblems of the heathen nations, but God is not moved by their fury. Whenever he utters His commanding voice, the earth melts.

-Herbert Lockyer, Sr.
(DP, pg. 330)

♦ No word is God's final word. Judgment, far from being absolute, is conditional. A change in man's conduct brings about a change in God's judgment.

-Abraham J. Heschel
(TP, pg. 247)

♦ The Lord wants to know if we love Him, or if we love a Jesus of our own mental creation. He's wondering, "If I begin to show you who I really am, will you still love Me?"

-Bob Sorge
(FDA, pg. 203)

♦ A sense of our own folly is a great step towards being wise, when it leads us to rely on the wisdom of the Lord.

-Charles Spurgeon
(MES, Sept. 1 (M))

♦ In prayer, in the evening I had such new and terrific views of God's judgment upon sinners in Hell, that my flesh trembled for fear of them. . .I flew trembling to Jesus Christ as if the flames were taking hold of me! Oh! Christ will indeed save me or else I perish.

-Henry Martyn
Missionary
(DP, pgs. 587-588)

♦ Those who delighted, as if by fire, to destroy innocent lives, will themselves be burnt up in the fiercest fire.

-Herbert Lockyer Sr.
(DP, pg. 619)

♦ There is to be a meeting of the United Nations, not in Paris, Geneva, or New York, or as they once met, at a place ironically called Lake Success, but in the plain of Megiddo in the north of Palestine.

-Donald Grey Barnhouse
(IW, pg. 282)

♦ Justice dies when dehumanized, no matter how exactly it may be exercised. Justices dies when deified, for beyond all justice is God's compassion. The logic of justice may seem impersonal, yet the concern for justice is an act of love.

-Abraham J. Heschel
(TP, pg. 257)

- Don't fool yourself; don't mislead yourself. Never think that God overlooks sins. Sins have to be dealt with, and the only way God ever deals with sin is to absolutely destroy its power.

  -Smith Wigglesworth
  (SWD, Nov. 23)

- It is because you know that justice and faithfulness are founded upon reasons that never vary or change, that have no dependence upon the merits of men, but are founded in the nature of things, in the laws of God, and are to be observed with an equal exactness toward good and bad men.

  -William Law
  (DHL, pg. 238)

The Winds Are Blowing

Winds are blowing,
  Diverse in purpose,
Moved by hands unseen,
  Touching the heart of the land.

Winds blowing on the currents of decision,
  Fair ones bringing the cool breezes of hope,
Contrary winds, times of testing,
  Storms of destruction, fear and uncertainty.

Winds blowing through the terrain of lives,
  Cool breezes touching the silent cries of the heart,
Contrary winds exposing character unseen,
  Stormy winds causing separation unspeakable.

Winds are blowing,
  Orchestrated by God,
No spirit untouched,
  No soul unchanged.

Some winds rage against man's resolve,
  E'er the wheat of God bows low,
Clinging to the ageless Rock of eternity,
  Purged of the chaff, but unmoved in hope.

Rayola Kelley

Winds of the age rage in wrath,
  Against the godless,
Shaking the shifting foundations,
  Exposing the foolish.
Winds are blowing, directed by Providence,
  Affronting my life with force,

Weathered indeed, but left standing,
  Free from the shifting sands of time.
The winds are blowing,
  God's instrument of judgment,
Proving sweetness to my spirit,
  And salvation to my soul.

-RJK

The wind bloweth where it listeth, and thou hearest the sound thereof, but canst not tell whence it cometh, and whither it goeth: so is every one that is born of the Spirit (John 3:8).

♦ If you are willing to receive it, God wants to use your season of affliction to reveal His love to you...God's discipline comes to us because of His great love for us. The fact that He leaves the wicked alone is part of their judgment. His correction truly is an expression of His love.

-Bob Sorge
(FDA, pg.108)

♦ Now, Christian, learn to distinguish between pride in a duty, and a proud duty; hypocrisy in a person, and an hypocrite; wine in a man, and a man in wine. The best of saints have the stirrings of such corruptions in them and in their services.

-William Gurnall
(CCA, Vol. 1, pg. 65)

♦ I have seen the liberal giver rise to wealth of which he never dreamed; and I have as often seen the mean, ungenerous churl descend to poverty by the very *parsimony by which he thought to rise.

-Charles Spurgeon
(MES, Oct. 26 (M))

♦ Shafts of *calumny may miss the mark, but not so the arrows of God. The coals of malice may cool, but not the fire of justice.
-Herbert Lockyer Sr.
(DP, pg. 619)

♦ Apart from Christ, everyone faces eternal death.
Extreme Devotion
(ED, pg. 235)

♦ If we do not resolutely cast out the natural, the supernatural can never become natural to us.
-Oswald Chambers
(DTD, Feb. 27)

♦ The Book of Life is the greatest and most magnificent volume in the world and in the universe. It contains the full and final census returns of all the glorified **human inhabitants** of Heaven!
-F. Ellsworth Powell
(KG, pg. 204)

♦ When it came to *Psalm 101:1* in regard to judgment and mercy, an 18th century expositor said this, "This song of Israel is peculiar to earth; they do not sing of *Judgment* in Heaven, for there is no sin there; they do not sing of *Mercy* in Hell, for there is no *propitiation for sin there.

♦ No man's destiny is made for him, each man makes his own. Fatalism is the deification of moral cowardice which arises from a refusal to accept the responsibility for choosing either the two destined ends for the human race—salvation or damnation.
-Oswald Chambers
(DTD, Nov. 2)

Not From the Same Cloth

When Jeannette and I realized that God was calling us to be missionaries in America instead of some foreign land, admittedly I argued with Him. In my mind I agreed with missionary James Elliot who wanted to go where there were no Bibles, no real light of the Gospel. As I considered the availability of Bibles in this nation and the seventeen churches that existed in our small community alone, I could not see any need for missionaries. Admittedly, in my initial ignorance it was easy for me to hold on to romantic notions about missionary work.

The Lord exposed the last abyss of my untamed zealous state of the old man: fanciful notions. In my zeal in my earlier years, I could see myself going off to whatever mission field with great zeal. Like Peter, I fancy myself willing to die for my Lord, as I "supposedly" gave all so that lost heathen could be saved. Obviously for those of us who hold to such notions, the nation of America does not feed into such a romantic concept.

Such a concept about missionary work may be noble, but not realistic. Most of missionary work entails pioneer work which can prove anything but romantic. When all is said and done, it is tedious work that involves drudgery and irritating challenges and hindrances that often find there source in the unseen world. The initial challenge for every missionary is not to die for Christ; rather, to learn how to live and be steadfast for Christ when the zeal, glamour, and imagined glory subsides, and they are left with the harsh reality that unless the Holy Spirit penetrates the darkness with the light of Christ, heathens will remain heathens regardless of the missionary's best attempts.

Every country and nation is a mission field. For Jeannette and me, we discovered back in 1996, America was the third largest mission field in the world. Whether the people have been refined by culture and defined by worldly education, if they have not been regenerated by the Holy Spirit, they still remain heathens at heart. At the heart of all heathenism is paganism. I have often stated that there is nothing as seductive as refined paganism, clothed in civilized garbs, dressed in silk robes, and hidden behind fig leaves of vain, godless education. In time, civilized garbs are torn away to reveal hypocrisy, silk robes stripped away discloses perversion, and fig leaves taken away reveal the utter foolishness and shame of the fallen, pagan man. It is for this reason Jesus stated in *John 15:22, "If I had not come and spoken unto them, they had not had sin: but now they have no cloke for their sin."*

After the Lord called us to be missionaries in America, we hit a ceiling of sorts while working under the auspice of a church. We recognized that we could not go any further in fulfilling our calling if we remained under such a covering. It was then that God showed us that we had to separate ourselves from under the hindering auspice, for He was going to prepare a door for us to walk through. As I look back at this separation almost three decades ago, I can see how He did indeed prepare a door just for us that would define much of the mission work we ended up doing in America.

The problem for servants of God is that much in the religious world has been organized in some way by man. Even though such organization may bring some discipline and can prove beneficial, it also can regress into an unfeeling system that simply deals within worldly facts and practices. If people do not operate within the systems of the organizations, they can easily be shunned or discarded. However, some of the greatest works of God has taken place through those who did not allow an unfeeling system to dictate to them about matters concerning souls. Such individuals are cut from another cloth. They do not necessarily fit any mold, for they have trusted God to mold them according to His capable hands. A couple of examples of missionaries who did not receive such backing or removed themselves from under such regulations were Hudson Taylor in China and Bruce Olson who has worked with the Motilone Bar Indians of Columbia and Venezuela since 1961. Another missionary who did not fit the regular mold set forth by a missionary board or organization was Amy Carmichael.

In the book about victorious Christians, the author Warren W. Wiersbe penned how the average church would probably have not supported Carmichael's work and that the average mission board would have dropped her after her first term. The reason was that her independence made her unpredictable. Wiersbe goes on to say, "We like the work of the ministry to be carried out in such a predictable way that there can be no surprises, no changes, no unexpected decisions that pioneer new territory for the Gospel. It might upset the donors."

In speaking about Carmichael's character, Wiersbe spoke how holy living was not a luxury to her, it meant sacrifice and ministry. She did not respect Christians who went from meeting to meeting and soaked up Bible truth, but failed to reach out to share Christ with others. It must be noted that in the 60 years she ministered as a missionary in India, she never took a furlough to touch base with her supporters. She understood that the work was God's work, and He alone could prosper it.

The amazing thing about Carmichael is that she was perhaps unpredictable to the Christian world, but in God's hands she was putty ready to be molded, shaped, and changed into a more usable vessel for His glory. For example, she had set out to be a missionary to Japan, but illness caused her to take what appeared as a detour to China for rest and then to Sri Lanka. She did return to England, but a year later on November 9, 1895, she landed in India and remained there among those she so loved until her death on January 18, 1951.

Amy's main goal was to preach the Gospel, however, God used different means to bring the life-saving message to those poor souls that came her way. Instead of literally preaching the Gospel, Amy first lived it. She started rescuing little girls from temple prostitution and took in orphans, and it was these tender souls she began to invest the life of Christ into, establishing a spiritual legacy that remains today.

To the world those who are cut from a different cloth such as Amy Carmichael may become unnerving, but to God it is an opportunity to take what appears to be unlikely and unpredictable, and turn it into an avenue where it becomes the incredible, the miraculous, and the extraordinary.

If a man therefore purge himself from these, he shall be a vessel unto honour, sanctified, and meet for the master's use and prepared unto every good work (2 Timothy 2:21).

♦ The *light from above* assures us that we are not bound to this age; rather, we are being prepared for the next. The *light from without* of God's Spirit and Word confirms that we do not walk in condemnation of the past, but in light of the resurrection power that will raise us up above the judgment that is already upon the world. The true *light from within* brings an inner knowing that we are not groping in darkness, while walking according to a false light that blinds us to God's wrath.

-RJK

♦ Bread of deceit is sweet to a man, but afterwards his mouth shall be filled with gravel.

-John Rusk
(FT, pg. 62)

♦ As the Roman soldier received provision—money which to sustain life so that he could fight and die for Caesar, so the unsaved receive provision—money from sin, spiritual death, so that they can serve it, then physical death and final banishment from the presence of God for all eternity. Neither receives wages, only enough sustenance to enable him to serve his master.

-Kenneth Wuest
(BNT, pg. 58)

♦ Let God's servant watch for souls and not for statistics. God keeps the books!

-Unknown

♦ Death quickly unrobes, not only judges, but all men. No position in society is too high for death's arrows, for it can bring down birds from the tallest trees.

-Herbert Lockyer, Sr.
(DP, pg. 272)

The Cult of the Caesar

At times I found the history surrounding the Roman Empire a bit confusing. It seemed that the Roman people had an array of gods and altars, thereby embracing what we would consider, "Political Correctness," but history revealed that Christianity was not tolerated by this empire. Christians were crucified, fed to the lions and made spectacles as a means of feeding the sensual appetites of people in the name of live, gory entertainment.

It was not until I read Kenneth S. Wuest's book, *"Bypath in the Greek New Testament,"* that I finally understood the real struggle that ensued between the Roman Empire and Christianity. Like then, the same type of struggle is now going on in America between the Liberal, Progressive Communist and the Christian.

It is true that the Roman Empire tolerated other gods and beliefs, but it did so in light of what Wuest called, *The Cult of the Caesar."* This cult allowed its subjects to retain their own religions as long as they recognized the Emperor worship in addition to their belief system.

In essence, Caesar was considered a god and he would demand worship that could only be expressed in absolute allegiance and devotion when people were called upon to show or confirm their devotion. Ultimately, if it came to a choice between their personal god or Caesar, Caesar would have to ultimately come out on top as the supreme god.

Christianity only recognizes the one true God of heaven. Believers can be patriotic and display loyalty in regard to such things as country, but if anything challenges or demands ultimately worship and consecration, they must reject it as idolatrous, profane, and unacceptable.

There was an incident in A. D. 286 where 6,666 men of the Theban Legion were ordered by Emperor Maximus to march to Gaul to assist in dealing with the rebels of Burgundy. The uniqueness of the group of soldiers was that they were Christians.

The struggle between the dark idolatrous, pagan cult of Caesar collided with the light of Christianity when Emperor Maximus demanded a general sacrifice to be offered before going into battle. Every Christian of the Theban Legion refused to betray their God.

Their action was considered insubordination. In order to gain control of the soldiers, the emperor ordered every tenth man slain with the sword. However, these tempered soldiers of the cross would not be persuaded. Once again the emperor tried to gain the upper hand by ordering his soldiers to go back through the Theban Legion once again and killed every 10th man. Each time these saints died with great poise and dignity.

The soldiers remaining decided to swear their loyalty to Rome, while declaring that their faith and dedication to God made them more loyal to the emperor. However, Maximus would have no part of it. He ordered all of them to be killed. (ED, pg. 283)

The Roman's tolerance towards diverse beliefs applied only if the cult of Caesar was mixed in the combination and ultimately exalted. It is for this reason we must consider what transpired between Jesus and Rome.

Pilate was assured that the kingdom Jesus was king over was no threat to the political machine of Rome. He stated as much, but it is obvious the unseen aspect of the kingdom of God was not considered until later when the believers refused to recognize the different Caesars as gods who deserved devotion and worship.

However, in an indirect way Jesus brought this conflict to the forefront. It was during the time the Pharisees were testing Him by asking Him whether He should pay taxes. The Lord cleverly asked for a coin. He asked whose image was on the coin. This is an important detail. Remember, the idea of Caesar was worship; therefore, his very image required a certain response.

Jesus told the religious leaders that they must give to Caesar what belonged to him, that which was of a physical nature, and give to God what belonged to Him. And, what belongs to the unseen God is all honor and worship for He alone is the sovereign Creator and God of heaven and earth.

Jesus made a clear distinction between the seen and unseen. He wisely silenced all debate, confirmed what was already established by heaven, and established the authority and place the cult of Caesar was to have in His people's lives. (BNT, pgs. 20-28)

Whosoever therefore shall confess me before men, him will I confess also before my Father which is in heaven. But whosoever shall deny me before men, him will I also deny before my Father which is in heaven (Matthew 10:32-33).

♦ Personality is the characteristic of the spiritual man as individuality is the characteristic of the natural man...Individuality is a smaller term than personality...a lamp unlighted will illustrate individuality; a lighted lamp will illustrate personality. The lighted lamp takes up no more room, but the light permeates far and wide.

-Oswald Chambers
(DTD, Jun. 19 & Aug. 23)

- There are just two parties in the world to-day, the confessed followers of Christ and the deniers of Christ, and you belong to one or the other.

    -R. A. Torrey
    (RA, pg. 170)

- As a footstool bears the whole weight of the body, so the enemies of the Lord are to bear the weight of His heavy and everlasting wrath upon their souls if they die unrepentant. The One sharing a glorious throne also has a footstool.

    -Herbert Lockyer, Sr.
    (DP, pg. 455)

- The whole diabolical delusion of a 'second chance' after death and of purifying, post-mortem fires to accomplish what the blood of Jesus failed (sic) to do is a blasphemous assumption of divine prerogative without any Scripture foundation whatever, and comes not "down from the father of Lights, with whom is no variableness, neither shadow of turning".

    -F. Ellsworth Powell
    (KG, pg.196)

- 'Tis paradise if Thou art here,
    If Thou depart 'tis hell.

    -Dr. Watts

In the Currents of Life

To me one of the great luxuries in the present religious world is to find a church whose pastor is a true shepherd and shows it by preaching and teaching the unadulterated Word of God. It is even a double blessing if the pastor's wife proves to have the same heart and vision he does. The proof of such leadership is found in the body that shows genuine love to one another. I have met some pastors that indeed fit this criteria, but they can appear to be far and few because it seems churches are falling into the modern day heresy that is taking America by storm.

Since moving to northern Idaho, I have encountered a few pastors who have an uncompromising attitude towards God's Word. If you can add a true shepherd's heart to that equation it is indeed a priceless combination.

It was at a church that I heard about a saint by the name of William Moore. He was born in Silver City, New Mexico. At age 14, he was diagnosed with tuberculosis. Due to his illness he was relocated from Fort Stockton, Texas to his grandmother's ranch in the dry mountains in New Mexico.

It was in his upstairs' attic room, at daybreak that he actually saw Jesus looking at him through the window. The Lord never spoke, but His look of love spoke volumes. From that moment, William Granville Moore, was entrusted with the incredible testimony of God's power to heal. For it was from that time that the problems and symptoms associated with tuberculosis ceased to be.

It was also during a time of meditation that Moore had an incredible encounter with the Holy Spirit. . He was thinking about how the people at his church had prayed, lifting their hand to God. It was at that time he decided to raise his hands and began to pray. As he lay in his bed, with his arms lifted towards God, the Holy Spirit suddenly took hold of him.

The only way that William Moore could describe what happened to him was that he had an out-of-body experience. He was taken to a river and as he looked into the river and along the shore he saw many people actually swimming in the water. The people were of all ages and nationalities. He also looked across the river and saw beautiful trees, flowers, and grass, and the people who were in the midst of such beauty were dressed in white. He realized that the place's beauty was brilliant and was clearly not of the present world. He quickly surmised that it was heaven.

As he considered the scene before him the Spirit said, "Watch." As he observed, he noticed that one of the swimmers looked across the river and saw heaven and started to swim towards it. Moore was then carried by the Spirit as a means to watch the swimmer. As the swimmer began his journey to the other side, he encountered various types of water from still water to rough water, as well as whirlpools. However, the swimmer would not be deterred from his mission, but when the swimmer came close to the other side the water became very swift.

It was at that time that Moore realized that this river represented life. As each individual travels through life to his or her final destination, he or she will encounter many different types of waters. Some water will prove pleasant, while other waters will become challenging and harsh. As the person's life begins to wind down, life with its currents will escalate as one seems to be catapulted towards their final destination.

When the swimmer finally reached the other side of the bank of the river, he encountered about a 4' to 5' high, muddy, slick slope. As the swimmer tried to claw his way up the formidable slope to enter heaven, he was further swept along the bank. Moore saw someone kneeling along the riverbank and reaching out over the water.

He knew that the man who was kneeling was Jesus. As the swimmer came up to Jesus, his eyes still were on heaven and not on the hand that was reaching to pull him up out of the entanglement of dangerous waters. As a result, the swimmer missed his opportunity to be saved and was taken over a bottomless waterfall to never be seen again.

Once again the Spirit transported Moore back to where the journey had begun for the first swimmer. He was again instructed by the Holy Spirit to, "Watch!" He saw another swimmer look across the water, but this person saw Jesus standing on the shore. Likewise, he began his journey across the river. He also encountered the same waters as the first swimmer, but he never took his eyes off of Jesus. When the swimmer reached the swift water, he swam directly to the outstretched hand of Jesus, where he grabbed it and was pulled out of the treacherous current to experience the brilliant glory of heaven.

Before the experience was over, the Holy Spirit showed Moore other swimmers. When he suddenly found himself back in his bed, he looked at the time and realized that this experience had lasted for three hours.

The river of life proves to be a great equalizer. It does not matter how rich or poor, your nationality, or walk of life, everyone must face the inevitable challenges of life. In its current, each person is nothing more than a swimmer trying to get to a particular destination in spite of the different waters. Even though each one of us might see the destination of heaven, and head towards it with great determination, we cannot reach it without the intervention of Jesus. We must put our focus on Him as our only lifesaver and push through any current and obstacle to grab a hold of His blessed hand in complete assurance that He will not only pull us up out of the river, but He will not allow us to succumb to the current. He is the only one in the right place that can lift us out of the treacherous currents of life to experience the beauty and glory of heaven.

And many of them that sleep in the dust of the earth shall awake, some to everlasting life, and some to shame and everlasting contempt (Daniel 12:2).

THE POWER OF
OUR HIGH CALLING

$$\dagger$$

A Simple Act

Homer Specter, a white missionary to Haiti was driving to a gospel service on a bumpy road when he saw a black man walking at the side of the road. He had a bag with a long rope handle slung over his shoulder. The missionary pulled up alongside the man and offered him a ride. The man looked a bit astonished since it was a rare thing for a white person to give a Haitian a ride, but he climbed in the Jeep. A few moments later he turned to the strange white man and asked him if he knew who he was. The man told the missionary that he was a hougan (voodoo priest), and that he was on his way to a voodoo ceremony.

The white man countered with, "Do you know who I am? I am a missionary, a man sent by the TRUE God to tell your people about Jesus and how He died to save them from sin." From that point, the hougan heard the Gospel story and how Christ came to heal sick bodies as well as save sin-darkened souls. When the missionary let the priest out at his destination he told the priest that if he was ever in trouble and could not get help from his voodoo gods, to call on the Lord Jesus Christ.

A year later, Specter was attending a convention at a church in Croix-des Bouquets. A strange man stood up in the back of the church and asked permission to say something. The missionary called him forward and asked him to speak into the microphone so everyone could hear. What the man said was also recorded on tape.

The man came forward and began to tell his story. He told how a year ago he was walking along the road to attend a voodoo ceremony. In fact, he was the houngan who was in charge of it. He related how a white man who turned out to be a missionary had picked him up in his Jeep and told him about Christ. He also shared how the missionary had instructed him that if he was ever in trouble to call out to Jesus. Months went by when things began to go wrong in his life. One of the challenges was that his wife became deathly ill. He called upon his voodoo gods and performed all of the required ceremonies, but nothing changed the situation. No matter what he did, things seemed to slide downward to the point that it was obvious his wife was dying. It was then that he remembered what the white missionary had told him. Since his gods appeared silent, he concluded that he had nothing to lose. He, therefore, called on Jesus.

In these words the man described what happened. "An amazing thing happened! When I confessed my sin and asked Him to save my soul, I felt CLEAN. He did save me and He healed my wife. He straightened up my tangled life. I renounced voodooism. Today I am living for Him because (and he turned to the white missionary at this point) you, Pastor Homer, told me the Gospel story. You were the man who picked me up that day a year ago!"

There was a great time of rejoicing, and afterwards the man came to the missionary and told him how he would never forget that he led him to Christ and wanted to show his appreciation. The born-again Haitian shared how he was now a tax commissioner for the government in the area of Kenscoff, a mountain resort, and since he had the power to do so, he wanted to give to him a beautiful piece of property that was worth several hundred dollars—which he did! (SFG, pgs. 98-99)

For whosoever shall call upon the name of the Lord shall be saved (Romans 10:13).

♦ This complete salvation is accompanied by a *holy calling*. Those whom the Saviour saved upon the cross are in due time effectually called by the power of God the Holy Spirit unto holiness; they leave their sins; they endeavor to be like Christ; they choose holiness, not out of any compulsion, but from the stress of a new nature, which leads them to rejoice in holiness just as naturally as aforetime they delighted in sin.

-Charles Spurgeon
(MES, Jun. 12 (E))

♦ Once more, when I thought about the need to be crushed and bruised in order to be used effectively for God, I knew it was but a small price to pay for the rewards God was giving me.

-Mikhail Khorev
(SPP, pg. 212)

Prayer: Our Heavenly Father: Let us see Thy glory, if it must be from the shelter of the cleft rock and from beneath the protection of Thy covering hand. Whatever the cost to us in loss of friends or goods or length of days let us know Thee as Thou art, that we may adore Thee as we should. Through Jesus Christ our Lord. Amen.

-A. W. Tozer
(KH, pg. 43)

♦ Without the example of godliness, there is no witness to verify the reality of Christ and His redemption in one's life.

-RJK

♦ The American Board of Missions, New York, has as its seal an ox, with an altar on one side, and a plough on the other, and the motto, *Ready for either*—ready to live and labor, or ready to suffer and die.

-Herbert Lockyer Sr.
(DP, pg. 533)

♦ The watchword against temptations of the flesh is: *flight.*
The watchword against the world is: *faith.*
The watchword against temptations from the devil is: *fight.*

-Donald Grey Barnhouse
(IW, pg. 180, 183, 184)

♦ Everyone is just as holy as he wants to be.

-A. W. Tozer

♦ It was Dr. Dale, I think, who said that we may change our difficulties in Christian work but we can never escape them. I, for one, thank God with all my heart that I am just where I am and in the work I am now in.

-James O. Fraser
Missionary to China
(MR, pg. 168)

♦ There is no hope for Pentecost unless we come to God in our brokenness.

-Smith Wigglesworth
(SWD, (TFT) Jun. 21)

♦ If heavenly affection and contempt of the world are necessary to the character of Christians, it is necessary that this mind-set appear in the whole course of their lives and in their manner of using the world, because it can have no place anywhere else.

-William Law
(DHL, pg. 12)

♦ One of the tests that many of the greatest saints have shared is to suffer a negative reputation—to have others who love and serve God decide that you're suffering because God's displeasure is upon you.

-Bob Sorge
(FDA, pg. 27)

♦ A person doesn't truly know how to love their friends until they learn how to love their enemies.

-Jeannette Haley

♦ If every Christian would pay a scrupulous regard to honesty, and always be conscientious to do exactly right, it would make a powerful impression on the minds of people of the reality of religious principle.

-Charles Finney
(LRR, pg. 142)

♦ What does the high calling entail for those who desire to reach their potential in Christ? It seems as if such people experience extremes in order to walk in the Spirit. They live in the heights of glory, but have learned to swim in the depths of despair as they become identified with the heart of God towards the lost. In his book about prophets, Abraham J. Heschel made this statement, "The prophet is a lonely man. His standards are too high, his stature too great, and his concern too intense for other men to share. Living on the highest peak, he has no company except God." (TP, pg. 127)

♦ He who would glorify his God must set his account upon meeting with many trials.

-Charles Spurgeon
(MES, Mar. (M))

***

There is no gain but by a loss,
You cannot save but by a cross;
The corn of wheat to multiply
Must fall into the ground and die.
Wherever you ripe fields behold,
Waving to God their sheaves of gold,
Be sure some corn of wheat has died,
Some soul there has been crucified;
Someone has wrestled, wept, and prayed,
And fought hell's legions undismayed.

-Samuel Zwemer
(1867-1952)

Verily, verily, I say unto you, Except a corn of wheat fall into the ground and die, it abideth alone: but if it die, it bringeth forth much fruit (John 12:24).

♦ One of the devices God uses to train His Davids is called "removal from ministry." Whether it's a forced removal or an inability to continue, the net effect is the same: cessation or limitation of ministry. His purpose is to test the heart motivations. God is wondering, "Are you in this thing for me or for yourself. Do you love to serve Me because it meets an ego need in yourself or is it because you really love Me?

-Bob Sorge
(FDA, pg. 65)

♦ One grand design of God in leaving Christians in the world after their conversion, is that they may be *witnesses for God.*

-Charles Finney
(LRR, pg.124)

♦ Be you a man with living principles within; never bow to the varying customs of worldly wisdom. Walk in your path of integrity with steadfast steps, and show that you are invincibly strong in the strength which confidence in God alone can confer.

-Charles Spurgeon
(MES, Sept. 1 (E))

♦ As far as the Holy Scriptures definitely tell us, the Holy Spirit has no way of getting at the unsaved world except through the agency of those who are already saved.

-R. A. Torrey
(PWH, pg. 83)

♦ The beauty about being the children of the light is that we know our identity is not attached to the present world of darkness. Our Christian life is a vocation that defines our responsibility, a high calling that distinguishes us, a way of walking that leads us, and a way of living that will bring satisfaction and contentment to our very souls.

-RJK

♦ The best gift the Son of God had was His Holy Manhood, and He gave that as a love-gift to God that He might use it as an atonement for the world. He poured out His soul unto death, and that is to be the characteristic of our lives. God is at perfect liberty to waste us if He chooses.

-Oswald Chambers
(DTD, Aug. 25)

♦ Suffering gladly borne for others convict more people than sermons.

Extreme Devotion
(ED, pg. 103)

♦ It is those who have been in the fight who can tell about the victories.

-Smith Wigglesworth
(SWD, (TFT) Oct. 20)

♦ Whatever we do to the glory of God must be done with a spirit suitable to that glory.

-William Law
(DHL, pg. 36)

♦ God had a very specific purpose in allowing Job to suffer as He did. His purpose was that Job would be a model for all generations after him of how God's ways are beyond comprehension, of how righteous do suffer, and of God's designs to bring them through to victory.

-Bob Sorge
(FDA, pg.38)

Prayer: Heavenly Father, here I am, I am your property. You have bought me with a price. I acknowledge your ownership and surrender myself and all that I am absolutely to you. Send me where you will; do with me what you will; use me as you will.

-R. A. Torrey
(PWH, pg. 212)

♦ Our religion is not to be confined to our closet; we must carry out into practical effect that which we believe. If a man walks in Christ, then he so acts as Christ would act; for Christ being in him, his hope, his love, his joy, his life, he is the reflex of the image of Jesus; and men say of that man, "He is like his Master; he lives like Jesus Christ."

-Charles Spurgeon
(MES, Nov. 9 (M))

Stir Me

Stir me, O stir me, Lord, I care not how,
But stir my heart in passion for the world:
Stir me to give, to go, but most to pray;

Stir, till the blood-red banner be unfurled
O'er deserts where no cross is lifted high.

Stir me, O stir me Lord till all my heart
Is filled with strong compassion for these souls,
Till thy compelling "must" drives me to prayer;
Till thy constraining love reach to the poles,
Far North and South, in burning deep desire;
Till East and West are caught in love's great fire.

Stir me, O Lord! Thy heart was stirred
By love's intensest fire, till Thou did'st give
Thine only Son, Thy best-loved One,
E'en to the dreadful Cross that I might live:
Stir me to give myself so back to Thee
That Thou can'st give Thyself again through me.

Stir me, O stir me, Lord; for I can see
Thy glorious triumph day begin to break;
The dawn already *gild the Eastern sky!
O Church of Christ, Awake!—Awake!
O, stir us, Lord, as heralds of that day!
The night is past, our King is on His way!

-Author Unknown

And that, knowing the time, that now it is high time to awake out of sleep: for now is our salvation nearer than when we believed (Romans 13:11).

♦ Trials are used to purify you; it is the fiery furnace of affliction that God uses to get you in the place where He can use you. The person who has no trials and no difficulties is the person whom God does not dare allow Satan to touch because this person could not stand temptation.

-Smith Wigglesworth
(SWD, Jan. 22)

♦ What people do not realize is the actual preparation time for up front preaching and teaching is about 95 percent, while actual up front time is about 5 percent!

-Jeannette Haley

♦ To suffer as a Christian is to suffer because there is an essential difference between you and the world which rouses the contempt of the world, and the disgust and hatred of the spirit that is in the world.

-Oswald Chambers
(DTD, Feb. 13)

♦ You are not called to have a religion suitable to your opinions, your business, or your pleasures; you are not called to a particular sort of piety that may be sufficient for gentlemen of fame or much property. Instead, you are called, first, to be holy, as "he which hath called you is holy"; secondly, you are called to be "holy in all manner of conversation," that is, to carry this spirit and degree of holiness into every part of your life.

-William Law
(DHL, pg. 10)

He Hath Sent Me

From the glory and the gladness,
From His secret place;
From the rapture of His Presence,
From the radiance of His face –
Christ, the Son of God, hath sent me
Through the midnight lands;
Mine, the mighty ordination
Of the pierced Hands.

-Author Unknown

As thou hast sent me into the world, even so have I also sent them into the world (John 17:18).

♦ It is manly to love one's country; it is Godlike to love the world.

-Unknown

♦ It is good for me to be afflicted that I may die wholly to this world and all that is in it.

-David Brainerd
(LDD, pg. 126)

♦ I am not going to hide the light that God has put into me. If I have to sacrifice everything I will.

-Rachel Scott
(ED, pg. 4)

♦ I will: Fight the good fight, die in the battle, but Jesus will win the war!

-Unknown
(BB)

I have only one candle to burn.
I would rather burn it
where people are in darkness
than in a land flooded with light.

-J. Oswald Sanders
(POG, pg. 119)

The people which sat in darkness saw great light; and to them which sat in the region and shadow of death light is sprung up (Matthew 4:16).

♦ The purpose of the desert (valley) season is that we be given the opportunity to build a highway in our hearts for God. If we build Him a highway, it will be the pathway upon which He will lead us out of the valley.

-Bob Sorge
(FDA, pg. 78)

♦ To be in the will of God is simply being willing to do His will without reference to any particular thing He may choose. It is electing His will to be final, even before we know what He may wish us to do.

-Lewis Sperry Chafer
(POG, pg. 41)

♦ Many people are satisfied with "good"—that is, with salvation. Other people are satisfied with "better"—a sanctified life, purified by God. Still other people are satisfied with the "best"—the fullness of God with revelation from on high. I am not satisfied with any of the three. I am only satisfied with the "best with improvement."

-Smith Wigglesworth
(SWD, Oct. 26)

♦ If therefore, we are to live unto God at any time or in any place, we are to live unto Him at all times and in all places.

-William Law
(DHL, pg. 50)

You Want Power?

Perhaps you have read about Betty's Bible in a previous section of this book. Betty Allen lent me her precious Bible that contained gems in the front and back part of it so I could record them in this book. Her Bible reminded me of my old Bible. As I opened it up she had a page from the "Daily Bread" devotion. This also brings memories back to me. I also had pages from the "Daily Bread" suck in my Bible as well as in the pockets of my Bible cover.

At the top of the page out of the "Daily Bread" dated November 28, she wrote the word, "POWER". The text related an incident about Bible scholar C. I. Scofield. He visited a psychiatric hospital in Virginia. While on tour of the facilities, the superintendent of the hospital pointed out a young man who was powerfully built and appeared to be a picture of health.

Scofield commented that due to the young man's strength, he must be difficult to handle if he became violent. The superintendent agreed with Scofield's evaluation but explained he never exerted his power. He went on to explain to the Bible scholar that the young man's delusion was that he had no strength. In fact, he always asked for medicine and complained about being weak.

It was with this premise in mind that Scofield later commented, "How many in the church are like that! Divinely gifted with the indwelling power of the Holy Spirit, they lacked the faith, knowledge, and consecration to use it. People are always praying for power. There is power enough. What they need is the willingness to be used in any humble position, and the faith to exercise the strength God has given."

Admittedly, in the past it was only when I came to the end of my own strength did I even consider the strength of God. It was only in absolute desperation did I allow myself to become a faucet in which that power could flow from the Spirit of God in and throughout my life. The problem with so many of us is that we are deluded by our self-sufficiency. The pride of our self-sufficiency sees no need to look upward and our fickle self-confidence can either make us hide in fear that we are too weak, or it drives us to exert ourselves in destructive ways.

Do you want power from God? Then know it comes through the weakness of humility, the meekness of submission, and the availability of sincere devotion.

Humble yourselves therefore under the mighty hand of God, that he may exalt you in due time (1 Peter 5:6).

♦ Do it now—suit up, show up, stand up, and speak up for Jesus.
-Unknown
(BB)

♦ Are you thinking of going to the mission field for thrilling and romantic experiences? If so, don't come! They aren't there. It's following Jesus, step by step, from the graveyard of selfish ambitions into the life of God.
-Gladys Aylward
Missionary to China

♦ I discovered that we don't really know what it's like for God to be the strength of our heart until our heart and flesh have failed.
-Bob Sorge
(FDA, pg. 125)

♦ ...no one can help us bear our cross but Jesus; it is one thing to surrender among tender sympathetic friends, but quite another to go back alone to the hut and its unwelcome presence.
-Isobel Kuhn
Missionary to China
(NAA, pg. 55)

♦ If you want to follow Jesus Christ, you must be ready to follow Him to the ends of the earth—for that is where He is going.

-Unknown

***

Jesus, I my cross have taken,
All to leave and follow Thee,
Naked, poor, despised, forsaken,
Thou from hence my all shalt be;
Perish ev'ry fond ambition,
All I've sought, or hoped, or known,
Yet how rich is my condition,
God and heav'n are still my own.

Let the world despise and leave me,
They have left my Savior, too;
Human hearts and looks deceive me—
Thou are not, like them, untrue;
Oh! While Thou does smile upon me,
God of wisdom, love, and might,
Foes may hate, and friends disown me,
Show Thy face, and all is bright.

-H.F. Lyte
(1793-1847)

And he said to them all, If any man will come after me, let him deny himself, and take up his cross daily, and follow me (Luke 9:23).

♦ I have never heard anything about the resolutions of the apostles, but a good deal about the ACTS of the apostles.

-Horace Mann

♦ I am not my own, nor would I choose for myself. Let God employ me where He thinks fit.

-William Carey
First Missionary to India

♦ Worship is priceless. Satan's whole idea is to rob God of it by ensnaring his people into some kind of idolatry. Idolatry claims another, besides God, to be worthy of worship. It is our privilege to counter this by holding it exclusively for God.

-Watchman Nee
(WN, Jun. 16)

***

For he that serves his Lord, must holy be,
And he that labors must be free from guile,
And he that sows be filled with purity;
And he that speaks the message of the Word
Must first receive the fullness of the Lord.

-M. B. Whiting

But as he which hath called you is holy, so be ye holy in all manner of conversation (1 Peter 1:15).

♦ Blessed is the man or woman who is willing to serve cheerfully in the second rank.

-Mary Slessor
Missionary to Africa

♦ Believer are not called we see
To sleep, nor play, but fight.

-Mr. Hart

Prayer: Lord Jesus, you be the needle and I will be the cotton thread. You go through first and I will follow wherever You may lead!

-Native from the Congo

♦ A call is a conviction that steadily deepens when faced with the facts of the case, so that sooner or later it becomes a matter of obedience or disobedience.

-L. T. Lyall
(POG, pg. 120)

♦ A missionary call is not a feeling but a conviction. The feelings follow the call, but are not always pleasant. Willingness to do God's will anywhere and at any times is a condition precedent to truly seeking guidance—and that condition is not always reached overnight.

-J. Oswald Sanders
(POG, pg. 129)

♦ Waiting on God is one of the highest spiritual disciplines...To wait quietly upon God is to refuse to save oneself.

-Bob Sorge
(FDA, pg.193, 196)

♦ It is more difficult, and calls for higher energies of soul, to live a martyr than to die one.

-Horace Mann

The Faithful Preacher

He held the lantern, stooping low,
So low that none could miss the way;
And yet so high, to bring in sight
That picture fair—the world's great Light:
That gazing up—the lamp between—
The hand that held it scarce was seen.

He held the pitcher, stooping low,
To lips of little ones below;
Then raised it to the weary,
And bade him drink when sick and faint.
They drank—the pitcher thus between—
The hand that held it scare was seen.

He blew the trumpet soft and clear,
To call the waiting soldiers near,
And then with louder note and bold,
To raze the walls of Satan's hold!
The trumpet coming thus between—
The hand that held it scarce was seen.

But when the Captain says, "Well done,
Thou good and faithful servant—come,
Lay down the pitcher and the lamp,
Lay down the trumpet—leave the camp,"

The weary hands will then be seen,
Clasped in His pierced ones—naught between!

-Author Unknown

He that is faithful in that which is least is faithful also in much: and he that is unjust in the least is unjust also in much (Luke 16:10).

♦ Those who understand authority recognize that they are leading people. They show those whom they lead the proper respect, consideration, and honor. They are genuinely concerned for the welfare of those who are following them. They see themselves as servants who must first regard the people under them in a proper way before they can expect to lead them in a successful way.

-RJK

♦ Once we realize that the fundamental call in the Bible is to follow Jesus Christ as Saviour and Lord, all of us are subject to the same conditions of discipleship, and we all recognize that God has the right to ask us to go anywhere and do anything at any time He chooses.

-Denis Lane
(POG, pg. 109)

♦ I had to learn the difference between planning to do God's work and being willing to work at God's plan.

-William P. Andrews
Missionary to Chile

♦ Here is the reason a saint goes through the things he (or she) does go through—God wants to know if He can make him (or her) good "bread" to feed other people with. The man—who has gone through the crucible is going to be a tremendous support to hundreds of others...

-Oswald Chambers
(DTD, Feb. 19)

Ministry

Not to sit on a lifted throne,
Not to rule superbly alone,
Not to be ranked on the left or right
In the Kingdom's glory the Kingdom's might;

242

Not to be great and first of all,
Not to hold others in humble thrall,
Not to lord it over the world,
A scepter high and a flag unfurled;
Not with authority, not with pride,
Vain dominion, mastery wide;
Nothing to wish for, nothing to do;
Not, in short, to be ministered to.

Ah, but to minister!
Lowly to sup with the servant's bread
    and the servant's cup;
Down where the waters of sorrow flow,
Full-baptized in the stream of woe;
Out where the people of sorrow are,
Walking brotherly, walking far;
Known to bitterness, known to sin,
To the poor and the wretched, comrade
    and kin;
So to be helper, the last and least,
Serf in the Kingdom, slave at the feast;
So to obey, and so to defer,
And so, my Saviour, to minister.
Yes, for never am I alone;
This is Thy glory, this is Thy throne;
Infinite Servant, well may I be
*Vassal and toiler with Thee!

-Amos R. Wells
(1862-1933)

But it shall not be so among you: but whosoever will be great among you, let him be your minister; And whosoever will be chief among you, let him be your servant (Matthew 20:26-27).

♦ Christians are like Tea: Their real strength comes out when they get into HOT WATER!

-Unknown

♦ A mission is never about a single person's responsibilities. It is singly focused on Christ and His Kingdom.

Extreme Devotion
(ED, pg. 29)

♦ A loving passion for Christ inevitably eventuates in a living passion for men.

-Unknown

Complete Surrender

We can hear about those who consecrate their whole lives to the Lord. It is not unusual for people, even in the Christian realm, to have different reactions. There are those who are convicted by such surrender. These are the people who want to hold on to certain aspects of their lives, while giving the hypocritical impression that they have committed all to Christ. Often these individuals become pouting or critical towards such commitment when they see it in others.

There are those who become fearful. Perhaps such consecration is catching and they do not want to be effected by it. They are content to live on the outer fringes of such devotion and simply be observers. They might display awe at it but they will never be "convinced" that it is for them. They will always give the impression of enthusiasm and support, but they will never make any real commitment to step outside of their comfort zones to become identified with it.

The third group of people is comprised of those who count such consecration as utter foolishness. They see it as fanatic and a complete waste of energy, time, and life. They will always present the worldly perspective and not the eternal reality of the Christian's commission.

There was a brilliant Oxford student who felt the call to be a missionary abroad. He met with logical opposition from one who presented the worldly argument: being that he would die in a year or two, thereby, throwing away his life.

The young man replied, "I think it is with missions as with the building of a great bridge. You know many stones have to be placed in the earth unseen to be a foundation for the bridge. If Jesus wants me

244

to be one of the unseen stones lying in an African grave, I am satisfied to be such."

Hardly two years passed and this young man became a martyr for Christ. He indeed became one of those unseen foundation stones for the African Church.

Wherefore, seeing we also are compassed about with so great a cloud of witnesses, let us lay aside every weight, and the sin which doth so easily beset us, and let us run with patience the race that is set before us (Hebrews 12:1).

♦ The word "missionary" is not in the Bible—the word "witness" is.
-Jim Elliot

♦ The purpose of Christian suffering is that it is a means whereby sin is put out of our lives and likeness to Jesus produced. "We must be found between the millstones of suffering before we can become bread for the hungry multitudes."
-Kenneth S. Wuest
(GN, pg. 17)

♦ Opposition never yet did or ever will hurt a sincere convert: nothing like opposition to make the man of God perfect. None but a hireling, who cares not for the sheep, will be affrighted at the approach of barking of wolves. Christ's ministers are as bold as lions: it is not for such men as they to flee.
-George Whitefield
(GW, pg. 216)

True Place of Refuge

Edith Searell was from New Zealand. In 1895, she became one of the first New Zealander to serve on the mission field in China. She labored with another woman in the Shanxi region. Besides teaching, they did practical ministry by caring for opium patients and visiting villages.

Even though Searell suffered from a painful, chronic lung inflammation she was faithful to work tirelessly among the people.

However, her devotion was tested during the Boxer Uprising. She was aware that she was in danger because Christian missionaries and converts were being targeted. On June 28, 1900, she wrote these words to her friend, "From the human standpoint, (all missionaries in Shanxi Province) are equally unsafe. From the point of view of those whose lives are hid with Christ in God, all are equally safe! His children shall have a place of refuge."

It was noted in the small insert about Edith's life that two days after her notation, she was beheaded.

The Voice of the Martyrs Magazine

I will say of the LORD, He is my refuge and my fortress: my God; in him will I trust (Psalm 91:2).

◆ The ministry that does not demand a price of us is not worth anything.

-Unknown

◆ The passion of Christianity is that I deliberately sign away my own rights and become a bondslave of Jesus Christ. Any fool can insist on his rights, and any devil will see that he gets them; but the Sermon on the Mount means that the only right the saint will insist on is the right to give up his rights.

-Oswald Chambers
(DTD, May 24)

◆ The call today needs to go beyond mere revival or holiness...it needs to be an urgent call or warning. If I were to make such a call it would be, *"People of God arise! Arise from your sleep, your complacency, and your lack of love. Arise from acceptable religious works and games. Arise to the call of God, to holiness, to serve, and to overcome!"*

-RJK

◆ Being on a mission means you are always on the alert for new opportunities to further God's kingdom.

Extreme Devotion
(ED, pg. 43)

246

The Compelling Fire of the Gospel

What does it take to be a missionary? It takes a burden for the lost, a vision that will not be quenched, a hope that will not be silenced, and the compelling love of God that will not let the fire of passion be consumed by indifference, loss, and sorrow.

One of the missionaries that possessed such calling and character was a woman by the name of Evelyn Constance (Harris) Brand. She became a legend because of her feats. Her story was recorded in a book by Dorothy Clarke Wilson called, *Granny Brand Her Story.* Evelyn (Evie) was the ninth of eleven children. As she grew in her life in God, she felt a call to India. She had no idea how it would materialized but in assurance she would not be deterred by what seemed as obstacles or logical arguments. She knocked on doors and the Lord faithfully opened them for her.

Even though she began her journey as a single woman, the Lord provided the perfect partner in her spiritual venture. She married Jesse Brand, August 28, 1913. Brand worked among the people of India who lived around and in what they called "The Mountains of Death." These mountains were hills but they received such a dreaded title because six deadly fevers inhabited them and would claim many lives each year.

Jesse Brand was a man of many talents. He was a doctor, but he was also a builder, teacher, preacher, naturalist, agriculturalist, and father. He faithfully labored among the people in many capacities with the hope of distributing the real Bread of life among them. It was because of this man's endeavor, churches and schools were erected and agricultural methods greatly improved. It was also because of this man's loving, faithful, tireless service that he was considered a father among the people. Jesse and Evie had two children of their own, but took many orphans in, adopting some, all to impart the precious life and hope of Jesus.

Although Brand only had a year of training in tropical medicine, his treatment of the ailments proved to be phenomenal. In one year the Brands treated 1500 patients. This couple did not remain stationary. They would travel by foot and horse to others who lived in the shadow and confines of the Kolli hills and set up camp among the people. In fact, it was Jesse's goal to one day live among the more backward people who inhabited the seven unreached hills that stood before them. His vision also became Evie's. It was burned in her heart.

However that vision would appear to die when Jesse Mann Brand died of blackwater fever at the age of 44. He was mourned not only by family and believers but by Muslims. His loving ways, sense of humor, meek attitude, and practical service served as an incredible testimony to those he had encountered. He had been in India for 22 years and had settled on the Kolli Hills in 1913. What would happen to Evie? What would happen to the vision to not only reach all the backward people on those unreached hills, but to live and minister among them?

In spite of the concerns of the Mission Board, Evie continued to be a missionary. She stayed close to the people she had grown to love. Granted, she was eventually sent elsewhere in India, enlarging her mission outreach. It is hard to say how many people this faithful woman reached with the precious seed of the Gospel. She was affectionately known as "Mother" to those she served, Babs to siblings and friends, and Granny Brand to her grandchildren.

She never lost the vision her husband had concerning the backward people that resided on the hills in the looming shadow of death. However, the mission board never gave her permission to make an inroad into the unreached hills. At age 70 she officially retired from her obligations with the mission she had been affiliated with for so many years and set out on her own to fulfill the vision that had been birthed in her spirit decades before.

Needless to say, Mother Brand left an incredible impact. Her feats were most likely repeated by those who witnessed her stamina, courage, and sometimes the miraculous. Her mode of travel was a horse, but that changed with an accident. She had to be carried to the different places on a dholi and used two poles to brace herself when walking. Eventually a jeep was purchased that helped in some of her traveling adventures.

Evie inspired a work camp that would prepare the younger generation for missionary work. She pointed out to the chaplain that the students lived in an artificial world, sheltered from the poverty and suffering all about them. She concluded that it would be good for them to get their hands dirty, to sleep in mud houses under thatch.

In 1968 at the age of 89, there were 33 people including herself, manning sixteen stations on the seven hills. She watched schools and a hospital being constructed. At the age of 90 she witnessed the construction of a road into the hill area that would make travel easier in the jeep. In fact, a trailer could be pulled behind it. A close associate of hers noted that Evie seem to become more youthfully buoyant than ever.

Evie was joyful over what had been accomplished in spite of the great loss of her husband, separation from her children, the presence of death, sorrow, uncertainty, political unrest, and old age. It was noted that the joy came from her wonderful faith in Jesus Christ. The Lord had granted her long life so that she could see with her physical eyes what she saw long ago with the eyes of faith.

At age 94, Granny Brand's body had become frail. Her physical strength was ebbing away. It was more difficult for her to walk and it became hard for her to rise in a standing posture without help. Her memory was failing her, but her inner zeal and spiritual vigor were still present. As her body begin to give way to the inevitable and her eyes became dim, there was still one member of her body that never lost it youthfulness until the end, and that was her voice.

In her 95th year on Dec 18th, 1974, she climbed her last and highest mountain to see her glorious Lord and be reunited with her precious Jesse. Sixty years had separated them on earth but now her lifeless body would be laid to rest besides his, signifying that she was finally home. Her epitaph would read, *"Trust and Triumph."* Even though much had challenged her along the way, it appeared that the latter of her life was more glorious than the former. Clearly, she had faithfully trusted her Lord with the details and challenges of life according to the call and vision He had given her, and as a result experienced triumph.

But as it is written, Eye hath not seen, nor ear heard, neither have entered into the heart of man, the things which God hath prepared for them that love him (1 Corinthians 2:9).

The Melodious Interlude

Heritage of the Psalms

It is important to realize and remember the rich spiritual heritage we have in Christ. As we take this interlude to remember, we must keep in mind that through the years the melodious messages of the Psalms have been used to see many through tears, trials, and triumphs. They are full of prophetical insight, hope, and promises. In them we can follow Christ from the cross to complete triumph. We are able to catch glimpses into the testings of Israel. We can find every emotion towards love, injustice, and despair being brought out in light of the constant abiding Hand of God.

We see how Psalms affected the understanding of man, shaping his attitudes and his discoveries. For example, Alexander von Humboldt, who died in 1859, acknowledged that Psalm 104 was an epitome of scientific progress, a summary of the laws which govern the universe.

The effects of Psalms upon the generations of history of God's saints are immeasurable. Until the end of the 18th century, the Psalms were exclusively sung in the churches and chapels of America. They have been considered, *The Hymnbook of Humanity"* and used by many to take courage, find consolation, secure victory, and come to rest. For example, the Wars of Religion that was provoked by the massacres of the Huguenots, resulted in the Huguenots using the Psalms as their war-songs. *Psalm 115:4-8* was used by Christians to defy the imperial order to sacrifice to Caesar. It is said that it was with a Psalm that Gwynllia the Warrior, father of Cadoc, turned from a life of violence and banditry to the austerities of a monastery *anchorite.

President Kruger of South Africa was the prominent leader of the Boers. He often appealed to the Psalms, arrogating to himself many of their promises. Although some of his actions were questionable, his confidence in the Psalms was not unwarranted. He knew that the words would reach into the heart of the people. In his speech on May 7, 1900, opening the Volsraads, he applied the words of the 83rd Psalm to his struggle with the British Empire.

Psalm 114 has been the Psalm used to celebrate the release from the bondage of sin in all ages of the Church. Therefore it became suited to be used as a hymn for Easter night.

Bishop of Edinburgh, George Wishart, a fearless defender of the faith was permitted to choose a Psalm to be sung before his martyrdom. He chose Psalm 119 and before two-thirds of it had been sung, a pardon arrived and his life was spared.

Throughout this section you will see how the Psalms have played a significant role in history. The following is a summary of the different aspects presented about the Psalms. The stories and the facts that are being presented in this section were taken from the extraordinary devotion written about the Psalms by Herbert Lockyer Sr. (DP)

Psalm 2 is known as the *Psalms of the King.*
Psalm 8 has been rightly styled, *The Song of the Astronomer.*
Psalm 16 has been named, *The Golden Psalm.*
Psalm 18 has been given the heading, *The Grateful Retrospect* by Charles Spurgeon.
Psalm 22, (The Psalm of the Cross): In it we have the *Cross* with the Messiah as *Savior.*
Psalm 23, (The Psalm of the Crook): In it we have the *Crook* with the Messiah as *Shepherd.* (Is considered the most popular Psalm.)
Psalm 24, (The Psalm of the Crown): In it we have the *Crown* with the Messiah as *Sovereign.*
Psalm 25 completes the four postures of piety that David took in the four Psalms beginning with Psalm 22 according to Thomas Fuller. In Psalm 22 he is *lying* all alone, in 23 he is *standing*, in 24 he is *sitting*, and in 25 he is *kneeling.*
Psalm 30 is *A Song of Dedication for the House.*
Psalms 32 has been named, *The Psalm of Matchless Grace.* In fact, Psalms 32, 51, 130, and 143 were considered the *Pauline Psalms* by Herbert Lockyer Sr. because they teach about forgiveness of sins that come outside of the Law and apart from works.

Forgiveness is a matter of receiving by faith, God's mercy and grace that is realized through the work of redemption. It is also part of *The Penitential Psalms,* along with Psalms 51, 130, and 143.

Psalm 35 has been entitled: *The Awful Utterance of the Righteous One Regarding Those That Hate Him Without Cause* by Andrew Bonar.

Psalm 39 was dedicated to Jeduthun who was the medium (seer) of Divine guidance to David.

Psalm 43 is considered one of the small pearls in the setting of the Psalter.

Psalm 45: A proper title assigned to it was, *The Nuptial Song of Christ and the Church.*

Psalm 51 has been fitly called, *The Sinner's Guide.* (Is considered the most plaintive Psalm.)

Psalm 56 is known as *the Second Golden* Psalm.

Psalm 62 used to be called, *The Only Psalm.*

Psalm 67 has been given the distinction of *The Missionary Psalm.*

Psalm 68 was known as the war-cry of the Britons at Mold and of the Knights Templars, of Demetrius of the Don.

Psalm 81 title included *upon Gittith,* which literally means, "upon the winepress."

Psalm 84 has been entitled, *The Pearl of Psalms.* (Is considered the most sweet of the Psalms of Peace.)

Psalm 88 stands out as "The saddest and most despairing of all the Psalms."

Psalm 90 stands out as one of the most sublime of human composition, describing the deepest feelings, the loftiest in theologic conception, and the most magnificent in its imagery.

Psalm 91 became the battle-song of the Huguenots.

Psalm 92 is believed to be sung on the Day of the Sabbath. The sequence of psalms that were sung by the Levites as follow, 1st day, Psalm 24, 2nd day Psalm 48, 3rd day Psalm 82, 4th day Psalm 114, 5th day, Psalm 81, the sixth day, Psalm 93, and the 7th day Psalm 92.

Psalm 93 was named *The Psalm of Omnipotent Sovereignty* by Charles Spurgeon.

Psalm 114 is known as one of the finest lyrics in literature. At 15, John Milson, an undergraduate at Christ's College in Cambridge, translated Psalm 114 into verse.

Psalm 100 was entitled, *A Psalm of Praise* because it appears that it was to be sung when the *sacrifice of thanksgiving* was offered.

Psalm 101 is described as *Gnomic and referred to as *The Householder's Psalm.*

Psalm 102 was named *The Patriot's Plaint* by Charles Spurgeon

Psalm 103 is considered the most joyful Psalm.

Psalm 104 was called an inspired *Oratorio* of Creation.

Psalm 106 was entitled, *National Confession* by Spurgeon.

Psalm 110 was designated as the *crown* of all the Psalms.

Psalm 111 can be named *the Psalm of God's Works.*

Psalm 113 through 118 were known as, *The Great Hallel,* meaning "to praise". Psalms 113 and 114 were sung before the second cup at the Passover Feast, and Psalms 115-118, after the fourth cup. Psalm 113 has been called, *The Magnificat of the Old Testament.*

Psalm 114 has earned the reputation of being "one of the finest lyrics in literature, and has many historical connections.

Psalm 116 is known as, *The Pronoun Psalm. I* occurs 19 times, *MY* 11 times and *ME* four times.

Psalm 117 is considered, *The Tom Thumb* of the Psalter. Must remember, "Little is much if God is in it."

Psalm 118 has the prophetic expression of that exultant strain of anticipative triumph when Christ, and the rejected Stone, becomes the Chief Corner Stone of His own Temple.

Psalm 119 is considered the most deeply experimental Psalm. This longest Psalm has been broken down in 22 sections according to the Hebrew alphabet.

Psalms 120-135: Songs of Decrees. It means after being abased or down, one now can ascend. They were composed to celebrate the return of the Jews from captivity in Babylon. They were also sung by pilgrims as they journeyed from all parts of the country to attend the yearly Feasts at Jerusalem.

Psalm 121 is known as *A Psalm to the Keeper of Israel.*

Psalm 122 is known as *The Pilgrim Odes.*

Psalm 123 has been called the *Rhyming Psalm,* as well as *Oculus Sperans*—THE EYE OF HOPE.

Psalm 127 is said to be written to Solomon, but there are those who believe that Solomon is really the author of it.

Psalm 128 has been called *The Home, Sweet Home* of Judaism.

Psalm 131 is one of the shortest Psalms to read, but is considered one of the longest to learn. Psalm 130 is considered a Psalm of forgiveness, but this one is considered a Psalm of humility. It is said of 130 that it celebrates pardon from transgressions, but this one celebrates a person who has become meek and lowly in spirit because of forgiveness.

Psalm 137 is said to be the grandest patriotic song which was ever written, linking God and country together.

253

Psalm 140 has been called *A Cry Of A Hunted Soul* by Spurgeon.
Psalm 145 has been called *TE DEUM* of the Old Testament.
Psalm 147 theme is Greatness of God, seen in what He has done, what He does, and what He can do.

And he hath put a new song in my mouth, even praise unto our God: many shall see it, and fear, and shall trust in the LORD (Psalm 40:3).

- In 1174, Henry II quoted Psalm 6 when he sought penance for the murder of Thomas 'a Becket at Canterbury in 1170. His profound humiliation was described in the chronicles at that time in this way, "The mountains trembled at the presence of the Lord." (DP, pg. 27)
- Mary, Queen of Scots quoted Psalm 11, while kneeling to be executed. Previously, her executioner asked her to forgive him for what he was about to do. Her reply was that, "I forgive all." (DP, pg. 42)
- Many martyrs sang different verses of Psalm 18, while looking towards heaven in anticipation of their homecoming. Four sons of the Huguenots, who suffered much because of their Christian faith sang Psalm 18:17-19 while on the scaffold. The last martyrs of the desert sang the same verses, and Francis Rochette along with three brothers also sang these verses while greatly suffering under the reign of Louis XV in 1762. (DP, pgs. 64, 65)
- Martyrs Thomas 'a Becket in 1170, John Hus in 1415, Jerome in 1416, and Jesus Christ had something in common. Upon their martyrdoms, they quoted Psalm 31:5, "Into thine hand I commit my spirit." (DP, pg. 119, 120)
- Cardinal John Fisher quoted Psalm 34:5 as he mounted the steps of the scaffold to embrace the ultimate revelation of the glory and grace of heaven. He was weak and emaciated from spending 14 months of imprisonment in the Tower of London. He owned one of the best private libraries in England in the 15th century, but what he possessed spiritually far outweighed anything the world had to offer. (DP, pg. 137)
- Before Communism took over Russia, the people of Moscow used the 46th Psalm as their memorial song of triumph. They witnessed triumph the night that 20,000 horses of Napoleon's army perished by frost, and the time the French army was driven back by an unseen hand into its disastrous defeat. (DP, pg. 185)
- Covenanter Richard Camerson preached on Psalm 46:10 three days before his martyrdom. Eight years later another Covenanter,

James Renwich was executed, and on him was found the notes of his two last sermons, one of which was Psalm 46:10. What words of comfort and confidence does this verse give to those facing the fiery trials of persecution, "Be still, and know I am God, I will be exalted among the heathen, I will be exalted in the earth." (DP, pg. 187)

♦ In the 18th century, Commander Gardiner who had been in the Royal Navy recorded fearful trails he, along with his party, had endured in their missionary work on Picton Island. Facing starvation, he took courage in his faith in the face of death and in his dairy dated June 16th, he quoted Psalm 57:1. (DP, pg. 214)

***

Making Sense Out Of the Obscure

Life brings so many unpredictable scenarios our way. It can be all quite confusing. As we strive to make sense out of it, we can become overwhelmed as we balance on what we can consider a mental abyss of dread and uncertainty.

However, our confidence cannot be found in what we understand but who we know. We can look at life and see what looks like a scribble mess. But, glory to God, He knows how to unscramble the matters of life and bring peace to our souls. He has even given us a book that can enlighten us about what we need to do or should do. The truth is that there are hidden lessons and messages that can be found in those confusing times that can bring resolution to our souls and peace to our minds. We need to stand still and allow God to illuminate what He wants us to understand.

Following are sentences from the book of Psalms (KJV) that have been scrambled. By looking up the Scriptural reference, you can identify which Scripture it is from and unscrambled its message of the ages that has touched, warmed, and changed many throughout the generations.

1. Psalm 10:1
2. Psalm 14:1a
3. Psalm 24:1
4. Psalm 27:1a
5. Psalm 42:1

8. Psalm 66:1
9. Psalm 70:1
10. Psalm 84:1
11. Psalm 99:1a
12. Psalm 106:1

15. Psalm 119:33
16. Psalm 123:1
17. Psalm 139:1
18. Psalm 140:1
19. Psalm 144:1

| 6. Psalm 54:1 | 13. Psalm 108:1 | 20. Psalm 149:1 |
| 7. Psalm 61:1 | 14. Psalm 116:1 | |

a. O GOD, my retah is fetsatsad; I liwl gins and veig pesiar, neve twih my logry.
b. velired em, O LORD, mofm het veil nam serrevep em ofrm the lotiven emn.
c. rhea my ryc, O God; dettan to ym rerayp.
d. raipse ey eth LORD! gins toun the dlor a ewn nosg, and ish srapie ni het nogrogacetin of nastia.
e. eht reath is het odrls, nad eht fneslus rethefo: the rowld dan hety hatt weldl nethrie.
f. aemk staeh, O God, to lieverd em! emak hetas to leph em, O drol.
g. tuon uyo I flit pu nime yese O huot that welslted ni het avehens.
h. sa het rath naptthe tefar eth rawet kroobs, os teanpth my luso feart ethe, O ogd.
i. sraipe ey eth dlor! O vegi kasnth tuon the LORD; rof eh is dogo: rof sih remcy duethren ofr reve.
j. hyw desantst hotu arfa fof, O LORD? hyw dehist uhot sheytlf ni metis fo brotule?
k. cheat em, O LORD, het ayw of tyh tetastus; and I halsl peke ti otun eth den.
l. het lofo ash dias in ish areth, "rethe is on dog."
m. O LORD hotu stah rhecades em, dan wonnk em.
n. who abilame era hyt natebascler, O LORD of shost!
o. keam a fujoly sinoe nout God, lal ey sland:
p. I evol eth LORD, cabeuse he ahth daerh my ciove dan ym placipustions.
q. vase em, O God, yb hty mean, nad dujeg me yb hyt gettshrn.
r. dlesseb eb eth rlod my tregtnhs, chiwh chethaet ym ahsdn to raw, dan my fegnirs to gifht.
s. The drol ginethers tle het leppoes bretlem.
t. The rold is ym gilht dan my latavsion; womh alshl I rafe?

See answers on page 330.

Thy statutes have been my songs in the house of my pilgrimage (Psalm 119:54).

♦ Navy Commander Allen Gardiner found consolation in phrases of Psalm 62. Gardiner was the means of forming the Patagonian

Rayola Kelley

Missionary Society. In his last painful hour he urged his friends not to neglect the missionary society he had so gladly sacrificed his life for. (DP, pg. 224)

- In his battle to emancipate the slaves, William Wilberforce loved to study the Psalms and would turn to them for consolation when the battle proved to be extreme. He wrote in a letter to his wife that the 71ˢᵗ Psalm, which he learned by heart, became a real point of comfort to him. (DP, pg. 240)

- Out of love and devotion to Christ, two brothers, Crispin and Crispinian, renounced all honors of birth and made shoes for the poor. They suffered during the Diocletian persecution at Soissons in 288. They were sustained by such verses as Psalm 79:9, 10. (DP, pg. 264)

- Ernest the Pious—The Duke of Saxe-Gotha took his queue from Psalm 101:2 when it came to his personal conduct. As a result of his life before the Lord he actually turned the tide in a battle that took place on the field of Lutzen and secured victory. When peace returned to Germany, the pious Duke set himself to bring restoration to the land. He was one of the first to show interest in foreign mission work such as in the reformation. (DP, pg. 376)

- The one-time philanthropist and manufacturer, John S. Huyler was deeply interested in a mission in New York. He recorded that he had many texts for certain occasions, but the most prominent one for general uses was Psalm 103:14, "He knoweth our frame; he remembered that we are dust."

- John Craig was a colleague of John Knox. Although a Dominican monk at Rome, he embraced the principles of Reformation which caused him to be cast into prison by the Inquisition. The night before he was to die at the stake, the Pope died and insurrection broke out. The prison doors were thrown open and Craig escaped through a series of remarkable deliverance. He became God's agent in the work of reformation in his native Scotland. One of his feats is that he wrote a version of Psalm 102, causing him to be considered the oldest Scottish Psalter. (DP, pg. 380)

- In 1568 the Huguenot leaders, along with families and followers experience great peril leaving their refuge at Rochelle and fleeing their enemies. They had to wade through a rising river in order to place a barrier between themselves and their pursuers. When they reached the farther bank, they felt a certain identification to Israel's plight from Egypt, and fell on their knees and gave thanks by singing Psalm 114. (DP. pg. 384)

Antidote for the Soul

What can soothe the restless soul?
Calm the anxious heart,
Temper the uncertain mind,
Tame the wandering spirit:
Songs of praises towards the God of heaven!

What can penetrate raging waves of turmoil,
Cause an overwhelming mountain to
    become a molehill,
Bring down giants of anguish,
Straighten out the crooked paths
    of confusion:
Songs of thanksgiving towards our Redeemer!

What can bring hope to those in utter despair,
Cause joy to arise in the midst of misery,
Bring peace to those in chaos,
Cause the downtrodden to rise up on
    currents of victory:
Songs of worship toward the One
    Who deserves all honor and glory.

God has provided an antidote for the
    struggling soul.
It is a crescendo that ascends to the
    heights of excellence,
A melody that is lifted up by notes
    of heavenly inspiration,
A harmony that emerges with the
    symphony of heaven,

A song from a humble heart,
    pure lips, and meek attitude.
It is a sacrifice that reaches heaven,
A sweet fragrance that floats on gentle breezes,
Marked by the inspiration of the throne of God,
A precious gift of the Lord, made priceless
    by sweet surrender,

Culminated in the beauty of the voice of song, anointed
      by His Spirit.

-RJK

And the ransomed of the LORD shall return, and come to Zion with songs and everlasting joy upon their heads: they shall obtain joy and gladness, and sorrow and sighing shall flee away (Isaiah 35:10).

- Why the meanest insect on earth had more power of locomotion than the greatest of the heathen gods, the Psalmist condemns! (DP, pg. 496)
- Psalm 116 was a burial song of the Early Church as they faced the certain death of this present world in light of the life waiting them in the next world. (DP, pg. 503)
- The 8th verse of Psalm 118 stands in the middle of the 31,174 Scriptures in the Bible. It epitomizes the whole emphasis of the Christian walk, "It is better to trust in Jehovah." (DP, pg. 521)
- The author of, *The Life of God in the Soul of Man,* Henry Scourgal died at the young age of 28 in 1678. It is said that he took *Psalm 119:9* to heart that as a young man he needed to cleanse his way. It led him to complete surrender to God and into the Christian ministry. He became Professor of Theology at King's College. Because of his consecration to the Lord, it is said of his life that he left behind a great fragrance, for generations to appreciate. (DP, pg. 543)
- Psalm 121 was the favorite Psalm of J.S. Watson, Rear Admiral of the U.S. Navy who succeeded Admiral Dewey. (DP, pg. 623)
- Psalm 125 was the psalm the Scotch frequently sung in the hours of danger during the Reformation Period. (DP, pg. 641)
- Psalm 130 had a special meaning for Martin Luther due to a happening that occurred May 6th, 1524. A poor old weaver sang it through the streets of Magdeburg. Since he was poor he offered to sell it at a price that was suitable for the poorest. However, he was cast into prison for singing, which caused an uprising in the community. Two hundred citizens marched to the city hall and would not leave until the poor weaver was released.
- When the early Christians met in catacombs to escape the danger of persecution, special Psalms were played. For example, in the morning, they would open with Psalm 73 and in the evening, they

sang Psalm 141. It is said of this Psalm that few Psalms such as this one, in so small a compass crowd together so many gems of precious and holy truth.

◆ Many of the Psalms were known as the *Hallelujah Psalms*. The final group of these Psalms include 146-150. When the Britons were about to be attacked by the Picts and Saxons, their leaders, Germanicus and Lupus commanded the small army to shout *Hallelujah* three times. When the enemy soldiers heard the sound caused by their shouting, they were struck with terror, and fled in confusion, leaving the Britons masters of the field. (DP, pg. 765)

A New Song

God's Word is a revelation of His Son. Jesus is hid in Scriptures in the Old Testament and is revealed in the New Testament. It is vital that we find Jesus in order to grow in the knowledge of Him. As we grow in our understanding, we will grow more in love with His Person, character, and ways.

The following is a story that conceals 32 names and titles of Jesus. Some are obvious, others are not. They are hidden in words or found in a combination of words. See how well you can identify them. The name or title may be used more than once, but the first place it is used is where it is highlighted in the story. If you need help to know what titles you are looking for, look on page 331 for a list of the names of Jesus. If you want to see if you found them or need to locate any of His names the solution to the puzzle follows the names on pages 330-333.

Bob Messia had lived for himself. His story was one of "rags to riches". He thought that if he had all the world had to offer, he would be happy. He would later discover that regardless of the many worldly successes, his life would prove far from being glorious.

When he considered his so-called successes, he always described himself in the same way, "I am a self-made man." He perceived that in his world, all matters found the beginning and the ending in his understanding and abilities. Even though he had partners, he felt that he had proved time and again that the words he spoke would stand true.

As a means to formula a plan, Bob read of life according to the most successful people in the world. He also carefully planned every move he made. He had acquired three business partners in college. They had been known as the four Musketeers. In a way Bob handpicked his associates. He had observed, listened, and asked questions. Once he identified those who possessed certain qualities, he worked his way into each of their worlds, eventually bringing them together as a team. They were all from the high end of society. There was Alfred Prince of Peaceful Heights Estates, where men lived who were of renowned reputations in their different fields, Carl Anson of Manly Court, an exclusive country club, and Charles Mason of Godfrey Estates, which was bordered by a famous golf course.

They had formed an elite group that was simply called "Alpha," and omega was a coded system they developed to manipulate programs and communicate with each other on their computers. Later they would team up to form a business, using the "omega code" to solve business problems in the computer world, and even opened new branches in other locations. In fact, they were considered the latest saviors when confronting technical problems.

In Bob's mind he had the first and the last say, in regards to what took place in the kingdom that he was establishing with these three men. Each partner had his own unique abilities. Alfred was the life of the party, but he had a side that proved to be clever and shrewd. He could take what appeared to be a dead company and could ultimately do the impossible by ensuring the resurrection of it. Carl had what they considered a "high priestly" quality about him. He often served as a mediator when there was a clash of personalities. When it came to Charles, he proved to be a motivator. He often was like a reliable, good shepherd who guided many through troubled waters and inspired them to accept new challenges.

When it came to Bob, he was considered the anointed one. Everything he touched seemed to turn into financial gain. At age 35, he had quickly climbed the ladder of success and from the heights of his particular ladder, he viewed himself as the king of the computer world, the lord of his business domain, and master of all that he was overseeing. In essence, he saw himself as being divine, a type of god. It was clear he was a savvy businessman. Granted he was a bit ruthless, but he saw it as being necessary to ensure the way of success.

However, one day Bob's world came crashing down around him, along with what he considered to be the light of the world in his life. In fact, his light became shrouded in darkness and called into question. He had thought himself to be infallible, above the law, and capable of beating the odds.

It started when he had socialized a bit too much. Even though he had drunk over his limit, he assumed as always that he was still in control of his faculties. However, he ended up in a car accident. Fortunately, no one was killed but he received a serious concussion. When he woke up, confusion was his reality and his sharp intellect was nowhere to be found; and, from all appearances it would not return to its original capacity anytime soon.

Bob quickly discovered the truth about being part of the human race. To his surprise he was like everyone else. He was not an exception after all, and when he had to stand before the judge at the county courthouse for driving under the influence of alcohol, he realized how foolish he had been. He was not the master of his destiny, and he had been quickly demoted from being the king of kings in his profession and the lord of lords in his personal domain to a statistic. He had to face the harsh reality that when one is stripped of the fickle power the world affords, he or she is like everyone else.

The judge showed some grace, but Bob still had to attend a program that dealt with alcohol abuse and to do community service. He was given three choices, to work with the parks department, which majored in litter and latrines, the street crews, which cleaned up the fall leaves left in the gutters after the residents raked their yards, or in one of the community kitchens that helped the homeless. He chose the latter.

As Bob looked back he could see where it was the providence of God that he chose the last option. It was while serving the homeless, that he finally recognized the barren vanity of his life and his fruitless ways. It was also there he met Josh. Josh was the counselor for the homeless that were served by the community kitchen, and he shared with Bob the reality of the Lord Jesus Christ. He told him how Jesus came to save people from their sinful, dead end lives and to give them forgiveness for going the ruthless way of idolatrous selfishness.

Bob felt the convicting power of the Holy Spirit. He knew that all of his successes would pass away with the world, and that only that which comes from and by the redemption of Christ would withstand the present world, and continue to stand in the midst of glory in the next. That day he made his peace with the Almighty by asking the Lord for forgiveness for his despicable, self-serving ways and inviting Jesus Christ to come into his life as his Lord and Savior.

Josh also gave him a Bible. It was only one book, but it all seemed so new and overwhelming to him. He did not know where to start to tackle God's Word. Josh told him to read the Gospel of John, which proved to be beneficial, but he discovered the Psalms and became captivated by them. He often found himself going on a journey of the heart and discovering spiritual remedies for his heart, spirit, and soul. He would find his heart singing while his spirit soared and his soul rejoiced. It was so incredible, so wonderful.

It was through his spiritual journey that Bob discovered that God puts a new song in the hearts of His people. He not only put within Bob a new song that not only played a glorious melody in his inner being, but it was causing him to walk in a whole new way. He did not know what the future would bring him as far as his business and partners, but he knew he was walking according to the drum beat of heaven and there would be no turning back to the barren, empty ways of his former life.

O sing unto the LORD a new song; for he hath done marvelous things; his right hand, and his holy arm, hath gotten him the victory (Psalm 98:1).

THE MATTERS
CONFRONTING
THE CHURCH

☦

Jelly-fish Christianity

It is hard for generations to realize the problems and issues that faced the preceding generations are similar to their own. The reason for such similarity is because man's spiritual plight remains the same. The issues of sin, death, repentance, and salvation do not change regardless of the generation or times as brought out in the following writing.

The following description of Christianity was written in the mid or late nineteenth century. The author was J. C. (John Charles) Ryle. He was a son of a wealthy banker, and was educated at Eton and at Christ Church, Oxford. He proved his athletic abilities by participating in rowing and Cricket at Oxford. He served as bishop, rector, vicar, honorary canon, and dean during his many years of service to the Lord. He retired from ministry in 1900 at age 83 and died that same year.

"The consequences of this widespread dislike to distinct biblical doctrine are very serious. Whether we like it or not, it is an epidemic which is doing great harm, and especially among young people. It creates, fosters, and keeps up an immense amount of instability in religion. It produces what I must venture to call, if I may coin the phrase, a *'jelly-fish Christianity'* in the land—that is, a Christianity without bone, or muscle, or power.

"A jelly-fish, as everyone who has been much by the seaside knows, is a pretty and graceful object when it floats in the sea, contracting and expanding like a little delicate transparent umbrella. Yet the same jelly-fish, when cast on the shore, is a mere helpless lump, without capacity for movement, self-defense, or self-preservation.

"Alas! It is a vivid type of much of the religion of this day, of which the leading principle is, "No dogma, no distinct beliefs, no doctrine." We have hundreds of ministers who seem not to have a single bone in their body of divinity! They have no definite opinions; they are so afraid of "extreme views," that they have no views at all. We have thousands of sermons preached every year, which are without an edge or a point or a corner--they are as smooth as marble balls, awakening no sinner, and edifying no saint!

"We have legions of young men annually turned out from our universities, armed with a few scraps of second-hand philosophy, who think it a mark of cleverness and intellect to have no decided opinions about anything in religion--and to be utterly unable to make up their minds as to what is Christian truth. Their only creed, is a kind of 'nothingism.' They are sure and positive about nothing!

"And last, and worst of all, we have myriads of respectable church-going people, who have no distinct and definite views about any point in theology. They cannot discern things that differ, any more than color-blind people can distinguish colors. They think . . .

> everybody is right--and nobody is wrong,
> everything is true--and nothing is false,
> all sermons are good--and none are bad,
> every clergyman is sound--and no clergyman unsound.

"They are "tossed to and fro, like children, by every wind of doctrine;" often carried away by some new excitement and sensational movement; ever ready for new things, because they have no firm grasp on the old; and utterly unable to 'render a reason for the hope that is in them.'"

"All this, and much more, is the result of that effeminate dread of distinct doctrine which has been so strongly developed, and has laid such hold on many pastors in these days.

"I turn from the picture I have exhibited with a sorrowful heart. I grant it is a gloomy one; but I am afraid it is only too accurate and true. Let us not deceive ourselves. Distinct and definitive doctrine is at a premium just now. Instability and unsettled notions are the natural result, and meet us in every direction.

"Cleverness and earnestness are the favorite idols of the age!
What a man says matters nothing—
however strange and *heterogeneous
are the opinions he expresses!
If he is only brilliant and 'earnest'--he cannot be wrong!

"Never was it so important for believers to hold sound systematic views of truth, and for ministers to 'enunciate doctrine' very clearly and distinctly in their teaching."

That we henceforth be no more children, tossed to and fro, and carried about with every wind of doctrine, by the sleight of men, and cunning craftiness, whereby they lie in wait to deceive; But speaking the truth in love, may grow up into him all things, which is the head, even Christ (Ephesians 4:14-15).

♦ In relationship to opening the door to more than half of the human race—India, China, and Japan nearly eighteen centuries after it was birthed in Jerusalem, James O. Fraser made this statement, "I believe that He tried the evangelizing of the heathen...many times in former centuries, but His church did not rise to the occasion: she was too encumbered with error and corruption, too powerless to nourish the children to which she gave birth."

♦ Has it come to thus, that the worst counteraction to the truth, and the greatest obstacle to the Spirit shall spring from the church?
-Charles Finney
(LRR, pg. 334)

♦ Christ is in the Gospel, and that Gospel is opposed to wickedness in every shape, Wickedness arrays itself in fair garments, and imitates the language of holiness; but the precepts of Jesus, like His famous scourge of small cords, chase it out of the temple and will not tolerate it in the Church.

-Charles Spurgeon
(MES, May 29 (M))

♦ If our Evangelism was not so dry-eyed, there would be fewer who are perishing in their sin.

Herbert Lockyer, Sr.
(DP, pg. 595)

♦ The low view of God entertained almost universally among Christians is the cause of a hundred lesser evils everywhere among us. A whole new philosophy of the Christian life has resulted from this one basic error in our religious thinking.

-A. W. Tozer
(KH, pg. vii)

Challenging Progression of the "C" Words

Most people's desire is to live without conflict because they associate it with peace. However, without conflict people would subside into a limbo state that would prove to be destructive in the end. The truth of the matter is that without conflict, people would fail to see their lost state before God and their need for Him. They would be void of character, and would have no edge to rightly judge a matter.

True peace is not a state that lacks conflict but one that finds complete contentment and satisfaction in having a right relationship with God. My co-laborer, Jeannette gave this valuable insight into the work of conflict in our lives to challenge unrealistic thinking.

Without conflict there is no confrontation,
Without confrontation there is no contrast,
Without contrast there is no conviction,
Without conviction there is no conversion,
Without conversion, there is no consecration,
Without consecration, there is no conciliation with God.

Confirming the souls of the disciples, and exhorting them to continue in the faith, and that we must through much tribulation enter into the kingdom of God (Acts 14:22).

♦ In relationship with the Church coming into an unholy agreement with the political and heretical forces of Rome, Donald Grey Barnhouse made this statement, "There were rich promises and possibilities which belonged to the Church, and she could have remained spiritually powerful and persecuted. But she dropped the wonderful reality of her true position to grasp at the phantom of temporal power which she saw in the crumbling empire, and thus lost both." (IW, pgs. 241-242)

♦ It is the wind blowing from the lakes that has brought life and health to the cities. Just so, when the Spirit ceases to blow in any heart or any church or any community, death ensues; but when the Spirit blows steadily upon the individual or the church of the community, there is abounding spiritual life and health.
-R. A. Torrey
(PWH, pg. 43)

♦ Many Christians come across the Alps of Atheism in the workplace. Towering peaks of persecution form their own governments overshadow believers in restricted nations. However, a beautiful view is just beyond each mountain of opposition that faces the church today.
Extreme Devotion
(ED, pg. 94)

♦ In employing a minister, a church must remember that they have only employed a *leader* to lead them on to action in the cause of Christ. People would think it strange if anybody should propose to support a general and then let him go and fight alone!
-Charles Finney
(LRR, pg. 215)

♦ Large numbers of people who give lip service to revival does not necessarily give evidence of it, *but rather, evidence of revival is changed lives.*
-RJK

♦ Sometimes we meet Christians who have the "ministry" of "nitpicking". They thrive on picking everybody and everything apart in the name of "ministry" because they feel contempt or disdain toward that which they consider inferior.

-Jeannette Haley

♦ My sweet Lord Jesus remembers well the garden of Gethsemane, and although He has left that garden, He now dwells in the garden of His Church: there he unbosoms himself to those who keep His blessed company.

-Charles Spurgeon
(MES, Oct. 30 (E))

♦ What a difference it would make to Church unity today if only a like spirit of brotherliness prevailed among churches fighting against each other instead of fighting together against one common foe.

-Herbert Lockyer Sr.
(DP, pg. 629)

♦ In the Great Commission to the Church, we were never commanded to preach a political message to salvage our nation. We were commanded to preach a saving Gospel to lost men.

-Marvin Rosenthal

♦ Always the most revealing thing about the Church is her idea of God, just as her most significant message is what she says about Him or leaves unsaid, for her silence is often more eloquent than her speech. She can never escape the self-disclosure of her witness concerning God...The first step down for any church is taken when it surrenders its high opinion of God.

-A. W. Tozer
(KH, pg. 1, 4)

♦ It is as dangerous and ridiculous for our theological professors, who are withdrawn from the field of conflict, to be allowed to dictate in regard to the measures and movements of the church, as it would be for a general to sit in his bedchamber and attempt to order a battle.

-Charles Finney
(LRR, pg.183)
Said in 1833

♦ Donald Grey Barnhouse related how the Protestant Church is trying to imitate Rome. He made this statement, "How else can we look upon the ecumenical movement that seeks to tie in the Greek Orthodox Church (with its veneration of Mary and it prayers for the dead), with the American church organization (with their unitarianizing liberalism, and the state churches of Europe (with their cold and dead formalism)? A leading French theologian, the late Doyen Emile Doumergue, once pointed out that fusion without a true theological basis was nothing but confusion. (IW, pg. 243)

♦ There are many in the church today who once knew the matchless joy of the Holy Spirit, but some sin or worldly conformity, some act of disobedience, more or less conscious disobedience, to God has come in and the fountain is choked. Let us pull out the old rags today that this wondrous fountain may burst forth again, springing up every day and hour into everlasting life.

-R. A. Torrey
(PWH, pg. 109)

♦ When hypocrites and the half-hearted can dwell in our midst without being convicted or made uncomfortable, then something's wrong. God intends for His fire to so envelop the local church that hypocrites will not be able to stay, and the devout will not be able to remain unchanged.

-Bob Sorge
(FDA, pg.15)

♦ Thus far the church in America, in its apathetic state, has the luxury of believing that it is immune to the challenging realities of life, above the persecution that will press against the godly, and will be spared the suffering of the times that will confront those who are truly heirs of salvation. However, the Word is clear, that those who enter the kingdom of God will do so through much tribulation.

-RJK

♦ Loving the good with infinite intensity we must hate evil with the same intensity.

-Herbert Lockyer Sr.
(DP, pg. 591)

♦ The reason the world is not seeing Jesus is that Christian people are not filled with Jesus. They are satisfied with attending meetings weekly, reading the Bible occasionally, and praying sometimes.
-Smith Wigglesworth
(SWD, Mar. 12)

♦ The holiness of Christianity requires us to aspire after a universal obedience, doing and using everything as the servants of God.
-William Law
(DHL, pg. 10)

♦ The saint with sin in his life is not in correct relationship to His Head and to the rest of the Body, just as an arm out of joint is not in correct relationship to the body and the head.
-Kenneth S. Wuest
(GN, pg. 24)

♦ If the world is to get back on its feet, the church has to get on its knees.
-Unknown
(BB)

♦ Religion without a relationship with God is only man's futile attempt to get to heaven on his own merits.
-RJK

♦ The stiff Wind of Legalism—it blows in the west too. Christians sink so easily into thinking that to follow Christ is just a set of do's and don'ts.
-Isobel Kuhn
(NAA, pg. 165)

♦ God never gives back the world to the Christian, in the same sense that he requires a convicted sinner to give it up. He requires us to give up the *ownership* of everything to him so that we shall never again for a moment consider it *as our own.*
-Charles Finney
(LRR, pg.162)

♦ The greatest enemies of Christianity are prime targets for prayer.
                                                    Extreme Devotion
                                                    (ED, pg. 58)

♦ Conformity. This can kill everything—everything spiritual regarding usefulness to the kingdom.
                                                    -E. A. Johnston
                                                    (NTB, pg. 45)

Practical Service

A missionary who had served in New Guinea for many years was once asked about what he found when he arrived at his mission station. The missionary related a vivid description of how hopeless the situation appeared. In fact, he felt as if he had been sent into a jungle full of tigers.

When the man asked for clarification of that statement,, the missionary shared how the pagan people had no moral sense and that they lived and responded worse than beasts. He went on to explain how mothers would throw their babies into ditches and let them die if they began to cry. If a son saw his father break a leg, he had no compassion to help him; he would leave him in his plight.

The man then asked the missionary what would he do with such people? Did he preach to them?

The missionary responded, "Preach? No! I lived."

"Lived? How did you live?"

The missionary went on to say that if he saw a baby crying, he picked it up and comforted it. When he saw a man with a broken leg, he mended it. His kind actions eventually caught the attention of the people who began to come to him and say: "What does this mean? What are you doing this for?" It was at that time the missionary felt it was the opportune time to preach the Gospel.

The man asked the missionary if he succeeded.

The missionary responded, "When I left, I left a church!"

For whosoever shall give you a cup of water to drink in my name, because ye belong to Christ, verily I say unto you, he shall not lose his reward (Mark 9:41).

♦ He who follows Christ for His bag is a Judas; they who follow for the loaves and fishes are children of the devil; but they who attend Him out of love to Himself are His own beloved ones.

-Charles Spurgeon
(MES, Dec. 27 (M))

♦ I think it might be demonstrated that almost every heresy that has afflicted the church through the years has arisen from believing about God things that are not true, or from overemphasizing certain true things so as to obscure other things equally true. To magnify any attribute to the exclusion of another is to head straight for one of the dismal swamps of theology; and yet we are all constantly tempted to do just that.

-A. W. Tozer
(KH, pg. 79)

♦ The churches are very sticklish for correct doctrine and very careless about correct living. This is preposterous.

-Charles Finney
(LRR, pg. 383)

♦ For Christians, however, if we are not serious about the Word of God, we may still be semi-clueless about God, about our moral condition, about our purpose in God's plan (or clueless about the plan itself), and ill-equipped to deal with the problems of life.

-T. A. McMahon

♦ The true Church is left here, not to perfume the dung heap of a fallen humanity, but to save as many individuals out of the wreck as is possible before the final destructive crash comes.

-Donald Grey Barnhouse
(IW, pg. 245)

♦ Prayer links the King on the throne with the Church at His footstool.

-Andrew Murray
(AP, Feb. 26)

♦ O' reader! Look well to the ground work; for, believe me, it is one thing to profess Christ, and another thing to possess Christ.

-John Rusk
(FT, pg. 25)

♦ ...we sacrifice to our own net, and make an idol of ourselves, by making ourselves, and not Christ, the spring of our actions;...such actions are so far from being accepted by God, that according to the language of one of the articles of our church, "We doubt not but that they have the nature of sin, because they spring not from an experimental faith in, and knowledge of, Jesus Christ."

-George Whitefield
(GW, pg. 289)

♦ There is so little *principle* in the church, so little firmness and stability of purpose, that unless the religious feelings are awakened and kept excited, counter worldly feeling and excitement will prevail, and men will not obey God.

-Charles Finney
(LRR, pg.10)

♦ One of the questions that is asked, where is the watchman, the prophet who will warn and contend with the Church?" I believe they exist but I do not think that many have the ears to hear. Watchmen's true inspiration and leading comes from the Spirit above and not from circumstances or out of need. Abraham J. Herchel in his books about Old Testament prophets made this statement, "The ultimate purpose of a prophet is not to be inspired, but to inspire the people; not to be filled with a passion, but to impassion the people with understanding for God. Yet the ears of this people were closed." (TP, pg. 146)

♦ Let us pursue the best things, and let God have His right-of-way.

-Smith Wigglesworth
(SWD, Jan. 25)

♦ Professional Christianity is a religion of possessions that are devoted to God; the religion of Jesus Christ is a religion of personal relationship to God, and has nothing whatever to do with possessions. The disciple is rich not in possessions, but in personal identity.

-Oswald Chambers
(DTD, Nov. 6)

♦ How shall the world believe religion, when the witnesses are not agreed among themselves? You contradict yourselves, you contradict one another, and you contradict your minister, and the sum of the whole testimony is, there is no need to being pious.

-Charles Finney
(LRR, pg.147)

♦ Christian thinking today is "man-centered". Its focus is on improving, empowering, and enlarging one's base of operation. Its "center" is oneself. Basically, it is humanism wrapped in sermons and printed in best-sellers with topics driven with "purpose" and egocentric teachings, wrapped up in a "feel good" type of Christianity.

-E. A. Johnston
(NTB, pg. 1)

♦ If God's people were only more willing and responsive in their gifts, the church would not be obliged to seek assistance from such questionable things as bazaars, *whist drives, to carry on its own work. "Freely ye have received, freely give."

-Hebert Lockyer
(MP, pg. 356)

♦ When it came to testing the effectiveness of preaching, evangelical leader of the Anglican Church, Charles Simeon presented these criteria, "Does it humble the sinner? Does it exalt the Savior? Does it promote holiness?"

♦ One of the statements I would make to those at our fellowship services is that every time we come together, we need to be prepared to do business with God. If we have no intention of doing business with God, or meeting with Him, why bother entering the doors. Jesus' ministry is one of reconciliation, not one that majors in religious knowledge, activities, or experiences. We must encounter God on a personal level if we are to experience the change and impact that is so necessary for our lives.

-RJK

♦ What is religion, but supreme love to God and a supreme purpose of heart or disposition to obey God. If there is not this, there is no religion at all.

-Charles Finney
(LRR, pg. 401)

♦ What the Lord delights in and takes pleasure in is people who fear Him and find hope in His mercy.

-Barry Stagner

♦ The temptation with man of refined thought and high education is to depart from the simple truth of Christ crucified, and to invent, as the term is, a more *intellectual* doctrine. This led the early Christian churches into Gnosticism, and bewitched them with all sorts of heresies.

-Charles Spurgeon
(MES, Sept. 25 (E))

♦ To regain her lost power the Church must see heaven opened and have a transforming vision of God. But the God we must see is not the utilitarian God who is having such a run of popularity today, whose chief claim to men's attention is His ability to bring them success in their various undertakings and who for that reason is being *cajoled and flattered by everyone who wants a favor.

-A. W. Tozer
(KH, pg. 114)

♦ The whole evangelical church recognizes, theoretically at least, the utter insufficiency of man's own righteousness. What it needs to be taught in the present hour, and what it needs to be made to feel, is the utter insufficiency of man's wisdom. That is perhaps the lessons that this century of towering intellectual conceit needs most of all to learn.

-R. A. Torrey
(PWH, pg. 141)

♦ In a somewhat similar fashion, many Christians go to the great architect of lives, not so much to discover and accept His plan as to seek His approval of their own. They are really seeking consent, not guidance and direction.

-J. Oswald Sanders
(POG, pg. 19)

♦ Sinners that live under the Gospel are often supposed to be gospel-hardened; but only let the church wake up, and act consistently, and they will feel. If the church were to live only one week as if they believe the Bible, sinners would melt down before them.

-Charles Finney
(LRR, pg.144)

♦ In relationship to the church of Laodicea, Bob Sorge made this statement, "Because of the multicultural toleration of their communities, the believers were tempted with materialism, hedonism (pleasure-seeking), and the apathy that comes from relative comfort and security. Interestingly, these are the chief besetting sins of the church today." (FDA, pg. 18)

♦ Glory is not an outside halo; glory is an inward conception.

-Smith Wigglesworth
(SWD, (TFT) Apr. 6)

♦ Some fellowships over-emphasize experience and become experience conscious, others over-emphasize doctrine and become doctrine conscious. But the life of blessing centers in Christ and becomes Christ conscious.

Israel's Remnant
(Magazine)

♦ Some people will tell us that there is a progressive holiness, and that the old man is made better and better; but I believe that I am a partaker of grace, and I feel no alteration in the old man, for I find it worse and worse, stronger and stronger, working in all directions, so that I am a continual fear of bringing a disgrace on the blessed cause of Christ.

-John Rusk

♦ (In regard to Satan): His FIRST MAIN DESIGN is to draw into sin. The SECOND MAIN DESIGN is to accuse, vex, and trouble the saint for sin.

-William Gurnall
(CCA, Vol. 1, pg. 71)

Three Kinds of Givers

Some witty person once said: "There are three kinds of givers—the flint, the sponge, and the honeycomb."

"To get anything out of a flint, you must hammer it, and then you can get only chips and sparks.

"To get water out of a sponge, you must squeeze it, and the more you squeeze, the more you will get.

"But the honeycomb just overflows with its own sweetness.

"Some people are hard and stingy; they give nothing away if they can help it. Others are good natured; they yield to pressure, and the more they are pressed, the more they will give.

"Many delight in giving, without being asked at all. Of these the Bible says, 'God loveth a cheerful giver'."

But this I say, He which soweth sparingly shall reap also sparingly; and he which soweth bountifully shall reap also bountifully (2 Corinthians 9:6).

♦ The test of your Christianity is not how high you can jump, or how loud you can shout, but how much you can love under pressure.

-Unknown

♦ If you continue to prophesy on your own, at the end of the anointing, you are using false fire.

-Smith Wigglesworth
(SWD, (TFT) Dec. 16)

- Christians must renounce this world to prepare themselves, by daily devotion and universal holiness, for an eternal state of quite another nature.

  -William Law
  (DHL, pg. 37)

- When sinners are careless and stupid, and sinking into hell unconcerned, it is time the church should bestir themselves. It is as much the duty of the church to awake, as it is of the firemen to awake when a fire breaks out in the night in a great city. The church ought to put out the fires of hell which are laying hold of the wicked.

  -Charles Finney
  (LRR, pg. 23)

- The moralists discuss, suggest, counsel; the prophets proclaim, demand, insist.

  -Abraham J. Heschel
  (TP, pg. 275)

- God is going to turn up the heat on His last days' church, because if He doesn't, His saints will succumb to apathy, greed, lukewarmness, materialism, and the self-indulgent spirit of the entertainment industry.

  -Bob Sorge
  (FDA, pg.21)

- The Lord loves His church so much that He cannot bear that she should go astray to others; and when she has done so, he cannot endure that she should suffer too much or too heavily.

  -Charles Spurgeon
  (MES, Feb. 24 (E))

- Every church should support two pastors—one for the thousands at home, the other for the millions abroad.

  -Unknown

- The enemies of the church are ofttimes men of the finest brains and deepest policies.

  -John Flavel
  (RR, pg. 92)

279

♦ There are a great many spiritual *epicures in the churches, who are all the while seeking to be happy in religion, while they take very little pains to be useful.

-Charles Finney
(LRR, pg. 387)

♦ The church has consistently spiritualized Israel's blessing while interpreting her judgments literally. Basilea Schlink considers the transfer of one without the other to be "untruthful and impossible."

-Paul Wilkinson

♦ We are called to be fruit inspectors—carefully examining the fruit of people's lives to reveal their motives.

Extreme Devotion
(ED, pg. 230)

♦ Don't be fanatically religious and don't be irreverently blatant. Remember that the two extremes have to be held in the right balance. If your religion does not make you a better man, it is a rotten religion.

-Oswald Chambers
(DTD, Nov. 26)

♦ God has left his cause here before the human race, and left his witnesses to testify in his behalf, and behold, they turn round and testify the other way! Is it any wonder that sinners are careless?

-Charles Finney
(LRR, pg. 144)

♦ There's a difference between catering to people and ministering to them. When we cater to them we draw them to ourselves. When we minister to them we draw them to the Lord. Catering to people leads them down a blind alley.

-Selected

♦ (Concerning the end of the last days): For many people, objective truth will have been replaced by feelings and experience. For others, intellectualism and skepticism will have justified what will seem to be a very reasonable improvement upon "Christianity."

-Dave Hunt

♦ The Great Awakening was the result of solid doctrinal preaching that addressed itself to both the heart and the mind. It was preaching that dared to expose sin in the church. And God used it to sweep thousands into his family.

-Warren Wiersbe
(VCK, pg. 117)

Spiritual Nerds

In our society, we have a group of people who do not seem to interact or fit in the world around them. The reason for it is because they operate only on an intellectual level. Such individuals fail to connect with the reality around them. They often lose respect and authority because others see them as being unrealistic, clueless, and ridiculous. They are referred to as "nerds."

As Christians, we will not fit in this world, and our ability to interact with it on its level will result in different forms of separation. The separation could come in the form of broken relationships, losses such as reputations, and persecution.

New Christian converts will initially find themselves falling into one of two categories, depending on what influences them. The first category points to those who have the fiery zeal of the Holy Spirit, but do not yet possess wisdom. The second group lacks the real fire and is basically ineffective and dead and will fall into the category of those who possess lifeless knowledge.

Those who represent zealous Christians must become flexible and teachable as God fine-tunes them. They must strive to never let their initial fire die out.

The second group who possess lifeless knowledge I refer to as "spiritual nerds". This slang word simply means an "ineffective person." There are three types of nerds in the kingdom of heaven.

The first group of spiritual nerds are those who spiritualize Christianity. They are unrealistic and live in a fantasy land that often presents the kingdom of heaven as a candy store. They must conjure up some religious experience to give them that high or zeal towards Christianity. To onlookers they come across as spiritual fanatics.

281

However, their reality is very fragile and will cause them to collide with the challenges of life.

The second group are made up of those who act like they are God's favorites. They come across with the attitude of having all the spiritual goods they have need of; just ask them. These people can appear to be apathetic because they feel they have fire insurance against hell. But on the other hand, they are disobedient towards the Word of God and stand on shifting sand. Like the people at Ephesus, they have left their first love (Revelation 2:2-4).

The attitude of the second group is pride clothed in self-righteous snobbery. They stand judging that which does not align to their particular take on religion. Their idea of love is a tolerance that has an edge to it. In other words, there is an edge of impatience towards that which seems inferior, stupid, and insignificant in light of their self-importance. It is unattractive to every onlooker.

The third group are those Christians who are out to find some kind of recognition in the kingdom of heaven. They want to appear zealous in their witnessing and service, but will come across as obnoxious, undesirable, and even insulting. Their greatest feat is not really salvation, but self-exaltation. Their attempts turn unbelievers off and embarrass believers.

It takes learning the lessons of both this present life and heaven to ensure that we do not remain in a state of utter cluelessness about what is going on around us. All truth must be properly applied if we are going to be set free to reach our potential in the kingdom of God.

Do you fit in any of the categories above? Give the Lord permission to grow you up in the knowledge of Jesus Christ.

Ever learning, and never able to come to the knowledge of the truth (2 Timothy 3:7).

♦ In every church there are spiritual and carnal Christians, and in every church practically the same class predominate.

-Isobel Kuhn

(NAA, pg. 122)

- The Lord Jesus Christ found it more difficult to get the people to yield up their false notions of theology than anything else.

  -Charles Finney
  (LRR, pg. 360)

- Thus Paul exhorts the saints not to assume as an outward expression the fashions, habit, speech expressions, and artificiality of this evil age, thus hiding that expression of themselves which should come from what they are intrinsically as children of God. How saints sometimes like to have just a dash of the world about them so as not to appear too unworldly. How a coat of worldliness can cover up the Christ within.

  -Kenneth S. Wuest
  (GN, pg. 27)

- See why so much preaching is wasted, and worse than wasted. It is because the church will not break up their fallow ground. A preacher may wear out his life, and do very little good, while there are so many stony-ground hearers, who have never had their fallow ground broken up. They are only half converted, and their religion is rather a change of opinion than a change of the feeling of their hearts. There is mechanical religion enough, but very little that looks like deep heart work.

  -Charles Finney
  (LRR, pg. 46)

- Real Christianity is lost when the pressures subside. Today America has only traces of real Christianity because we have been so coddled in our modern luxuries, conveniences, and ease. Our prayers are without tears, our worship is a ritual; our study of the word is done at convenience, our evangelistic efforts are embarrassing.

  -Bob Sorge
  (FDA, pg. 111)

- It is amazing to see how many Christians are fleshly in their lifestyles. It is not unusual to hear about all kinds of works of darkness operating among Christians. Sexual immorality, pornography, abortions, and sensual pursuits of every imaginable kind are often bragged about or condoned by Christians. Either

283

the world has come so much into the Church that there is no discernment between what is clean and unclean, or we are spiritually dull because of compromise and pride. If the world has come in, then Christians' lifestyles are being determined by the world, and not by the Word of God and the example of Christ.

-RJK

♦ The crisis is the shallowness of the Christians themselves who desire candy over meat. There exists today in Christendom a vacuum of thought. A vacuum of spirituality. A vacuum of true discipleship.

-E. A. Johnston
(NTB, pg. 23)

♦ If we are ever going to make any progress in the divine life, we will have to have a real foundation.

-Smith Wigglesworth
(SWD, Jan. 15)

♦ What soft flabby lives we Christians live. How little of stern soul—discipline do we know.

-Kenneth Wuest
(BNT, pg. 54)

♦ The church is mighty orthodox in *notions*, but heretical in practice, but the time must come when the church will be just as vigilant in guarding orthodoxy in practices as orthodoxy in doctrine, and just as prompt to turn out heretics.

-Charles Finney
(LRR, pg. 383)

♦ The majority of the most fanatical intolerant people in the world are in religious circles.

-Manfred Haller
(CA, pg. 32)

♦ More people are lost in Christian land by neglecting than in any other way.

-R. A. Torrey
(RA, pg. 95)

♦ The satanic assault that America has experienced over the last 60 years were battles that Christians have lost by default.

> -Dr. David Schnittger

♦ There are Christians today who are ruled by their head. Historically our Goliath was overthrown at Calvary, but spiritually Saul lives on in us still.

> -Watchman Nee
> (WN, May 8)

♦ There are three kinds of straits wherein he (Satan) labours to entrap the Christian—nice questions, obscure scriptures, and dark providences.

> -William Gurnall
> (CCA, Vol. 1, pg. 95)

♦ Christians are bound to show by their conduct, that they are actually satisfied with the enjoyments of religion, without the pomps and vanities of the world; that the joys or religion and communion with God keep them above the world.

> -Charles Finney
> (LRR, pg. 137)

♦ Where there is great persecution, there is only one category of Christian: disciples (Acts 19:30). Where there is no persecution, there are two categories—believers and disciples. The westernized work has many believers and few disciples.

> -Bob Sorge
> (FDA, pg. 111)

The Universal Body

The Church of Jesus Christ is living and universal in scope. Some of His Church is being persecuted; part of it is being tested, while aspects of it know the abundance of blessing. That which is being blessed must share with that which is being tested and persecuted. That which is being tested must pray for those who are being persecuted, and those who are being persecuted must maintain their testimony and pray for those who have not yet been tested.

As we consider those of the Church who are being persecuted, they understand what it means to consecrate all to Christ, while those who are being tested are beginning to understand the trials of the fiery ovens and how such trials are designed to enlarge faith; and, those who are bless must carefully guard their attitude and conduct to ensure a realistic perspective of the Christian life.

I often read about the lives of missionaries and the persecuted Church to keep a realistic perspective about the Christian walk. In America, we can believe that we are immune from the challenges that other Christians face, and adopt the heretical philosophy of elitism, but the reality is if a truth cannot be realistically applied to the persecuted Church it cannot be applied to the part of the Church that has been lulled to erroneously believe that they are an exception to such challenges.

When I study the lives of those who are part of the persecuted Church, many of them understand what it means to offer the best to God out of their need, while those who are in trials are learning what it means to offer the sacrifice of praise, and those who are in the midst of blessing must remember where they have come from to ensure they are fruitful in the knowledge of Jesus.

This brings us to the matter of sacrifice. The Church in America often offers leftovers and calls them sacrifices, those being tested must leave the old life behind to gain what is real, while those of the persecuted Church will count the cost and often choose to pay it for the sake of furthering the kingdom of God. This is true when it comes to smuggling the Word of God into countries that consider it contraband. Those who are caught smuggling face torture, jail time, and even death.

If you read about those who smuggle Bibles, there is as much suspense in their escapes as in any mystery novel. Sometimes their experiences almost seem surreal, but nevertheless, it is their reality.

There is the story about a Romanian man named Gheorghe. He was part of the chain that smuggled Bibles into Russia. Another man, Codrean was one of the individuals who was also part of this valuable chain, but one day he was struggling with a headache that would keep him from his mission.

Codrean needed intervention from above. Those in the room knew who to turn to, but before they prayed for the intervention from above, a story was related to Codrean to stir up his faith.

Gheorghe had been exposed to God, but he had not committed his life to him until he came face to face with his spiritual emptiness. Nothing filled the emptiness, from his work to his marriage or new daughter. His wife had suffered health issues after the birth of their daughter, Luci. In the time of uncertainty, he found himself remembering what he had learned about God. He had been praying that God would reveal Himself to him, but this time he remembered what he had learned, and He once again called on the Lord. The room filled with light and Jesus stepped inside.

It was after his encounter with the Living Christ that Gheorghe felt drawn to be part of the ministry that smuggles Bibles so that they could be placed in the hands of the hungry, thirsty sheep of the Lord's Church. Gheorghe found opposition from his wife, but God had a plan that would not be thwarted by any opposition.

Gheorghe's wife, Lidia once again became very ill after the birth of their second daughter, Claudia. Gheorghe had reluctantly left his home to attend church, leaving Luci and the baby home with their sick mother. Lidia began to recognize she was in trouble. Her cries reached her four-year-old daughter Luci, who ran to her mother's side. Lidia cried that she was dying and to please get her help.

In her child-like mind, Luci knew there was only one source to go to and that was Jesus. She sent this prayer, "Lord Jesus, I am a little girl, I have a little sister, Claudia. If Mama dies, who will feed the baby? Heal my mama, Jesus! I know you can do it."

Lidia felt something like electricity go from the top of her head to the bottom of her feet. She immediately felt relief and knew God had healed her. She became a believer and not only joined her husband in his faith but was ready to serve the Lord with him.

After Codrean heard the story, he submitted to the group in prayer. Power came down in the form of electricity that went from his head to his feet and he immediately felt relief.

However, Gheorghe knew that he had been followed by the police and that any further involvement past the night might endanger those who were involved with smuggling Bibles. Sure enough the police did come through the front door of his home, but it was after the two servants escaped through the window of the back room with the precious cargo. (IH, pgs. 72-78)

Today, some believers are risking everything to get the Word of God into the hands of the persecuted Church. These deprived members value it like a most precious treasure.

These people's work reminds me that as Christians, we each are members of a living organism in which we have our place and function. Jesus said He would send us out among wolves. Such a thought can be frightening and overwhelming. However, if we ignore our calling or are hindered from fulfilling our destiny, the furtherance of His kingdom will be somewhat thwarted. Praise the Lord, He knows how to go around boulders and obstacles in order to put His Living Words in the hand of His thirsty people. The key is how open, available, and willing are you to be part of the work and move of God?

So shall my word be that goeth forth out of my mouth: it shall not return unto me void, but it shall accomplish that which I please, and it shall prosper in the thing whereto I sent it (Isaiah 55:11).

THE TRAVESY
OF MAN

The Failure of Each Generation

As Christians we possess a spiritual heritage that is meant to be passed down to the next generation. Sadly, it is hard to keep the torch burning bright as it is handed off to those who are coming behind us. For example, you cannot pass down passionate devotion where there is no real vision. You cannot stir up where there is no purpose. You cannot spur on when there is no compelling drive, and you cannot convince one who has no heart to hear, see, or believe.

Consecrated servants of God not only are willing to lose all they know to pick up the torch, but they are aware that if it is not passed on to others that the light will eventually go out. Therefore, they live and sacrifice all to pass on the torch, to keep the flames of the Holy Fire of God alive and burning for others to be drawn to in the dark night of hopelessness and death. However, regardless of their burning desire to see the kingdom of God go forth, there is the realization that they cannot pick up the torch for another.

Missionary Isobel Kuhn made reference to passing the spiritual legacy on in her book, *Nests Above the Abyss.* She stated, "But when God's providence takes an unexpected turn, shallow thinkers make shallow and dishonoring remarks. I believe that in each generation God has 'called' enough men and women to evangelize all the yet unreached tribes of the earth. Why do I believe that? Because everywhere I go, I constantly meet with men and women who say to me, 'When I was young I wanted to be a missionary, but I got married instead.' Or, 'my parents dissuaded me,' or some such thing. No, it is not God who does not call. It is man who will not respond!"

Then saith he unto his disciples, The harvest truly is plenteous, but the labourers are few; Pray ye therefore the Lord of the harvest, that he will send forth labourers into his harvest (Matthew 9:37-38).

♦ Man is forever trying to bring God down to his understanding instead of allowing God to bring him to the excellent heights of His wisdom, which would give him the far-reaching perspective of eternity.

-RJK

♦ Worldly conformity, in any degree, is a snare to the soul, and makes it more and more liable to presumptuous sins.

-Charles Spurgeon
(MES, Aug. 20 (E))

♦ The consistent testimony of Scripture is that those who worship helpless idols shall become helpless themselves.

Herbert Lockyer, Sr.
(DP, pg. 497)

♦ They that make them *images*, show their ingenuity, and doubtless are sensible men; but they that make them *gods* show their stupidity, and are as blockish things as the idols themselves.

-Matthew Henry

♦ The essence of idolatry is the entertainment of thoughts about God that are unworthy of Him.

-A. W. Tozer
(KH, pg. 3)

♦ Unregenerate man is not in the image of God...The false idea that all men still retain the divine image is so entrenched in the thoughts of men that they are more than startled when the fresh winds of the Word of God would blow the mind clear of the heresy of man's natural goodness and divinity.

-Donald Grey Barnhouse
(IW, pg. 42)

♦ Man-devised religions in the past have often missed the truth and man-devised religions in the future will doubtless do the same.

-R. A. Torrey
(PWH, pg. 101)

♦ As important as the content of our thinking about God is our way of thinking about Him...There are two pitfalls in our religious understanding; the humanization of God and the anesthetization of God. Both threaten our understanding of the ethical integrity of God's will.

-Abraham J. Heschel
(TP, pg. 351, 353)

♦ God wants to annihilate our inbred tendency to depend upon our own innate strengths. This is no small task and requires great breaking in our lives. We naturally think far too highly of ourselves. The Scripture says, "to God who alone is wise" (1 Timothy 1:7).

-Bob Sorge
(FDA, pg.107)

♦ Have you not so envied some that you have been pained to hear them praised? It has been more agreeable to you to dwell upon their faults, than upon their virtues, upon their failures, then upon their success. Be honest with yourself, and if you have harbored this spirit of hell, repent deeply before God, or *he will never forgive you*.

-Charles Finney
(LRR, pg. 42)

♦ Today, man thinks he knows best. In many arenas he has substituted worship of knowledge over worship of God. He often thinks he has the answers. He looks within rather than upward. He draws from his worldly sources only to fall into a vacuum that has no real answer or hope.

-RJK

♦ He who is content has enough. He who complains has too much!

-Unknown
(BB)

♦ In the name of freedom and right of choice, our most blessed of nations has condemned its unborn to the cruelest of deaths, has made a mockery of the sanctity of marriage, entertains itself with films and music centered on themes of violence, Satanism, and sexual perversions, has all but destroyed millions of its youth with drugs, and has created an urban war zone and a poisoned planet. Evil will soon be ripe for harvest.

-Dave Hunt

♦ It may be what you are pleased to call a *small* sin, but there are no small sins. There are sins that concern small things, but every sin is an act of rebellion against God. Therefore no sin is a small sin. A controversy with God about the smallest thing is sufficient to shut one out of the blessing.

-R. A. Torrey
(PWH, pg. 208)

♦ To be conformed to this world is all loss, but to be transformed from this world is all gain.

-Smith Wigglesworth
(SWD, May 11)

♦ A man who worships an image is but the image of a man, his senses must have left him. He who boasts of an idol makes an idle boast.

-LXX Version of Deuteronomy 32:43
(DP, pg. 356)

♦ The sin of hating or despising any one man is like the sin of hating all God's creation; and the necessity of loving any one man is the same necessity of loving every man in the world.

-William Law
(DHL, pg. 234)

♦ Obstinacy in an hour of imminent disaster is uncanny, irrational…When the wicked is spared, he does not learn righteousness; in the land of uprightness he deals perversely and does not regard the majesty of the Lord.

-Abraham J. Heschel
(TP, pg.115)

♦ Yet we should beware of any teaching that advocates a passive and blank mind while seeking guidance. That smacks more of demonism and the use of mediums than divine leading.

-J. Oswald Sanders
(POG, pg. 78)

♦ There's no one quite as insensitive to the poor as the one who has always enjoyed wealth. Theirs is no one quite as insensitive to the sick as someone who has always enjoyed relatively good health. There's no one quite as insensitive to the feeble as the one who has always been strong.

-Bob Sorge
(FDA, pg. 110)

♦ It is common for those ministers who have been to the seminaries and are now useful, to affirm that their course of studies there did them little or no good, and that they had to *unlearn* what they had there learned, before they could effect much.

-Charles Finney
(LRR, pg. 179)

♦ We are seeing where more and more individuals appear as if they have no conscience as to the destruction of their wicked deeds. Those who are void of such conscience are also void of being afraid of the consequences that will eventually follow their actions.

-RJK

♦ Those who seek to defame and destroy the righteous are "worse than cannibals, for they only eat men after they are dead, but slanderers eat them up alive.

-Herbert Lockyer Sr.
(DP, pg. 619)

♦ The reason a lot of people "drop the ball" (responsibilities) is because they were not carrying them in the first place. They were busy doing their own thing.

-Jeannette Haley

◆ Secularism, materialism, and the intrusive presence of things have put out the light in our souls and turned us into a generation of zombies.

-A. W. Tozer
(KH, pg. 18)

Prayer: Oh, God, Thou hast formed us for Thyself; and our souls can know no rest until they rest in Thee.

-Augustine
(IW, pg. 93)

◆ Human intelligence does not suffice to fathom the will of God. The mortal is a stranger on the earth; both time and strength are wanting to attain to knowledge which only Divine wisdom can teach.

-Herbert Lockyer Sr.
(DP, pg. 545)

◆ ...the most awful and dangerous characters are those who are well furnished in the head with gospel truth, and the devil deceived them with a fictitious experience; for they are full of lightness and levity, and never were in heart separated from this world, nor the spirit of it, nor yet from themselves.

-John Rusk
(FT, pg. 40)

Opinions!

Opinions, opinions, opinions,
Covered by fig leaves of nonsensical oratory,
Often robed in self-righteous zeal,
Clothed in incessant arrogance.

Always touted as truth,
Constantly upheld as THE standard,
Clearly maintained as THE way,
Declared from narrow pinnacles of ridiculousness.

Forever cascading from broken dams of ignorance,
Falling into whirlpools of indifference,

Forming hard rocks of criticism,
Always colliding with the waves of reality.

Incapable of floating with currents of truth,
Blocked by concrete anchors of indoctrination.
Entangled by weeds of delusion,
But always standing tall in judgment.

Having no substance to withstand,
Void of the light of reason,
Lacking the penetrating love of God,
Quenching the clarity of the Spirit.

Standing on shifting sand of prejudice,
Taken out by the changing tides of perverted imagination,
Opinions always forming a rushing river,
Descending into the Dead Sea of vanity, stagnation,
    and foolishness.

Opinions, opinions, opinions,
Drowning out all rationale and wisdom,
Proving, empty, unsettled, destined to crumble in utter ruin
Ultimately, falling into the endless abyss of silence,
    never to be heard from again!

-RJK

Wherefore let him that thinketh he standeth take heed lest he fall (1 Corinthians 10:12).

♦ There is no limit to cruelty when man begins to think that he is the master.
-Abraham J. Heschel
(TP, pg. 211)

♦ Those who assume that whatever 'vision' fills the blank is from God, have no defense against the invasion of obsessive, grandiose, self-serving imaginations spawned by their own conceit.
-J. I. Packer
(POG, pg. 30, 31)

♦ The main symptom of spiritual pride is sincere decision making without consulting God.

-Bob Sorge
(FDA, pg.137)

♦ Wherever a sinner is entrenched, unless you pour light upon him there, you will never move him.

-Charles Finney
(LRR, pg.191)

♦ Modern ethical teaching bases everything on the power of the will, but we need to recognize also the perils of the will. The man who has achieved a moral victory by the sheer force of his will is less likely to want to become a Christian than the man who has come to the moral frontier of his own need.

-Oswald Chambers
(DTD, Jan. 2)

♦ Can you hold God? Yes you can. Sincerity can hold Him, dependence can hold Him, weakness can hold Him. I'll tell you what cannot hold Him; self-righteousness cannot hold Him; pride cannot hold Him; assumption cannot hold Him; high-mindedness cannot hold Him—thinking you are something when you are nothing, puffed up in your imagination.

-Smith Wigglesworth
(SWD, Jan. 6)

♦ The philosopher and the scientist will admit that there is much that they do not know; but that is quite another thing from admitting that there is something which they can *never* know, which indeed they have no technique for discovering.

-A. W. Tozer
(KH, pg. 26)

♦ Self-respect is the fruit of discipline; the sense of dignity grows with the ability to say no to oneself.

-Abraham Joshua Heschel

♦ There is danger in selecting counselors we are sure will not run counter to our desires

-J. Oswald Sanders
(POG, pg. 86)

♦ If thou doest worship God, and that devoutly, but not by Scripture rule, thou art but an idolater. If according to the rule, but not in spirit and truth, then thou art a hypocrite, and so fallest into the devil's mouth.

-William Gurnall
(CCA, Vol. 1, pg. 41)

♦ Man can only spend his millions in peace conferences that *eventuate in further seeds of war. He can create his leagues of nations and his united nations, which leave wonderful buildings in Geneva and New York like the tower of Babel, monuments to the folly of man's attempts to do that which can be done only by God.

-Donald Grey Barnhouse
(IW, pg. 263)

♦ The flesh has its worship as well as its lusts. The worship that the flesh prompts is an abomination to God. In this, we see the folly of any attempt at a conference of religions where the representatives of radically different religions attempt to worship together.

-R. A. Torrey
(PWH, pg. 149)

♦ Lying lips are bad enough for they suck away the character of the one lied against, downright falsehood is worse than a lie. Deceitful tongues that fawn and flatter but are ready to destroy a life are to be feared, even as the Devil is when he appears as an angel.

-Herbert Lockyer, Sr.
(DP, pg. 618)

♦ Custom, reputation, praise, advancement, and other flies, are the small game which hypocrites take in their net.

-Charles Spurgeon
(MES, Aug. 8 (M))

Prayer: Lord, lead us ever lest our enemies trip us up!

-Charles Spurgeon
(MES, Sept. 11 (E))

♦ It is almost as presumptuous to think you can do nothing as to think you can do everything.

-Phillips Brooks

♦ Finitude is our excuse rather than our shame. We could not bear being infinite. There is a stigma in being reckless, in forgetting that we are finite, in behaving as if we were infinite.

-Abraham J. Heschel
(TP, pg. 341)

♦ But I have resolved this much: I will not adjust my theology to accommodate my experience. That would be "subkingdom theology." I will not adapt my expectations or faith stand or view of God's word because I'm still not healed or because someone else is still not healed.

-Bob Sorge
(FDA, pg. 216)

♦ *Parleying with temptation is always fraught with danger. The serpent should be killed, not stroked.

J. Oswald Sanders
(POG, pg. 54)

♦ No sinner ever had an idea that his sins were greater than they are. NO sinner ever had an adequate idea of how great a sinner he is. It is not probable that any man could live under the full sight of his sins.

-Charles Finney
(LRR, pg.322)

♦ Grudges against others are like babies—the longer they are nursed the bigger they grow.

-Herbert Lockyer, Sr.
(DP, pg. 396)

♦ Woe, woe, woe, to the man who would live disentangled life in my century.

-Jim Elliot
(SOA, pg. 117)

♦ Many people put their human wisdom in the place of God, and God is not able to give the best because the human is confronting God in such a way. God is not able to get the best through us until the human will is dissolved.

-Smith Wigglesworth
(SWD, Jan. 12)

***

Spiritual pride that rampant beast,
Would rear it haughty head;
True faith would soon be dispossess'd,
And carelessness succeed.

-Mr. Hart
(FT, pg. 53)

But in vain they do worship me, teaching for doctrines the commandments of men (Matthew 15:9).

♦ What we call the irrational nature of man, they (prophets) called hardness of heart.

-Abraham J. Heschel
(TP, pg. 241)

♦ They who have laid great stumbling blocks in others' way, by the *open transgression*, are bound to remove them, by their *open repentance.*

-Charles Finney
(LRR, pg.280)

♦ (The enemy) usually speaks to us in the first person, so we think the thoughts are our own, when in fact they are his...And the temptation is always the same. He wants us to get mad at God, get bitter over our circumstances, and quit. He wants us to crawl into a cocoon of self-pity and resentment.

-Bob Sorge
(FDA, pg.15)

♦ The emotions of the soul are as important as the acts of life, for they are the fountain and spring from which the actions proceed.

-Herbert Lockyer Sr.
(DP, pg. 584)

♦ Racism is man's gravest threat to man - the maximum of hatred for a minimum of reason.

-Abraham Joshua Heschel

♦ Temperament has been defined as a person's nature as it controls the way he or she behaves, feels, and thinks. It is the soul's essential response to its surroundings.

-J. Oswald Sanders
(POG, pg. 94)

♦ No sins speak a higher attainment in wickedness, than those which are the result of deliberate counsel and deep plottings.

-William Gurnall
(CCA, Vol. 1, pg. 83)

♦ Where the sacred writers saw God, we see the laws of nature. Their world was fully populated; ours is all but empty. Their world was alive and personal; ours is impersonal and dead. God ruled their world; ours is ruled by the laws of nature and we are always once removed from the presence of God.

-A. W. Tozer
(KH, pg. 66)

♦ Man's greatest problem today, whether he recognizes it or not, is how to push aside every other allegiance but the eternal one.

-Donald Grey Barnhouse
(IW, pg. 37)

♦ An alluring world is more dangerous to the soul than a frowning world, or the malice of the ungodly.

-John Rusk
(FT, pg. 65)

♦ Some people GROW under responsibilities; others merely SWELL!

-Unknown

♦ The largest cemetery in the world is the one containing buried talents.

-Unknown

♦ All the impossibility is with us when we measure God by the limitations of our unbelief.

-Smith Wigglesworth
(SWD, (TFT) Jan. 26)

♦ The local seat of antichrist is called by three names—*Egypt*, in regard to *idolatry,* Rev. 2:8—*Sodom* in regard to her *filthiness,* Rev. 2:8—*Babylon*, in several places, in regard to her *cruelty.*

-Bishop Thomas Westfield
16th Century Writer

♦ Sometimes it is cowardly to speak and sometimes it is cowardly to keep silence. In the Bible the great test of a man's character is his tongue.

-Oswald Chambers
(DTD, Jun. 18)

♦ Satan has a Friend-at-Court in the heart of youth. Often my zeal was mixed with my own wildfire.

-Samuel Rutherford

♦ He is a weak fencer that lays his soul at open guard to be stabbed and wounded with guilt, while he is lifting up his hands to save a broken head. Our fear commonly meets us at that door by which we think to run from it.

-William Gurnall
(CCA, Vol. 1, pg. 83)

***

Dead to the world and its applause,
    To all the customs, fashions, laws,
Of those that hate the humbling Cross
    So dead that no desire may rise
To appear good, or great, or wise
    In any but my Saviour's eyes.

-Unknown

I protest by your rejoicing which I have in Christ Jesus our Lord, I die daily (1 Corinthians 15:31).

♦ We have learned to live with unholiness and have come to look upon it as the natural and expected thing. We are not disappointed that we do not find all truth in our teachers or faithfulness in our politicians or complete honesty in our merchants or full trustworthiness in our friends.

-A. W. Tozer
(KH, pg. 103-104)

♦ The opposite of freedom is not determinism, but hardness of heart. Freedom presupposes openness of heart, of mind, of eye, and ear...Freedom is not a natural disposition, but God's precious gift to man...Hardening of the heart is the suspension of freedom.

-Abraham J. Heschel
(TP, pg. 243)

♦ The fact is, the anxious sinner is seeking a hope, he is seeking pardon, and comfort, and deliverance from hell. He is anxiously looking for some one to comfort him, and make him feel better, without being obliged to conform to such humiliating conditions as those of the Gospel

-Charles Finney
(LRR, pg. 319)

♦ Emptiness, inability, frustration, dust: these are the portion of the man who walks his own way. Satisfaction is not to be found outside of God as revealed in Jesus Christ, and obedience to His will. There is no other source of joy.

-Donald Grey Barnhouse
(IW, pg. 60)

♦ *"The* [natural] *heart is deceitful above all things, and desperately wicked; who can know it?"* (Jeremiah 17:9), and there is nothing in which the inbred deceitfulness of our hearts comes out more clearly than in our estimations of ourselves.

-R. A. Torrey
(PWH, pg. 78)

♦ There is no such thing as purifying the impure. Evil things never get purer, but more vile. All impurity, all evil must be cast out. You can never make Satan holy.

-Smith Wigglesworth
(SWD, May 15)

♦ We are so slavishly bent on explaining ourselves that we sell cheaply ourselves and God's purposes.

-Manfred Haller
(CA, pg. 16)

♦ Life is clay, and righteousness the mold in which God wants history to be shaped. But human beings, instead of fashioning the clay, deform the shape.

-Abraham J. Heschel
(TP, pg. 253)

♦ The delicate mechanism of conscience was thrown off balance at the Fall, and now it requires constant adjustment to God's standards. The reactions of our consciences will vary according to the accuracy of the adjustment.

-J. Oswald Sanders
(POG, pg. 82)

♦ The world is full of people who hate to think and because they hate to think they go into things blindfolded, and come out with blighted hope and broken hearts and blasted lives.

-R. A. Torrey
(RA, pg. 145)

♦ The greatest lie the Devil ever told was that you could win souls with entertainment.

-Charles Spurgeon

♦ The real attitude of sin in the heart towards God; it is pride, the worship of myself, that is the great atheistic fact in human life.

-Oswald Chambers
(DTD, Apr. 1)

♦ Man's sin is in his failure to live what he is. Being the master of the earth, man forgets that he is the servant of God.

-Abraham Joshua Heschel

♦ A proud heart and a lofty mountain are never fruitful.

-William Gurnall
(CCA, Vol. 1, pg. 41)

♦ When the roots of our inward being reach no farther than our own thoughts, they find but dry ground.

Isobel Kuhn
(NAA, pg. 42)

♦ Vice, like virtue, advances by degrees.

-Unknown

♦ The focal point of man's interest is now himself. Humanism in its various forms has displaced theology as the key to the understanding of life.

-A. W. Tozer
(KH, pg. 116)

♦ Now, when we show that the Bible teaches the doctrine of total depravity, we are not claiming that there is no good in man, but that there is no good in man *that can satisfy God.*

-Donald Grey Barnhouse
(IW, pg. 115)

♦ Satan so subtle to trouble the saint's peace? This proves them to be the children of Satan, who show the same art and subtlety in vexing the spirits of the saints, as doth their infernal father; not to speak of bloody persecutors, who are the devil's slaughter-slaves to butcher the saints, but of those who more slyly trouble and molest the saint's peace.

-William Gurnall
(CCA, Vol. 1, pg. 92)

♦ The spirit of ecumenism without the deity of Christ is, of course, a Satanic spirit in the light of all that we have seen in these studies.

-Donald Grey Barnhouse
(IW, pg. 272)

♦ The heart conceives, the mind reflects, and the mouth is operated. But you must not try to reverse the order. Some people are all tongue, neither head nor heart. But when He comes, there is perfect order...The heart believes and then like a ventilator, it flows through and quickens the mind. Then the tongue speaks of the glory of the Lord.

-Smith Wigglesworth
(SWD, Jun. 18)

The Enemy

The Bible is clear that we are in a battle. As believers we know who will win the war in the end, but meanwhile, we find ourselves in various skirmishes and battles in our lifetime. The battles vary because the enemies vary. On the home front we must battle the flesh with its various appetites and overcome it. On the social scene, we must discern the entanglements of the world and separate from its various lies and influences. However, on the unseen spiritual front, we must battle Satan and take authority over Him in the power of God and with the authority of His Word.

Satan uses the world to entangle us, the flesh to entice us, and the systems of the world to enslave us. He uses lies to seduce us, lustful pursuits to pervert us, and worldly knowledge to blind us. It is for this reason that the Apostle Paul tells us we must not be ignorant of the devil's various devices.

When James O. Fraser went to China as a missionary, he was not prepared to meet the enemy that had cleverly taken the people captive with superstition and witchcraft. He had to learn to fight the enemy while in the midst of the battle that was taking place over their souls. He realized that the aim of Satanic power was to cut off communication with God.

He shared what he learned about this matter and fortunately his daughter recorded it in her book she wrote about him. As you consider his heavenly gems about this matter, perhaps you can discern where the enemy might be causing you some problems.

- (To cut of communication with God): To accomplish this aim he deludes the soul with a sense of defeat, covers him with a thick cloud of darkness, depresses and oppresses the spirit, which in turn hinders prayer and leads to unbelief. (MR, pg. 126)
- Each time your spirit goes under and faints in the testing and trials which come to you, you lose mastery over the powers of darkness, i.e., you get below them instead of abiding above them in God. (MR, pg. 125)
- The devil knows this (the power of earthly entanglements), and pours earthly things upon you to keep you down so that you go under and not over when the battle comes. (MR, pg. 126)
- The enemy is delighted to have us so occupied incessantly with secondary and trivial concerns instead of attacking and resisting in the true spirit of the conflict. (MR, pg. 127)
- Every time you take the earth standpoint—think as men think, talk as men talk, look as men look—you take a place below the powers of darkness. (MR, pg. 125)
- The mastery of them depends upon your spirit abiding in the place above them, and the place above them means knowing God's outlook, God's view, God's thought, God's plan, God's ways, by abiding with Christ in God. (MR, pg. 125)
- (In regard to new converts): They have not yet grown to military age in this spiritual warfare; they are babes in God's nursery, not warriors in God's army. The vast difference between you and them is that you are "grown up" in Christ, while they are babes and sucklings; and the work of pulling down Satan's strongholds requires strong men, not infants. (MR, pg. 188)

- My weapon these days against sin and Satan — or rather, sin alone — is the love of God. . . "The love of Christ constraineth us." (MR, pg. 164)

Lest Satan should get an advantage of us: for we are not ignorant of his devices (2 Corinthians 2:11).

♦ Without putting off and burying the old, the new man cannot be awakened or quickened in us to properly respond to the light. The ways of the "old man" often serve as our grave clothes that bind us to the stench and decaying conduct of the old life. Like the raising of Lazarus in John 11, Jesus may raise us out of the grave with resurrection power, but we cannot walk in the new way until we are loosed from the old. Such rotting clothing will cause us to be spiritually inept to properly see, hear, or know the life that awaits us. For this reason, the Bible clearly tells us we must put off the old in order to put on the new.

-RJK

♦ It's a natural tendency of our fallen human condition to be religious. Before the fall, Adam and Eve had fellowship with their Creator. After the fall, however, this relationship was lost and fallen man substituted religion for relationship. Adam and Eve sewed fig leaves together to form a covering for their nakedness. Ever since that time, down through the centuries, people have naturally depended upon their own "coverings" and works of righteousness.

-Jeannette Haley

♦ Our problem is a hearing problem. Our problem is a seeing problem. Our problem is a doing problem. We do not wish to hear, to see, or to do if it entails a denying of self. We want the Saviour of the world to get us into heaven. But we shy away from the Lord of Life when it comes to counting the cost of discipleship.

-E. A. Johnston
(NTB, pg. 9)

♦ People who turn Christianity into a cause run the risk of confusing violence for obedience.

Extreme Devotion
(ED, pg. 76)

- If we make our life a muddle, it is to a large extent because we have not discerned the great underlying relationship to God.

  -Oswald Chambers
  (DTD, Dec 1)

- Only let the Lord withdraw, and lay a particular cross upon us, and we soon get light and trifling, joking, jesting, can mix with the world, take an advantage, overreach, set up idols, and our corrupt affections will run after every object that takes the eye, and such an uncommon inordinate affection will work, dressed up in a religious garb—a covetous, selfish spirit also—shut up against the Lord's family, as well as others.

  -John Rusk

- It is possible that sometimes when we think we are standing for principle, in reality we are falling for prejudices.

  -J. Oswald Sanders
  (POG, pg. 100)

- In these days a man cannot afford to make any mistakes. Every decision a man makes shapes his entire life.

  -John R. Mott
  (POG, pg. 133)

- Civilization has become an elaborate way of doing without God, and when civilized life is hit a smashing blow by any order of tyranny, most of us have not a leg to stand on.

  -Oswald Chambers
  (DTD, Nov. 4)

- Man is a messenger who forgot the message.

  -Abraham Joshua Heschel

- Satan is such an archer as can shoot at a penny breadth. If all the man be armed, and only the eye left without, Satan can soon shoot his fire-balls of lust in at that loophole, which shall set the whole house on flame.

  -William Gurnall
  (CCA, Vol. 1, pg. 58)

The Sum Total of Foolishness

One of the difficulties of living in the last of the end days is to watch your world as you know it slide into utter destruction. Granted, there are still decent people and a semblance of sanity can be detected, but the philosophy that is taking over the "so-called" civilizations is nothing more than insane foolishness.

As I consider this present environment, I can see how people are being encouraged to sell the truth for lies, sell their liberty for a false peace, sell their autonomy for bondage, and sell their soul for false hope. It is clear they have been indoctrinated by Hollywood and the liberal, communistic school system and media. Their consciences have been seared by a total divorce from truth and decency. They have no sense of honor and sacrifice, and from all appearance they do not retain any knowledge of God that could be appealed to or reasoned with.

This insane foolishness has vexed my spirit. I have a sense of how Lot felt in Sodom when he watched the men of his community become more coarse and ruthless in their abominable ways. He probably wondered if there was any end to such insanity, and that such an end would most likely not be good or pleasant. I even wondered if he could look down the road and see that if God did not judge it in His righteousness that it indeed was doomed to eventually cave in on itself.

This insane foolishness is referred to by a couple of names in this present age: "Political Correctness, Social Justice, Collective Salvation, Tolerance, and the latest digression is Woke." These wicked philosophies of Satan has been promoted by every liberal, anti-God, progressive, humanistic mover and shaker. Its greatest affront is against moral integrity. It calls for tolerance for every immoral practice, while showing total intolerance towards anyone or anything that would advocate any form of morality, righteousness, and judgment. These individuals call evil good and good evil, causing an insane reality that drips with utter absurdity.

In June 2013 in *The Berean Call's* News Watch section, the concept of tolerance was addressed. It was stated that, "America is becoming a more tolerant nation, we are told. Each new thing that we learn to tolerate makes us more progressive. But tolerance is a relative thing. For every new thing we learn to tolerate, there is a thing that we must stop tolerating." The article goes on to say that the problem with tolerance is that it is others who decide what needs to be tolerated by the rest. The truth is that a free society is responsible and does not tolerate that which disrupts the healthy order of things; therefore a tolerant society is not free. Rather, a tolerant society becomes a dictatorship of virtue that is intolerant towards that which holds to moral integrity. Ultimately, such liberal values prove to be at odds with reality and those who adhere to them are not about to let reality win.

Today these people get around the moral aspect of matters by putting immoral practices under the guise of "civil rights". It was stated in an article by Dr. David Schnittger that, "Civil rights protections have not historically been applied to lifestyle choices, especially immoral lifestyle choices. Put simply, civil rights apply to persons, not behaviors!" He also pointed out that history has demonstrated that the widespread acceptance and practice of homosexuality in a culture is one of the last mileposts prior to the destruction of that society. He cited the fall of Rome to the Vandals in A. D. 455 as an example of this principle.

We know that since allowing homosexuals to openly flaunt their lifestyle in the military there have been as many as 85,000 reports of men raping men, ripping and tearing at the effectiveness of our military, leaving this nation unprotected. Since there are no real boundaries nothing will be held sacred, and yet these radicals have the audacity to declare that this lifestyle is upright and can fit into that which is complementary to the general welfare of a society as a whole. Granted, not all homosexuals resort to animalistic depravity, but it would behoove people to honestly consider that like Sodom of the Old Testament, this blatant behavior is leading this nation down a path of no return, and nothing will be left including people's wicked lifestyles.

The harsh reality is that without moral integrity, man will give into his base disposition of rebellion. He will do what he thinks is right in his own eyes without any regard as to whether it is honorable or not. Since man will not morally police himself according to his God-given conscience to prevent utter chaos, he must be oppressed by police states or such despotic governments like Communist. Or, on the other hand, he will find himself a victim of total anarchy as fanatics and gangs rule with an iron fist. Perhaps at one end such blatant lifestyles may be ignored and tolerated but at the other end of the spectrum these very lifestyles will be judged with malicious swiftness. Either way there will be no real quality of life. People will live like substandard humans or animals that have no real hope or purpose.

Clearly, these individuals have become deluded by the god of this world, Satan, and cannot see how insane, hypocritical, and destructive their logic is. They believe that they are moving towards an utopia, which will eventually require them to get rid of anyone who does not line up or agree with their take on matters. Blood will flow and eventually pour from their hands like a fountain, but they will continue to insist that they are right. However, the Lord says of such individuals, "Woe unto you!"

As a Christian I become more and more aware that my hope and future is not in the present world. I am a citizen of an unseen kingdom and have before me a future that will never be threatened by such insane rhetoric and wicked philosophies again. For Christians, we are looking forward to the real utopia, while those of this world are blindly heading towards the wrath of God, to taste the eternal damnation of the lake of fire.

As a people we need to come back to center as to that which is righteous. There is no such thing as tolerance towards that which has already been deemed as wicked and unacceptable by the Judge of this universe. Granted, man can declare there is no such God; therefore, there is no real just standard by which he will be judged. He can even use worldly laws to redefine morality, but the immutable God of heaven remains unchanged and His standard will be lifted up against evil. In the end, the rebel will be brought low, the lawless will be stopped in his tracks, the arrogant will be humbled, the militant will be defeated, and the despot will be silenced, as all of their evil deeds are proven to be the sum total of vanity and foolishness that already stands judged and condemned by the one true Righteous Judge of all.

And even as they did not like to retain God in their knowledge, God gave them over to a reprobate mind, to do those things which are not convenient (Romans 1:28).

♦ Hot heads and cold hearts never solved anything.

-Billy Graham

◆ The old life is unmanageable in its thinking, undisciplined in its emotions, unyielding in its ways, and unruly in its plans. It may appear as if it is under control, but it is only a matter of outward compliance, reformation, performance, and conforming. Sadly, without transformation the inward man continues to be ruthless and treacherous as it watches out for its own self-interest and purpose.

-RJK

◆ Passion does not compensate for ignorance.

-Samuel Chadwick
(VCK, pg. 121)

◆ The proper seat of sin is the will, of comfort the conscience.

-William Gurnall
(CCA, Vol. 1, pg. 85)

◆ Most people want to be regarded as grownup, but they do not want to go through the process of actually growing up to reach maturity. Such people prove to be naïve about life, spoiled when it comes to having life their way, obnoxious in action, and foolish in character.

-RJK

◆ Any associations that tend to make sin less sinful are to be shunned.

-J. Oswald Sanders
(POG, pg. 134)

◆ Religion does not consist in *desires to do good actions*. Desires that do not result in right choice and action are not virtuous.

-Charles Finney
(LRR, pg. 394)

◆ The history of man is as the history of grass—*Sown, Grown, Blown, Mown, Gone.*

-Herbert Lockyer, Sr.
(DP, pg. 310)

◆ When there are no absolutes, justice will be absent. Without justice, there will be no fear of consequences. Without consequences, rights or wrongs become a matter of personal opinions or preference. Since there is no real standard of right and wrong, chaos will ensue, lawlessness will be the order of the day, and fear will be the byproduct.

-RJK

♦ Union with Jesus is so strong, that nothing can break it. Communion with Jesus is so fragile that the slightest sin can break it.

-Unknown
(GN, pg. 105)

♦ Satan works in various ways. sometimes by the ungodly, sometimes by professors of religion, and sometimes by hypocrites in Zion; but none of these are so trying as when he works by God's children, and he certainly does this, which we may see in Job's three friends.

-John Rusk
(FT, pg. 19)

♦ Though the devil throws the stone, yet it is the mud in us which *royles (roils) our comforts. (Parenthesis added.)

-William Gurnall
(CCA, Vol. 1, pg. 94)

♦ "Calvary" means "the place of the skull;" and that is where our Lord is always crucified, in the culture and intellect of man, who will not have self-knowledge given by the light of Jesus Christ.

-Oswald Chambers
(DTD, Nov. 30)

The Man of Sin

Every generation and every age must contend with the seductive lies and heresies of Satan. The subtly of Satan is that he cleverly intertwines seeds of lies and heresies in the philosophies and cultures of the present day. Each point of man's failure in the different ages for Satan simply means he takes the lies, repackage it for that time, and finds receptive ground to once again bring forth his deception. Each package will fit into the present scene, indoctrinating the next generation, dulling the people down in such a way that truth and righteousness will become fuzzy.

313

For example, during Charles Finney's time, he had to contend with Universalism; for Spurgeon, it was Higher Criticism, and for Smith Wigglesworth it was Christian Science. Wigglesworth related how a person came to him and pointed out that Christian Scientists must be right because people were following them due to their beautiful buildings.

It was clear that Wigglesworth was not intimidated by such challenges. His reply to this individual showed that he was not responding from a human perspective, but from a heavenly one. The heavenly one is that there are no disciplines or cost to taking the broad way, except your soul. Hence, Wigglesworth response, "Yes everybody can belong to it. You can go to any brothel you like, you can go to any theater you like, you can go to any race course you like, you can be mixed up with the rest of the people in your life and still be a Christian Scientist. You can have the Devil right and left and any where and still belong to Christian Science. "

As we approach the end days, we are being inundated with various lies from the New Age to ideologies of Social Justice and Collective Salvation. We have Muslim radicals bent on taking over the world and Hindu gurus that have massed people and finances to ensure their own little worlds, while those with a Communist philosophy are licking their lips as they see their oppressive, insidious philosophy render the youth of this generation as sheep ready to be taken to the slaughter.

Wigglesworth lumps much of the heresy into one term. He made this distinction, "Theosophy, which is based on theories of reincarnation and other falsities, has a new man. Nothing but theosophy could have a new man. The foundation of this Theosophy has always been corruptible. The formation of Theosophy was connected to one of the greatest atheists of the day. Theosophy sprang out of atheism." (SWD, Apr. 3)

Who will be considered the greatest atheist of all times? The Bible refers to him as, "The Son of Perdition" or "The Man of Sin." We certainly live in the days that many so-called "shakers and movers" of the world would foreshadow this individual. However, when this individual comes, he will usher in a one world government, economic, and religious system by using the false front of promising peace. Even though this individual will use oppressive methods like the Communist, be unforgiving like the radical Muslims, and serve as the ultimate guru, he will not tolerate any competition that will mirror any other cause or agenda but his own.

The Bible warns that if it were possible, even the elect would be deceived. The reason is that great signs and wonders will be present that will seduce and deceive those who do not love the truth. There are books out there outlining how some of the greatest seduction will come by way of the sky. In other words, UFOs will play a major role in this deception. Today we have various programs on TV about UFOs. People are clearly being conditioned to accept the possibilities of beings from another planet, galaxy, or universe. Are there really beings from other planets? The answer is no, but there are beings from another dimension. They are called demons. The Bible is clear that Satan will be behind the lying signs and wonders. The realm of the demonic will be busy and active in these end days.

As Christians we know the end of this man of sin as well as those who foolishly follow him. Clearly, we must be informed about the days and times we live in, but we must above all else know our God in order to do exploits that will counteract the advances of the demonic and confirm the truth about salvation that can only be obtained in Christ Jesus.

And then shall that Wicked be revealed, whom the Lord shall consume with the spirit of his mouth, and shall destroy with the brightness of his coming: Even him, whose coming is after the working of Satan with all power and signs and lying wonders. (2 Thessalonians 2:8-9).

BITS AND PIECES

The Largest Bible

Our lives are made up of bits of memories and pieces of experiences. Our understanding is made up of bits of information and pieces of facts. Our emotions are made up of bits of sorrow intermingled with pieces of happiness. Our motives are comprised of bits of worldly agendas and pieces of fleshly priorities.

Bits and pieces often represent how limited or fragmented our lives and understanding can prove to be. As the Bible clearly states, "we know in part." In our spiritual walk we pick up bits of truths along the way and try to properly place them into the pieces of God's promises to produce a recognizable mosaic. Our hope is to bring life-changing revelation to our dulled spirits and our undisciplined, restless souls.

Admittedly, at times the bits and pieces of my life frustrate me. God's bits and pieces seem like broken glass or confusing puzzle pieces strung out all over the floor of my chaotic life. I possess a heart's desire to know how to put the different parts or images together in order to take care of challenges. I would love all the pieces of life to fall into place at once to be spared from the growth pains that often come my way, but through the years I had to confess that I would not see any need to trust God to resolve the matters that challenge my spirit, soul, and life without the bits and pieces.

The beauty about God is that He has put into one book all the bits and pieces that I need to work with. Granted, the pieces are spread out in His Word and the bits can sometime remain hidden from my limited understanding, but they form a clear picture once the Holy Spirit puts them together. There is no inconsistency or fluctuation in them.

As I thought about God's precious Word, I discovered a bit of information that caught my attention. It was about the largest known Bible in the world. It is located in the Vatican in Rome. It is in Hebrew manuscript and weighs 320 pounds. (DP, pg. 565)

While thinking about the weight of this enormous book, I had to rejoice that even though I could never physically carry such a Bible, I do carry His Word in my heart. There is nothing heavy about His Word. His precious words are not written on my heart by ink, but by His Spirit. Because of where it is written, it proves to be light and because of the author, it brings such liberty and joy to my spirit. In essence, its revelations give me the means to soar above the challenges of this present age.

The largest Bible might be in Rome, but the Living Word resides in my heart, and the teacher of it dwells in my inner being.

For verily I say unto you, Till heaven and earth pass, one jot or one tittle shall in no wise pass from the law, till all be fulfilled (Matthew 5:18).

♦ A man's thoughts dye his soul.

-Marcus Aurelius
(SOA, pg. 52)

♦ The past is gone, the future is unknown. God gave us today that's why it called the present.

-Unknown
(BB)

♦ Knowledge compasses inner appropriation, feeling, a reception into the soul. It involves both the intellectual and an emotional act.

-Abraham J. Heschel
(TP, pg. 70)

♦ Remarkable words often come from people of few words.

-Unknown

- In seeking the Best, we soon find that our enemy is our good things, not our bad.

  -Oswald Chambers
  (DTD, Jan. 5)

- Age is a question of mind over matter. If you don't mind, it doesn't matter.

  -Leroy "Satchel" Paige

- It is better to light a candle, than to curse the darkness.

  -Chinese Proverb

- He who can take advice is sometimes superior to him who can give it.

  -Von Kneble

- The devil always wants to make it believed that God's people, who are the most loyal people in the world, are rebels to the government under which they live.

  -George Whitefield
  (GW, pg. 328)

- In relations to Communism, Edward E. Erickson, Jr., made this statement, "But if I were asked today to formulate as concisely as possible the main cause of the ruinous revolution that swallowed up some 60 million of our people, I could not put it more accurately than to repeat: 'Men have forgotten God; that is why all of this happened'"

- Four things come not back to man or woman: the sped arrow, the spoken word, the past life, and the neglected opportunity.

  -Robert Louis Stevenson

- Opportunity knocks once. Temptation leans on the doorbell.

  -Church Reader Board

- Life by the mile is hardly worthwhile. Life by the inch is a cinch!

  -Unknown
  (BB)

♦ Nobody grows old merely by living a number of years. We grow old by deserting our ideals. Years may wrinkle the skin, but to give up enthusiasm wrinkles the soul.

-Samuel Ullman

♦ It is said that Spurgeon would occasionally preach in his sleep, and that his diligent wife was always ready with pencil and pad to capture her husband's sublime, unconscious, yet God-given thoughts, thereby supplying him with material for a Sunday sermon. (DP, pg. 654)

♦ History is where God is defied, where justice suffers defeats. God's purpose is neither clearly apparent nor translatable into rational categories of order and design. There are only moments in which it is revealed. God's power in history does not endure as a process; it occurs at extraordinary events.

-Abraham J. Heschel
(TP, pg. 214)

Who Am I

I always enjoy learning new things about those who make up the great cloud of witnesses that have gone on before us. Some of them are well known, while others, it is either their works or examples that we learn about. Still there are those you may have never heard of until now, but consider how such unknown servants have made an impact on generations.

See how well you know those who have left name, reputation, and works behind them to serve as a witness to us.

1. Before his conversion this man was known as a swearing tinker from Bedford, and later became mentally challenged in his prison cell because of His faith for he feared what might overtake his family, especially his blind child in his absence. He spent twelve years in prison but wrote a much beloved classic.
2. This poet suffered much from despondency and was even placed in an asylum but recovered. It is said that joy, like his previous despair for him was clothed in the language of the Psalms.

3. He was spiritually awakened in 1838 while hearing Ephesians 2 being read in church. At age 64, he became the first bishop of Liverpool, at the recommendation of Prime Minister Benjamin Disraeli.
4. He not only became the founder and leader of a ministry that is still in operation today in many cities in America, but was a street-corner preacher and ordained minister who preached two sermons a day until his death.
5. Due to his awkward style of speaking, this man's gifted wife, Polly, preached and evangelized long before he was empowered by the Holy Spirit to preach, which materialized in a worldwide evangelistic and healing ministry.
6. This China's missionary's father began to pray for China two years before he was even born?
7. This Scottish pastor learned the Greek alphabet and was able to write the letters on his slate at age four while recovering from an illness.
8. This prolific Gospel songwriter wrote under more than a hundred pseudonyms.
9. He was a noted missionary to the Muslims and the minister that missionary William Borden planned to study under when he traveled to Egypt. He was the one who preached at Borden's funeral.
10. This Bible expositor, preached his first sermon at age 12 and almost 67 years to the day, he preached his last sermon at Westminster Chapel, in London.
11. Referred to as the apostle of the haphazard by some, this Scottish preacher, teacher, and one of the most quoted authors' parents were baptized by Charles Spurgeon, and Spurgeon also had ordained his father to the Baptist ministry.
12. This neglected evangelical leader of the eighteenth century, was an aristocrat who used his money and position to further the cause of the Gospel at a difficult time in the church history.
13. This Walsh revival minister was stabbed, nearly drowned, and lost his right eye. As a result he had to daub the empty socket with laudanum to ease the pain the rest of his life.
14. Two years after he entered Yale Divinity School in 1875, this preacher, Bible Scholar, and founder of a Bible institute, lost both of his parents. Even though his father was a well-to-do banker, his parents' estate had all but disappeared by the time they died. He stated, "I'm glad I did not inherit a fortune. It would have ruined me."

15. Even though John and Charles Wesley are accredited with the founding of the Methodist Church, it is really this English evangelist and outdoor preacher of the 18th century that founded it, but turned over the leadership of the movement to the Wesleys.
16. This late 17th and 18th century expositor of Scriptures lost his first wife in childbirth, and later married again. He and his second wife had nine children, eight of them girls.
17. This India missionary at one time was in danger of serving seven years in prison for "assisting in the kidnapping of a child."
18. He lived from 185-253 A.D. He dominated the century as much by his character as by his genius. He was a son of a martyr, the master of disciples who braved martyrdom, a confessor who endured imprisonment and the torture of the chain, the collar, and the rack.
19. He was known as one of the greatest orators and theologians in the fourth century.
20. He was known in the 6th century as the Apostle of Switzerland.
21. This blind Scotsman was an 18th century poet.
22. It is said of this man that bloody Queen Mary feared his prayers more than all the armies of Europe.
23. This President as a young Whig was part of a movement in the United States that slashed alcohol consumption by three fourth by 1850.
24. This great revivalist presided over the Oberlin College during the time it produced America's first female college graduate.

For the answers to these questions see page 334.

***

♦ Do the duty that lies nearest to you which you know to be your duty. Your second duty will already have become clearer.

-Thomas Carlyle
(POG, pg. 56)

♦ It takes a miracle to give a positive response in a negative situation.

-Unknown
(BB)

♦ Children are well-called *arrows*, for if they are well bred, they will shoot at their parent's enemies, and if evil bred, they shoot at their parents.

-15th Century Writer
(DP, pg. 655)

♦ The young may close their ears to our advice, but will open their eyes to our example.

-Unknown

♦ If you're going to lift anybody you'll have to stoop.

-Gypsy Smith

♦ The past is history, the future is a mystery, and today is the present (gift).

-Unknown
(BB)

♦ There are still far too many of these grinders in the world, and *totalitarianism* is one of them with its determination to beat both Jews and Christians to pieces.

-Herbert Lockyer, Sr.
(DP, pg. 334)

♦ In their work, *The Lessons of History,* The Durants made these statements: "Democracy is the most difficult of all forms of government, since it requires the widest spread of intelligence...Ignorance is not long enthroned, for it lends itself to manipulation by the forces that mold public opinion." (pg. 77)

♦ The more you learn about God, you realize the less you know, and the more you think you know about Him the less you will know.

-RJK

♦ Often times we need not be taught so much as to be reminded.

-Unknown

♦ He who is his own pupil, has a fool for his master.

-Saint Bernard

♦ I have often repented of having spoken, but never of having been silent.

-Xenocrates
(DP, pg. 731)

♦ Triumph is just "umph", added to TRY!

-Unknown

Message to America

As a nation, America is in big trouble. I am sure this is nothing new to those who are reading this message. However, it is not where we are as a nation that is most disturbing to me; it is where we are heading. We must change direction because we are heading for a cliff and if we go over the cliff there is no turning back or reversing the devastation that will occur.

The other equation to this matter is that those who could do something about it appear to have blinders on. They are either operating in total delusion or wishful thinking. Either way, they are blinded to the suicidal cliff that is before the people of this nation. And, since there is a righteous, just God, these blind leaders will ultimately be held responsible for their devious leadership.

To me the best description of where this nation is can be summed up in the essay that Paul Harvey wrote in 1965, 47 years ago. Even though Harvey would not declare himself to be a prophet, his essay is proving to be prophetic. It is for this reason his essay serves as a formidable warning to present day America. He described how he would destroy us (America) if he were the devil.

"If I were the devil, I wouldn't be happy until I had seized the ripest apple on the tree—Thee. So I'd set about however necessary to take over the United States. I'd subvert the churches first—I would begin with a campaign of whispers. With the wisdom of a serpent, I would whisper to you as I whispered to Eve: "Do as you please." "Do as you please." To the young, I would whisper, "The Bible is a myth." I would convince them that man created God instead of the other way around. I would confide that what is bad is good, and what is good is 'square'.

323

And the old, I would teach to pray. I would teach them to pray after me, 'Our Father, which art in Washington...'

"And then I'd get organized. I'd educate authors on how to make lurid literature exciting, so that anything else would appear dull and uninteresting. I'd threaten TV with dirtier movies and vice versa. I'd pedal narcotics to whomever I could. I'd sell alcohol to ladies and gentlemen of distinction. I'd tranquilize the rest with pills.

"If I were the devil I'd soon have families that war with themselves, churches that war among themselves, and nations that war with themselves; until each in its turn was consumed. And with promises of higher ratings I'd have mesmerizing media fanning the flame. If I were the devil I would encourage schools to refine young intellects, and neglect to discipline emotions—just let those run wild, until before you knew it, you'd have to have drug sniffing dogs and metal detectors at every schoolhouse door.

"Within a decade I'd have prisons overflowing, I'd have judges promoting pornography—soon I could evict God from the courthouse, and then the schoolhouse, and then from the houses of Congress. And in His own churches I would substitute psychology for religion, and deify science. I would lure priests and pastors into misusing boys and girls, and church money. If I were the devil I'd make the symbols of Easter an egg and the symbol of Christmas a bottle.

"If I were the devil I'd take from those who have, and give to those who wanted until I had killed the incentive of the ambitious. What do you bet I could get whole states to promote gambling as the way to get rich? I would question against extremes and hard work, and Patriotism, and moral conduct. I would convince the young that marriage is old-fashioned, that swinging more fun, that what you see on the TV is the way to be. And thus I could undress you in public, and I could lure you into bed with diseases for which there is no cure. In other words, if I were the devil I'd keep on doing what he's doing."

Today, Paul Harvey is correct. We can point the finger where we wish, but the truth of it is that much of the spiritual condition of this nation will rest at the door of our churches. Charles Finney summarized the Church's part in a nation in this statement, "God cannot sustain this free and blessed country, which we love and pray for, unless the church will take right ground" (LDD, pg. 282). Granted, the church cannot change the direction of man, but it can influence the tone towards God, life, and morality that a nation takes on. However, instead of being a light in America, the world has come into the Church, dulling it down, dumbing it down, and rendering it into another worldly organization.

In the book, *A Small Price to Pay,* in the, "Afterword," it told how Evangelist Mikhail Khorev, of Romania, came to America to assist the Russian immigrant churches in America. Thousands of Russian Baptists immigrated to America seeking religious freedom (SPP, pg. 240). Khorev, himself had suffered under communistic oppression for years. It included spending years in prison for his faith. In order to continue his evangelism, he even had to go into hiding for a couple of years before the old Soviet Union was band by the Romanian authorities.

The question is why did the Russian immigrants asked for Khorev's assistance? It is because when many of them arrived in America, they often found it difficult to know how to relate to tolerant, "Christian" America. The most significant danger came from the public schools. Sadly, many of these individuals slipped into the general flow of American society. For those recognizing the dangers they were facing to their spiritual wellbeing, they requested to be allowed to rejoin their former brotherhood. It was their way of making themselves accountable by becoming identified with the same standards of holiness as in the past.

With such knowledge the question is, as a church what have we done to try to remedy this condition? Many in the visible church are trying to solve the problems of the world with the methods of the world. By tacking Christ on the unholy, they believe that they are making it acceptable to God. We can see in some cases where some of the people of the churches have become politically involved, a few more radical in some of their stands, and others more socially minded, but the fruit of such attempts lack substance. What is often promoted is not the Gospel Paul preached, but a social gospel of "tolerance towards abominable acts" and "good works" that hopefully will make the pigpens of the world more tolerable for those who are drowning in the miry waters of despair, hopelessness, and spiritual death. This brings me to considering the message to the church.

When I read the epistles, I have often wondered what kind of letter Paul would have written to the American Church. Would it deal with the Gospel and the Law like he did in the epistle to the Romans, contains rebuke for carnality such as he did to the Corinthians, condemn the legalistic agenda in Galatians, speak of our inheritance like he did to Ephesus, or would he speak of what it would mean for us to neglect the Gospel?

As a missionary called to America, I have some definite ideas of what I would like to say to the Church. Often times my concerns for what I see are confirmed by others. Like Paul I would also have to probably break down my concerns according to those I would be speaking to. There are usually four attitudes found within the Church. These are: the legalist who lacks a right spirit, the liberalist who lacks the disciplines of the truth of the Word, the moderate who compromises by trying to bring both the world and spiritual truths together, and those who love the Word of God because they love the author behind it.

To begin this letter I would have to start in general terms. The Church has always had its enemies and challenges. What we are confronted with in America is not new and the Bible clearly addresses it. However, the problem rests with the fact that many in the American Church have no standard by which to examine themselves. The Word of God has been downplayed, justified away, ignored, and adjusted to fit the latest movements and gospels. There are so many Bible versions that are adjusted and twisted to placate not only the worldly taste that has become outlandish in the visible church but to appeal to abominable moral preferences. The watered-down or blasphemous versions give the impression that God has flung His holiness to the wind as He regresses into the moral cesspool of the age, all in the name of profane love.

God has not changed and even though the present age continues to blast an onslaught of lies as a means to change the times, seasons, and laws, God remains God, holy, just, and immovable. Scripture is clear His ways are higher than ours. He will never lower Himself down to our small-minded profane level to convince us He is God; rather, He requires us by faith to look up and began to ascend to the heights of His holy ways by the power of the Spirit which enables us to obey His Word.

This brings us to the real challenge of the Church in America. In some countries where persecution is great, the choice is clear, "Am I willing to suffer and die for the sake of Christ." However, the challenge in America has been different, "Am I willing to live for the sake of Christ."

This brings us back to the four groups found among the visible Church. Three of them are failing to live for the sake of Christ. In most cases they have failed to add faith in the equation. They have put their confidence in something other than the God of heaven. As a result, the Word will have no real power to change them and the Spirit will not be able to transform them.

For those who are simply legalist you need to know you are missing the mark. Granted, some of your facts and doctrines may be Scriptural, but they lack dimension. They have no life, which means you may know a matter to be true, but you have failed to make it a personal reality by walking it out in your life. In a way you are simply being a convert to your own form of religion. You are the ones who have a form of godliness but are denying the power thereof. As a result of only possessing an outer shell of religion, you will not have the heart revelation that will produce a loving, compassionate attitude in you towards others. As Jesus stated, it will be easy to tell His true disciples because they have love for one another, and in your rigid judgmental legalism you will ultimately fail the test of love. You need to repent of your lifeless, unloving, judgmental religion and truly be converted to embrace the humble attitude of your Lord and Savior.

Those who hold to a liberal view of God, they need to know that they are WRONG in their perspective, and they need to repent of their casual attitude towards God and be converted to that which speaks of God's holiness. God's holy ways cannot be adjusted to fit into broad ways that are profane and wicked in His sight. He will have no part of it. Even though you may be doing good works, they will be considered reprobate because they lack purity of motive.

For those who are moderate in their beliefs, they need to know they are lukewarm towards the things of God. Jesus said of such Christians that He would spit them out of His mouth. If you are a moderate, you need to realize that you might be living in the misty flats of comfortable compromise with the world, but you will never bring any real distinction between the Christian life and the pigpens of the world.

You will be void of the fragrance of Christ as the stench of the world becomes more prevalent in all you do. You need to awaken yourself to your real condition and repent of settling for the misty flats of worldliness and compromise, and choose that which is excellent according to the glory of God.

To those who are part of those who have not yet compromise or come into agreement with the presentation of Modern Day Christianity, you need to know you are not alone. The sorrow for this nation is not your burden alone. The despair over the visible church in America is not yours alone to carry. There are many that are shedding tears on bended knee for this church and the nation. No doubt the tears have merged into a stream, and the water is being bottled by the hand of God and set before His throne; and, take heart in knowing that those tears that remain will be wiped away on that glorious day.

As for the message of encouragement to those who have not bowed to the god of this age, bought the lie of the worldly philosophy, succumbed to the misty flats of compromise, and flowed with the false waves of religion, be of good cheer! Even though you feel alone, know that the Lord has not forsaken you; therefore, do not be weary in doing good in relationship to serving the Lord, for in due time you will reap. If you are being persecuted because you will not come in agreement with the matters of the world, rejoice and know that such testing will only last for a season. Be true to what you know, stand on what is eternal, choose the ways of righteousness, and advance forward by trusting in who God is.

As His true church, we believers are facing dark times, but His light is ever shining in our hearts and will not be snuffed out by the darkness around us. In fact, it will shine in greater ways if we choose to trust Him in the grave darkness coming on this world. Even though everything will be shaken in the end, our foundation of Christ will continue to stand, the truths of His Word will endure the testing, and His glorious coming will put the final exclamation mark on what will be according to the eternal, righteous judgments of heaven.

Many will say to me in that day, Lord, Lord; have we not prophesied in thy name? and in thy name have cast out devils? and in thy name done many wonderful works? And then will I profess unto them, I never knew you: depart from me, ye that work iniquity (Matthew 7:22-23).

SOLUTION TO PUZZLES

Making Sense Out of
the Obscure

Answers to page 255-256

a. 13	h. 5	o. 8
b. 18	i. 12	p. 14
c. 7	j. 1	q. 6
d. 20	k.15	r. 19
e. 3	l. 2	s. 11
f. 9	m. 17	t. 4
g. 16	n. 10	

A New Song

Answers to pages 260-263

Bread of Life	Good Shepherd	Messiah
Wonderful	The Life	King of kings
King	High Priest	I AM
The Resurrection	The Anointed One	Branch
Prince of Peace	God	Lord of lords
The Truth	Son of Man	Mediator
The Way	Son of God	Lord
The Word	Alpha and omega	Jesus Christ
The Light of the World	Master	Savior
Counselor	Judge	The first and the last
The Beginning and the Ending	Almighty	

Bob Messia had lived for himself. His story was one of "rags to riches". He thought that if he had all the world had to offer, he would be happy. He would later discover that regardless of the many worldly successes, his life would prove far from being glorious.

When he considered his so-called successes, he always described himself in the same way, "I am a self-made man." He perceived that in his world, all matters found the beginning and the ending in his understanding and abilities. Even though he had partners, he felt that he had proved time and again that the words he spoke would stand true.

As a means to formula a plan, Bob read of life according to the most successful people in the world. He also carefully planned every move he made. He had acquired three business partners in college. They had been known as the four Musketeers. In a way Bob handpicked his associates. He had observed, listened, and asked questions. Once he identified those who possessed certain qualities, he worked his way into each of their worlds, eventually bringing them together as a team. They were all from the high end of society. There was Alfred Prince of Peaceful Heights Estates, where men lived who were of renowned reputations in their different fields, Carl Anson of Manly Court, an exclusive country club, and Charles Mason of Godfrey Estates, which was bordered by a famous golf course.

They had formed an elite group that was simply called "Alpha," and omega was a coded system they developed to manipulate programs and communicate with each other on their computers. Later they would team up to form a business, using the "omega code" to solve business problems in the computer world, and even opened new branches in other locations. In fact, they were considered the latest saviors when confronting technical problems.

In Bob's mind he had the first and the last say, in regards to what took place in the kingdom that he was establishing with these three men. Each partner had his own unique abilities. Alfred was the life of the party, but he had a side that proved to be clever and shrewd. He could take what appeared to be a dead company and could ultimately do the impossible by ensuring the resurrection of it. Carl had what they considered a "high priestly" quality about him. He often served as a mediator when there was a clash of personalities. When it came to Charles, he proved to be a motivator. He often was like a reliable, good shepherd who guided many through troubled waters and inspired them to accept new challenges.

When it came to Bob, he was considered the anointed one. Everything he touched seemed to turn into financial gain. At age 35, he had quickly climbed the ladder of success and from the heights of his particular ladder, he viewed himself as the king of the computer world, the lord of his business domain, and master of all that he was overseeing. In essence, he saw himself as being divine, a type of god. It was clear he was a savvy businessman. Granted he was a bit ruthless, but he saw it as being necessary to ensure the way of success.

However, one day Bob's world came crashing down around him, along with what he considered to be the light of the world in his life. In fact, his light became shrouded in darkness and called into question. He had thought himself to be infallible, above the law, and capable of beating the odds.

It started when he had socialized a bit too much. Even though he had drunk over his limit, he assumed as always that he was still in control of his faculties. However, he ended up in a car accident. Fortunately, no one was killed but he received a serious concussion. When he woke up, confusion was his reality and his sharp intellect was no where to be found; and, from all appearances it would not return to its original capacity anytime soon.

Bob quickly discovered the truth about being part of the human race. To his surprise he was like everyone else. He was not an exception after all, and when he had to stand before the judge at the county courthouse for driving under the influence of alcohol, he realized how foolish he had been. He was not the master of his destiny, and he had been quickly demoted from being the king of kings in his profession and the lord of lords in his personal domain to a statistic. He had to face the harsh reality that when one is stripped of the fickle power the world affords, he or she is like everyone else.

The judge showed some grace, but Bob still had to attend a program that dealt with alcohol abuse and to do community service. He was given three choices, to work with the parks department, which majored in litter and latrines, the street crews, which cleaned up the fall leaves left in the gutters after the residents raked their yards, or in one of the community kitchens that helped the homeless. He chose the latter.

As Bob looked back he could see where it was the providence of God that he chose the last option. It was while serving the homeless, that he finally recognized the barren vanity of his life and his fruitless ways. It was also there he met Josh. Josh was the counselor for the homeless that were served by the community kitchen, and he shared with Bob the reality of the Lord Jesus Christ. He told him how Jesus came to save people from their sinful, dead end lives and to give them forgiveness for going the ruthless way of idolatrous selfishness.

Bob felt the convicting power of the Holy Spirit. He knew that all of his successes would pass away with the world, and that only that which comes from and by the redemption of Christ would withstand the present world, and continue to stand in the midst of glory in the next. That day he made his peace with the Almighty by asking the Lord for forgiveness for his despicable, self-serving ways and inviting Jesus Christ to come into his life as his Lord and Savior.

Josh also gave him a Bible. It was only one book, but it all seemed so new and overwhelming to him. He did not know where to start to tackle God's Word. Josh told him to read the Gospel of John, which proved to be beneficial, but he discovered the Psalms and became captivated by them. He often found himself going on a journey of the heart and discovering spiritual remedies for his heart, spirit, and soul. He would find his heart singing while his spirit soared and his soul rejoiced. It was so incredible, so wonderful.

It was through his spiritual journey that Bob discovered that God puts a new song in the hearts of His people. He not only put within Bob a new song that not only played a glorious melody in his inner being, but it was causing him to walk in a whole new way. He did not know what the future would bring him as far as his business and partners, but he knew he was walking according to the drumbeat of heaven and there would be no turning back to the barren, empty ways of his former life.

Who Am I?

Answers to pages 319-321

1. John Bunyan
2. William Cowper
3. John Charles Ryle
4. General William Booth
5. Smith Wigglesworth
6. Hudson Taylor
7. Robert Murray McCheyne
8. Fanny Crosby
9. Dr. Samuel Zwemer
10. George Campbell Morgan
11. Oswald Chambers
12. Charles Simeon
13. Christmas Evans
14. R. A. Torrey
15. George Whitefield
16. Matthew Henry
17. Amy Carmichael
18. Origen
19. Gregory Nazianzea
20. Gall
21. Thomas Blacklock
22. John Knox
23. Abraham Lincoln
24. Charles Finney

BIBLIOGRAPHY

(GN) Golden Nuggets from the Greek New Testament, © 1940 by Kenneth S. Wuest, WM. B. Eerdmans Publishing Company

(GTL) Great Truths To Live By from the Greek New Testament, © 1952 by Kenneth S. Wuest, WM. B. Eerdmans Publishing Company

(FT) The Fiery Trial, John Rusk, Pietan Publications

(DP): A Devotional Commentary Psalms, Herbert Lockyer, Sr., © 1993 by Kregel Publications

(RR): The Righteous Man's Refuge, John Flavel, Old Paths Gospel Press

(GW): Sermons of George Whitefield, © 2009 by Hendrickson Publishers Marketing, LLC

(RA): Revival Addresses, R. A. Torrey, © 1903 by Fleming H. Revell Company

(SOA): Shadow of the Almighty, © 1958 by Elisabeth Elliot, Harper and Row Publishers

(CA): God's Goal, Christ as All in All, © 1996 by Manfred Haller, Published by The SeedSowers

(DTD): Daily Thoughts For Disciples, Oswald Chambers, © 1990 by Oswald Chambers Publication Association

(BNT): Bypaths in the Greek New Testament, Kenneth S. Wuest, © 1940, Wm B. Eerdmans Publishing Co.

(NAA): Nests Above the Abyss, Isobel Kuhn, © by Overseas Missionary Fellowship, First published in 1947 and reprinted May 1980

(ED): Extreme Devotion

(KG): Knothole Glimpses of Glory, F. Ellsworth Powell; © 1963 by Osterhus Publishing House

(NTB): No Turning Back, E. A. Johnston, © 2005, Gospel Folio Press

(SFG): Sent Forth By God, © 1980 by Ruth Specter Lascelle; Bedrock Press

(MA): Memories of Miracles in Africa, Carol Zurcher, © 1989 by Nazarene Publishing House

(ISL): I Saw the Lord, Chester and Lucille Huyssen, © 1977, 1992 by Chester Huyssen, Chosen Books

(BKY): Before We Kill and Eat You, H.B. Garlock with Ruthanne Garlock, © 2003 by Ruthanne Garlock, Regal Books

(SWD): Smith Wigglesworth Devotional, Smith Wigglesworth, © 1999 by Whitaker House

(VCK): Victorious Christians You Should Know, Warren W. Wiersbe, © 1984 by Baker Book House Company

(DHL): A Devout Holy Life, William Law, © 1996 by Whitaker House

(MES): Morning & Evening Daily Devotional by Charles Spurgeon, © MCMXCVII by Barbour Publishing. Inc.

(SPP): A Small Price to Pay, Harvey Yoder, © 2006 by TGS International

(ENS): Evidence Not Seen (A Woman's Miraculous Faith in the Jungles of World War II), Darlene Deibler Rose © 1988 by Darlene Rose, Revised © by Dr. William and Jan Henry

(KH): The Knowledge of the Holy, © 1961 by A. W. Tozer, Harper Collins Publishers

(IW): The Invisible War, Donald Grey Barnhouse, © 1965 by Zondervan

(PWH): The Presence & Work of the Holy Spirit, R. A. Torrey, © 1996 by Whitaker House

(FDA): The Fire of Delayed Answers, © 1996 by Bob Sorge, Published by Oasis House

(LRR): Lectures on Revivals of Religion, Charles G. Finney, Fleming H. Revell Company

(TP): The Prophets, © by Abraham J. Heschel, Harper Perennia Modern Classics

(POG): Every Life is a Plan of God, © 1992 by J. Oswald Sanders, Discovery House Publishers

(CCA) The Christians in Complete Armour, William Gurnall; Hendrickson Publishers Marketing, LLC; The first edition of this work was published in Scotland in 1865.

(IH) Into Their Hands, Harvey Yoder, © 2009 by TGS International, a wholly-owned subsidary of Christian Aid Ministries, Berlin, Ohio

The Hand of God, In the Life of a Country Preacher, © 2009 by Daniel Moore

The Great Pyramid Prophecy in Stone, © 1996, 2010 by Noah Hutchings, Defender Publishing

Glossary

anchorite: one who lives in seclusion for religious reasons.
aphorism: a concise statement of a principle, a truth or sentiment.
aye: yes, or ever, always, continually.
cajoled: to persuade with flattery in the face of reluctance.
calumny: the act of uttering false charges or maliciously misrepresenting something to incur damage of reputation.
canonical: relating to a general rule or text that has been accepted.
chequer: it is the British word for "check."
corollary: something that naturally follows which produces results.
deftly: marked by facility and skill, dexterous.
epicure: one devoted to sensual pleasure.
eventuates: contingent, conditional, taking place at an unspecified later time.
exegesis: to explain or interpret.
exigency: a state of affairs that make urgent demands.
gild: to give an attractive but often deceptive appearance.
Gnomic: poetry characterized by aphorism or a concise statement of a principle or a terse formulation of truth or sentiment—an adage.
gratis: favor, free, without charge or recompense
heterogeneous: pointing to mixed or dissimilar ingredients.
inexorable: to prevail upon, but will not be persuaded.
lapidary: engraver on stone or the art of cutting them.
lutenist: a lute player.
mettle: quality of temperament or disposition.
parleying: to confer, to discuss terms with an enemy.
parsimony: the quality of being careful or stingy with money and resources.
precipitancy: falling, flowing or rushing with steep descent, headlong and abruptly.
propitiation: to gain good-will, appease, conciliate, an atoning sacrifice in place of something.
Pyrrhic: in reference to the king of Epirus who sustained heavy losses in defeating the Romans. A victory won at excessive cost.
quintessence: the essence of a thing in its purest form, the most typical example or representative of something.
royles: If this word is roils it means to churn up or stir up..
sere: to wither or make threadbare.

shoal: shallow

stratagem: general maneuver, an artifice or trick in war for deceiving and outwitting the enemy.

succour: to run as a means to aid or help in order to relieve.

timorous: a timid disposition.

theorems: an idea accepted or proposed as a demonstrable truth often as a part of a general theory.

vassal: one in a subservient or subordinate position.

veracity: truthfulness—the power to convey truth or fact.

whist: whisking up the tricks in relationship to a card game for four players. It is also used in reference to hush or enjoin silence.

wont: habitual way of doing something.

(The majority of definitions were taken from Webster's New Collegiate Dictionary © 1976 by G. & C. Merriam Company.)

About the Author

Rayola Kelley, an ordained minister of the Gospel, was born again and saved out of a cult in 1976 while serving in the U.S. Navy. Her spiritual journey continued through extensive discipleship, before following the Lord's call upon her life into full-time ministry since 1989, when, with Jeannette Haley, founded Gentle Shepherd Ministries.

Through the years, Rayola's gift of teaching the Word has opened many doors for her to teach adult Sunday school, oversee a fellowship for over 15 years, hold evangelistic meetings in churches, conduct seminars, and speak at retreats. She has served in jail ministry, and is well known for her gift of spiritual insight and counseling. Upon being called to be a missionary in America, Rayola, along with Jeannette Haley established different fellowships where intense Bible Studies and discipleship training were conducted to equip believers for the ministry. These different mission fields in America entailed working in various churches as well as working with other cultures such as Korean and Hispanic nationalities.

Rayola, along with co-laborer Jeannette Haley, (professional artist, author of Christian novels, Bible Studies and stories for children) began sending out a monthly newsletter containing articles for the Body of Christ in 1997 which continues to grow. Ms. Kelley has authored over 50 books, and numerous Bible Studies including an advanced Discipleship Course (available in both English and Spanish) that is being used in countries such as Africa, Bulgaria, Israel, Ireland, India, Cuba, and Pakistan. Among her many books is *"Hidden Manna"* which deals with destructive cycles in people and relationships, and *"Battle for the Soul"* which presents a clear picture of the battle that rages in the soul. She has written six in-depth devotional books, including both the Old Testament and New Testament devotional study which takes the reader through the entire Bible in one year. All of her books are hard-hitting, bottom-line spiritual food for the hungry and thirsty soul to "chew" upon in order to *"grow strong in the Lord, and in the power of His might."*

Rayola currently resides in Oldtown, ID. She continues to fulfill Christ's commission to make disciples through teaching, spiritual counseling, and writing.

Please visit Gentle Shepherd Ministries Web Site at: www.gentleshepherd.com for further information, and to access her challenging and informative audio sermons.

Other books by Rayola Kelley:

Hidden Manna (Original)
Battle for the Soul
Stories of the Heart
Transforming Love & Beyond
The Great Debate
Post to Post: (1) Establishing the Way
Post to Post: (2) Walking in the Way
Post to Post: (3) Meditations Along the Way

Volume One: Establishing Our Life in Christ
My Words are Spirit and Life
The Anatomy of Sin
The Principles of the Abundant Life
The Place of Covenant
Unmasking the Cult Mentality

Volume Two: Putting on the Life of Christ
He Actually Thought it Not Robbery
Revelation of the Cross
In Search of Real Faith
Think on These Things
Follow the Pattern

Volume Three: Developing a Godly Environment
Godly Discipline
Prayer and Worship
Don't Touch That Dial
Face of Thankfulness
ABC's of Christianity

Volume Four: Issues of the Heart
Hidden Manna (Revised)
Bring Down the Sacred Cows
The Manual for the Single Christian Life
Parents are People Too

Volume Five: Challenging the Christian Life
The Issues of Life
Presentation of the Gospel
For the Purpose of Edification
Whatever Happened to the Church?
Women's Place in the Kingdom of God

Volume Six: Developing Our Christian Life
The Many Faces of Christianity
Possessing Our Souls
Experiencing the Christian Life
The Power of Our Testimonies
The Victorious Journey

Volume Seven: Discovering True Ministry
From Prisons and Dots to Christianity
So You Want To Be In Ministry

Devotions
Devotions of the Heart: Books One and Two
Daily Food for the Soul: Books One and Two

Gentle Shepherd Ministries Devotion Series:
Being a Child of God
Disciplining the Strength of our Youth
Coming to Full Age

Nugget Books:
Nuggets From Heaven
More Nuggets From Heaven
Heavenly Gems
Heavenly Treasures

Gentle Shepherd Ministries Series:

The Christian Life Series
What Matter Is This?
The Challenge of It
The Reality of It
The Leadership Series
Overcoming
A Matter of Authority and Power
The Dynamics of True Leadership

Other Books By:
Jeannette Haley
Books co-authored with Rayola Kelley:
Hidden Manna (original)
The Many Faces of Christianity (Volume 6)
Discovering True Ministry: Volume 7
Post to Post 3: Meditations Along the Way
Other Books:
The Pig and I
Reflections of Wonder (Devotional)
Children's Books:
Little Stories for Little People
Traveler's Tales
The Adventures of Zack and Mira
The Adventures of Paul and Dana
(A House on the Beach)
The Monster of Mystery Valley

www.ingramcontent.com/pod-product-compliance
Lightning Source LLC
Chambersburg PA
CBHW031233090426
42742CB00007B/186